Resurrection

Resurrection

Extraordinary Evidence for an Extraordinary Claim

NICK MEADER
Foreword by Luke Ijaz

RESOURCE *Publications* · Eugene, Oregon

RESURRECTION
Extraordinary Evidence for an Extraordinary Claim

Copyright © 2024 Nick Meader. All rights reserved. Except for brief quotations in critical publications or reviews, no part of this book may be reproduced in any manner without prior written permission from the publisher. Write: Permissions, Wipf and Stock Publishers, 199 W. 8th Ave., Suite 3, Eugene, OR 97401.

Resource Publications
An Imprint of Wipf and Stock Publishers
199 W. 8th Ave., Suite 3
Eugene, OR 97401

www.wipfandstock.com

PAPERBACK ISBN: 978-1-6667-8305-6
HARDCOVER ISBN: 978-1-6667-8306-3
EBOOK ISBN: 978-1-6667-8307-0
VERSION NUMBER 09/11/24

All Scripture quotations, unless otherwise indicated, are taken from the Holy Bible, New International Version®, NIV®. Copyright ©1973, 1978, 1984, 2011 by Biblica, Inc.™ Used by permission of Zondervan. All rights reserved worldwide. www.zondervan.com The "NIV" and "New International Version" are trademarks registered in the United States Patent and Trademark Office by Biblica, Inc.™

Contents

List of Tables | vii
List of Figures | viii
Foreword by Luke Ijaz | ix
Acknowledgments | xi
List of Abbreviations | xiii
Introduction | xv

Part One: What is Extraordinary Evidence? | 1
    Chapter 1   What is Extraordinary Evidence? | 3
    Chapter 2   Probability Theory and Theology | 11
    Chapter 3   Worldviews | 22

Part Two: The Nature of Reality | 33
    Chapter 4   Existence of the Universe | 35
    Chapter 5   Intelligibility and the Success of Science | 43
    Chapter 6   Suffering and Evil I | 52
    Chapter 7   Suffering and Evil II | 60
    Chapter 8   Summary of Evidence on the Nature of Reality | 65

Contents

Part Three: Hebrew Bible and the Messiah | 73

    Chapter 9   The Word (*Memra*) Made Flesh | 78
    Chapter 10   The Tabernacle and Temple | 84
    Chapter 11   The Suffering Messiah | 90
    Chapter 12   Resurrection in the Hebrew Bible | 97
    Chapter 13   Son of Man, the Ascended King | 104
    Chapter 14   Jesus the Promised Messiah | 111

Part Four: The Evidence for Jesus' Resurrection | 119

    Chapter 15   First Corinthians 15, An Early Creed | 122
    Chapter 16   Mark and Matthew | 130
    Chapter 17   Resurrection Accounts in Luke and John | 136
    Chapter 18   Summary of Evidence for Jesus' Resurrection | 145

Part Five: Naturalistic Explanations | 151

    Chapter 19   Naturalistic Explanations for the Empty Tomb | 155
    Chapter 20   Visions or Hallucinations? | 162
    Chapter 21   Conversion Disorder and "Mass Hysteria" | 172
    Chapter 22   Distorted Memories and Other Explanations | 180
    Chapter 23   Cognitive Dissonance Theory | 189
    Chapter 24   A Summary of Alternative Explanations | 200

Part Six: Modelling Resurrection Evidence | 207

    Chapter 25   Resurrection Model | 209
    Chapter 26   Exploring the Robustness of the Model | 223
    Chapter 27   Resurrection and Redemption | 229

Appendix 1: Summary of Major Rabbinic Jewish Writings on Isaiah 52:13—53:12 | 233
Appendix 2: Studies Included in Bereavement Hallucination Estimates | 242
Bibliography | 251
Subject Index | 261

List of Tables

Table 1. Comparing Eden and the Tabernacle/Temple | 25

Table 2. Comparison between four worldview categories and Christianity | 27

Table 3. Comparisons between the Genesis creation account, Mount Sinai, and the Tabernacle | 86

Table 4. Summary of key aspects of the resurrection narrative in the four Gospels | 146

Table 5. Summary of minor differences between resurrection accounts in the four Gospels | 146

Table 6. A summary of evidence for Jesus' resurrection | 147

Table 7. Prevalence of group visions | 167

Table 8. Alternative explanations for empty tomb | 201

Table 9. Alternative explanations for postmortem appearances | 201

Table 10. Varying natural theology judgments | 225

Table 11. Varying judgments about the evidence | 226

Table 12. Summary of major Rabbinic literature on Isaiah 52:13—53:12 before 1000 CE | 237

Table 13. Summary of major Rabbinic literature on Isaiah 52:13—53:12 from 1000 CE | 238

Table 14. Summary of studies used to estimate median prevalence of bereavement hallucinations | 243

Table 15. Studies excluded with reasons | 247

List of Figures

Figure 1. Bayesian network of Hume's theoretical miracle | 9

Figure 2. Intelligibility as a confounder of the association between naturalism and the success of science | 48

Figure 3. Network diagram summarizing Part Two | 74

Figure 4. Main factors impacting on the prior for Jesus' resurrection | 120

Figure 5. Three Stages of Cognitive Dissonance | 193

Figure 6. Model of evidence for the resurrection | 213

Figure 7. Prior probabilities for the nature of reality | 214

Figure 8. Model results on the probability of Triune God, Jesus is the Messiah, and Jesus was raised from the dead | 221

Foreword

You are about to embark on reading a book quite unlike any other. In these pages we are released from the methodological strait-jacket which hinders so many evidential approaches to Jesus' resurrection. It is all too readily assumed that it is possible for both the reasonable naturalist and the reasonable Christian to reach the same conclusion simply through a careful weighing of pertinent evidence. But neither has unhindered access to raw "facts". Each is deeply wedded to underlying worldview assumptions which have all but decided the conclusion, which no consideration of evidence can modify. The naturalist and the Christian are talking past one another, because their feet are firmly planted in different worlds.

These chapters bring the field of biblical theology into conversation with the field of statistics. The use of probabilities in these pages is a novel one, to me at least. Nothing so crude as an attempt to give some mathematical proof of Jesus' resurrection. The use of numbers here is to help us *think*. It provides a means for us to move around within contrasting worldviews; enabling us to weigh up their underlying assumptions and better grasp their internal consistency—or inconsistency. The promise is held out of the naturalist and the Christian now talking *to* one another about which world provides the firmer footing for our feet.

What follows reframes our thinking about Jesus' resurrection; especially the "extraordinary" nature of it. Where the naturalist and the Christian are often seen to be in agreement on a belief that Jesus' resurrection is extraordinary to the extreme. By this, both have already conceded too

Foreword

much. Part 1 helpfully unpacks why. Central to the argument of this book is the belief that resurrection is deeply grounded in the theology of the Hebrew Bible—and hence the worldview arising from it. Far from resurrection being an unexpected denouement at the close of the narrative, the logic of the resurrection is fully congruent with the way this world works. It has a prior probability. Moreover, Part 3 helps us appreciate that Jesus' resurrection is no incoherent final flourish, easily dismissed as a dispensable "bolt-on" to his life. Rather, it is central to the identity of Israel's Messiah. The contention is: If we can reasonably conclude that Jesus "fits the bill" of this long-expected Messiah, then it is also reasonable to conclude that he was raised from the dead.

This book is written with an admirable clarity and simplicity. Complex and weighty concepts and ideas, which are seldom brought into conversation let alone made comprehensible, are here made accessible. I am no statistician, but I could easily follow the thread—with the short work proving something of a page-turner. This book has also been structured in such a way that, whatever has led you to pick it up (be it biblical theology or probability theory), you can dip-in on the various parts according to interest and still follow the argument. If numbers are a limited aid to helping you think, do not be put off by them—and vice versa.

You are about to embark on reading a book quite unlike any other. Who knows? When you disembark at the other end, you may find your feet newly planted in a world quite unlike any other.

Revd Luke Ijaz
Wimbledon, London
June 2024
1 Peter 1:3

Acknowledgments

As with any book, there are many people that have helped me along the way. I would like to thank Luke Ijaz for all his encouragement, for helpful comments and suggestions on the book, and for writing the foreword. He was there with me at the beginning of my Christian faith, and I'm glad that he remains a great friend almost three decades later.

I'm extremely grateful for all those that took the time to read the manuscript. For Warren Beattie and Ian Shaw's wise comments on the draft—their experience and feedback had a huge impact on this work. For James Wright and Alastair Jakeman reading sections of the draft and encouraging me to keep going. I also want to thank Andrew Loke, James Anderson, and Priyan Dias for reading the draft and sharing their expertise. I'm also thankful to Wipf and Stock for their patience—giving me a little extra time to finish off—and giving me the opportunity to publish with them.

I'm so thankful to Mami, Emma, and Mike. Writing has taken far more work than I expected. I have spent too much time being brain dead and distracted around the house. Mami's comments on the draft have been very insightful. Her Japanese perspective helped me try thinking beyond the traditional divides of naturalism and Christianity. Mami's faith, hard work, and strength continue to be an inspiration to me. For Emma and Mike, I continue to pray that, "he who began a good work in you will carry it on to completion until the day of Christ Jesus." (Philippians 1:6)

List of Abbreviations

BCE: before the common era (equivalent to BC)
CDT: cognitive dissonance theory
CE: common era (equivalent to AD)
DSM-5: Diagnostic and Statistical Manual-Version 5
DSS: Dead Sea Scrolls
ECREE: extraordinary claims require extraordinary evidence
FNSD: functional neurological symptom disorder
GR: general relativity
H': HaShem (the divine name)
HH model: Hartle-Hawking model
HI: hypothesis of indifference
ICD: International Classification of Diseases
1QIsa^a: The Great Isaiah scroll
KRA: Kripke-Ross argument
Lbs: pounds (weight)
MPI: mass psychogenic illness
NIV: New International Version
NT: New Testament
p: probability

Introduction

Growing up in London, to a non-religious family, "extraordinary claims require extraordinary evidence [ECREE]"[1] was self-evident to me. Miracle claims, like Jesus' resurrection, were remnants of a superstitious past. Any other explanation for the "evidence" was more likely.

When I now read Christian responses to ECREE, or to Hume (who likely inspired the phrase), I often have mixed feelings. I am disappointed with how closed-minded I was. But these "refutations" are frequently little more than a sidestep. As John Frame points out, "unbelievers demand that we consider the facts of their experience, which seem to them to refute Christianity."[2] For many, Carl Sagan and David Hume have shown miracle claims fail. Why think Jesus' resurrection is any different?

The aim of this book is to explore whether Sagan and Hume have really shown miracle claims fail. At times, it feels like I am having a conversation between my former self (when I was an atheist) and present self (now a Christian). But, of course, there are other conversation partners. Muslims, Rabbinic Jews, Hindus, Buddhists, and animists all have different ways of thinking about this evidence.

I will explore how ECREE has been defined—with the help of David Hume and probability theory. This will require us to consider how wider beliefs impact judgments on what is extraordinary. Should we act as if the laws of nature are fundamental—until proved otherwise? Or do the

1. Sagan, *Broca*, 75.
2. Frame, *Apologetics*, 58.

regularities of the universe point to a creator God? How do these assumptions impact how we view evidence for Jesus' resurrection? As Andrew Loke points out, investigating Jesus' resurrection requires methods that "move beyond discipline-specific approaches."[3]

Historians, philosophers, and theologians are rightly at the centre of this debate. But scholars have applied Bayesian approaches to these questions since the eighteenth century. In addition, many naturalistic theories employ psychological explanations (e.g., bereavement hallucinations, cognitive dissonance, the unreliability of memory) to account for the disciples' experience.[4] We will reflect on how perspectives from statistics and psychology, my areas of academic research, contribute to this discussion. We will also consider insights from several other disciplines including philosophy, theology, Biblical studies, and religious studies. In this chapter, we will explore the following themes:

- naturalist and Christian approaches to Jesus' resurrection;
- how assumptions about reality impact our conclusions;
- an overview of the book.

NATURALISM AND CHRISTIANITY

As historian, Tom Holland, points out: "To live in a Western country is to live in a society still utterly saturated by Christian concepts and assumptions ... its trace elements are to be found everywhere in the West."[5] Christian concepts were both familiar and alien to me. I took it for granted the triumph of Christianity led to "an age of superstition and credulity."[6] I was unaware of repeating a familiar narrative of Western history. Charles Taylor, a Canadian philosopher, calls it a subtraction story.

My path to Christianity began by reading Luke's gospel, given by my flatmate at that time, who also wrote the foreword to this book. We both became Christians at University College London, the "Godless Institution of Gower Street," founded in 1826 as an atheist alternative to Oxford and Cambridge. Like many of us, Christianity and naturalism have shaped me:

3. Loke, *Resurrection*, 2.
4. We will explore these arguments in Part Five.
5. Holland, *Dominion*, xxv.
6. Holland, *Dominion*, xxvii.

INTRODUCTION

our age is haunted. On the one hand, we live under a brass heaven, ensconced in immanence. We live in the twilight of both gods and idols. But their ghosts have refused to depart, and every once in a while we might be surprised to find ourselves tempted by belief . . . most of us live in this cross-pressured space, where both our agnosticism and our devotion are mutually haunting.[7]

A Naturalist Illustration of Miracle Claims

Arif Ahmed, a philosophy professor at the University of Cambridge, provides a useful illustration of how naturalists often view evidence for miracles.[8] Imagine you are measuring the temperature of water in a bucket:

- you have five thermometers;
- each states the temperature is 10 C (50 F);
- the water feels a little cold to the touch.

You agree the water is 10 C. What if all five thermometers find the water is 30 C (86 F)? You might expect the water to feel warmer but are willing to give them the benefit of doubt. What if they all suggest the temperature is 600 C (1112 F)—yet the water is not boiling and in a liquid state? There is important background knowledge we draw upon from school days:

- water boils at temperatures over 100 C;
- no one has observed water in a non-boiling and liquid state at 600 C;
- thermometers sometimes malfunction.

Evidence from five thermometers is insufficient—it is far more plausible that they are broken.

WORLDVIEW AND EVIDENCE

Ahmed applies similar reasoning to Jesus' resurrection. Dead people do not rise from the dead. When a group of people claim to see a resurrected man, it is more likely they were mistaken or lying. Even for me, a Christian, his analogy has intuitive power. Why? Ahmed is invoking worldview

---

7. Smith, *Secular*, 3–4.
8. Ahmed, *Debate*, 9:12 to 11.00.

assumptions we are unaware of imbibing. He presents, "an unchallenged framework, something we have trouble often thinking ourselves outside of, even as an imaginative exercise."[9] Jesus' resurrection is viewed through the lens of an eighteenth century subtraction story.

> And so we come to understand our lives as taking place within a self-sufficient immanent order; or better, a constellation of orders, cosmic, social and moral . . . these orders are understood as impersonal. This understanding of our predicament has as background a sense of our history: we have advanced to this grasp of our predicament through earlier more primitive stages of society and self-understanding. In this process, we have come of age.[10]

Jesus' resurrection, if it occurred, would violate our assumptions of an impersonal universe, "a kind of punctual hole blown in the regular order of things from outside, that is, from the transcendent."[11] From a naturalist perspective, this is close to impossible.

African Christianity and the Subtraction Story

In the West, we tend to view these assumptions as the direct result of our scientific development. For example, when Christian missionaries left Africa after the collapse of colonialism, Western scholars assumed the continent would follow a similar path to widespread non-belief observed in Europe. Lamin Sanneh, a scholar of World Christianity, argued many failed to understand the culturally contingent nature of their predictions:

> According to Africans, whether Christian or not, we are not alone in the universe, which is inhabited by the devil and by a host of spirit forces that are ever attentive to us. We should also be ever attentive to them if we are sensible . . . That small, disinfected universe of the West is fine for the conventional rhythms of the regular day, but not when the legion of ancestors, the spirits, and the living dead come calling . . . people are surrounded by an active, dangerous spirit world that requires constant and vigilant intervention to be safe and whole.[12]

---

9. Taylor, *Secular*, 549.
10. Taylor, *Secular*, 543.
11. Taylor, *Secular*, 547.
12. Sanneh, *Christianity*, 7–8.

INTRODUCTION

The inevitability of naturalism triumphing over the miraculous, self-evident to numerous Westerners, made little sense to many Africans. Of course, some of Hume's ancestors may retort that Sanneh is describing an "ignorant and barbarous people"[13] who have not yet "advance[d] nearer the enlightened ages."[14] Yet there is a dilemma. It is possible to interpret the decline in religious belief among Western countries as support for subtraction stories. But how should we interpret data in the opposite direction—the rise of African Christianity after the retreat of colonialism?

The Importance of Background Beliefs

Evidence for the resurrection cannot be assessed in isolation from our background beliefs. The naturalist view, asserted by Hume and his descendants, is one way of interpreting these data. But we should not assume its neutrality—or its validity:

> In general, we have here what Wittgenstein calls a "picture", a background to our thinking, within whose terms it is carried on, but which is often largely unformulated, and to which we can frequently, just for this reason, imagine no alternative. As he once famously put it, "a picture held us captive". We can sometimes be completely captured by the picture, not even able to imagine what an alternative would look like; or we can be in somewhat better shape: capable of seeing that there is another way of construing things, but still having great difficulty making sense of it.[15]

A key aim of this book is to reflect on how these pictures of reality impact conclusions on Jesus' resurrection. For Christians, the resurrection shows he is God's king and judge: "For he has set a day when he will judge the world with justice by the man he has appointed. He has given proof of this to everyone by raising him from the dead" (Acts 17:31, NIV).[16] In contrast, for naturalists, his resurrection is close to impossible. There are thousands of other worldviews, each providing a different lens.[17] Am I going to consider them all? Of course not. But nor will I dismiss them all. This approach can be summarised as follows:

13. Hume, Enquiry, Section X: Part I: 94.
14. Hume, Enquiry, Section X: Part I: 94.
15. Taylor, Secular, 549.
16. All subsequent Bible references use the NIV translation unless stated otherwise.
17. E.g., Barrett, Encyclopedia, 1–12.

INTRODUCTION

But they [Christians] can place themselves upon the position of those whom they are seeking to win to a belief in Christianity for the sake of the argument. And the non-Christian, though not granting the presuppositions from which the Christian works, can nevertheless place himself upon the position of the Christian for the sake of the argument.[18]

OVERVIEW OF THE BOOK

Part One provides a framework for viewing Jesus' resurrection from a range of perspectives. I will focus on naturalism and Christianity because these are the dominant options in the West. But I will also consider a range of other worldviews such as Islam, Hinduism, Buddhism, and animism. *Part Two* outlines the Christian story of creation and fall. The Triune God creates a universe where he will dwell with his people. Humans made in God's image, can (at least partially) understand our world. Yet we are fallen, prone to error, bias, and evil. I will compare this Christian view of reality with alternative worldviews to assess how well they account for the existence of the universe, the success of science, suffering, and evil. *Part Three* looks at the life of Jesus and how he meets the promises of the Messiah in the Hebrew Bible. If Jesus is the divine Messiah, who lays down his life for us, then it is likely that God will raise him from the dead. *Part Four* focuses on the resurrection accounts. *Part Five* considers the main naturalistic explanations for these events. *Part Six* represents data from Parts One to Five, in a graphical model of evidence for Jesus' resurrection.

Although this argument is built up consecutively, each part is self-contained enough to dip in and out of sections. I have several kinds of reader in mind. I expect the primary audience will be seminary students, pastors, and those with an interest in philosophy and apologetics.

But I also hope the book is accessible to serious-minded Christians. Some may want to understand why their friends consider evidence for the resurrection insufficient. The first two parts of the book, outlining the Bayesian approach and prior probabilities, will be a good place to start. For others, you may have friends who have no doubt there is a God; yet it is inconceivable to them that the Messiah could be divine or could suffer. In this instance, the first and third parts of the book are most relevant.

---

18. Van Til, *Knowledge*, 11.

Introduction

Others may want to explore the evidence for the resurrection as an argument for Christian theism. In this case, Part Two and Part Six are most relevant for them. Some readers may want a refresher on the resurrection. Parts Four and Five summarise the evidence and responses to several naturalistic explanations. It is also important to note this is not only a book for Christians. I have met many non-Christians who are well-informed about the Bible and theology. Perhaps you are curious why Christians believe in the resurrection?

This book seeks to offer reflections for people in all the above categories—whether from inside the Christian church or connecting to those beyond who have an interest in exploring and addressing the philosophical questions that the New Testament raises.

PART ONE

What is Extraordinary Evidence?

"Extraordinary claims require extraordinary evidence (ECREE)"[1] is a popular phrase among sceptics. But what does it mean? ECREE is sometimes used as a marker of group identity.[2] Yet there are more productive interpretations rooted in probability theory. Getting this clear now will help reduce misunderstanding later—when we assess evidence for Jesus' resurrection (for a plan of Part One, see Box 1).

BOX 1. SUMMARY OF PART ONE

Chapter 1. What is extraordinary evidence? How did David Hume define extraordinary (or sufficient) evidence? The importance of prior probabilities to "extraordinary claims require extraordinary evidence".

Chapter 2. Probability theory and theology. This chapter considers objections to the application of probability theory to theology and apologetics.

---

1. Sagan, *Broca*, 75.
2. To set apart "sceptical" atheists from "naïve" religious people.

PART ONE: WHAT IS EXTRAORDINARY EVIDENCE?

BOX 1. SUMMARY OF PART ONE

Chapter 3. Worldviews. This chapter briefly compares Christianity with four alternative worldviews:

- physical-first (necessary) (e.g., naturalist views that the universe has always existed);
- physical-first (contingent) (e.g., naturalist views that the universe emerged from nothing);
- unipersonal theism (e.g., religions such as Islam or Judaism that believe the universe was created by a single person God);
- mind-first (e.g., animist and Buddhist religions that deny a creator God, but believe there are many finite gods).

Chapter 1

What is Extraordinary Evidence?

1.1 INTRODUCTION

WHAT SAGAN MEANT BY extraordinary evidence has been widely debated. He never explicitly defined the term. God painting "I am here!" in the sky? But that could be easily faked. Others may argue, if God is omniscient, he would know what evidence would convince them. He has failed to convince, so evidence is insufficient.

However, these ways of framing extraordinary are open to bias. Hume, although sharing some limitations with Sagan, was more explicit in his definitions. I will take Hume's understanding of sufficient evidence to be synonymous with Sagan's extraordinary evidence.[1] The aim of this chapter is to present a rigorous definition of these terms including:

- Hume's approach to miracles: the likely inspiration for Sagan's slogan;
- Hume's theoretical miracle: he aimed to minimize false positives (believing there is a miracle, when there was no miracle); but is his approach vulnerable to "false negatives" (believing there is no miracle, when a miracle happened)?
- Bayes's rule: building on Arif Ahmed's illustration I will explore how Bayesian methods can help evaluate Hume's approach;

---

1. Because for Hume, sufficient evidence to support a miracle (for him, a violation of nature) needed to be extraordinary.

Part One: What is Extraordinary Evidence?

- Hume's rationalism and irrationalism: I will argue that his "empirical" approach is unamenable to evidence.

1.2 HUME ON MIRACLES

Hume's approach to miracles has dominated naturalist views for over 250 years. On the popular level, atheist YouTubers like Paulogia and Matt Dillahunty continue to be indebted to him. I do not reject everything Hume wrote. His famous maxim is, in my view, uncontroversial: "That no testimony is sufficient to establish a miracle, unless the testimony be of such a kind that its falsehood would be more miraculous, than the fact which it endeavours to establish."[2] Carl Sagan's "extraordinary claims require extraordinary evidence"[3] was likely inspired by Hume.

Agnostic philosopher, Philip Goff, argues "without bringing in Bayesian notions, this is just a rhetorical slogan."[4] Atheist philosopher J.H. Sobel's work is a solid foundation to build upon.[5] He interpreted Hume's maxim to mean the prior probability of a miracle[6] must be greater than the probability of testimony about a miracle—if there was no miracle.[7] For example, the probability of Jesus' resurrection (before we have considered any evidence) must be greater than the probability of observing the empty tomb and appearances of Jesus—if Jesus was not resurrected.[8] At first glance, this sounds like Hume is ignoring evidence for a miracle. Yet Sobel showed mathematically that Hume's maxim is consistent with an event being more likely than not.

Scholars debate Hume's position on miracles. But his conclusion, that all miracle claims have failed, is not in doubt.[9] All testimony about miracles is like the third scenario in Ahmed's analogy. The prior probability is close

---

2. Hume, *Enquiry*, Section X: Part I:91.
3. Sagan, *Broca*, 75.
4. Goff, *Miracle*, lines 70–71.
5. Sobel, *Hume*, 230.
6. Which Hume considered a violation of the laws of nature.
7. $p(A) > p(a \ \& \sim A)$. Where A=miracle, a=testimony about a miracle, and $\sim A$=a miracle didn't happen.
8. That may sound dense and confusing. But I hope, when we consider Hume's theoretical miracle below, this will become clearer.
9. Hume, *Enquiry*, Section X: Part I:92.

to zero, and evidence insufficient. Hume claimed his conclusion was based on empirical evidence:

1. the probability of a miracle must be greater than the probability that the testimony is false;
2. no miracle claims in the past have ever met this criteria;
3. therefore we should act as if miracles do not happen unless sufficient evidence changes our conclusion.

1.3 HUME'S THEORETICAL MIRACLE

It is often suggested Hume assumed miracles were impossible, or at least, that it was impossible to demonstrate their validity. But he was clear, "there may possibly be miracles, or violations of the usual course of nature, of such a kind as to admit of proof from human testimony."[10] Hume proposed a scenario, an eight-day period of total darkness in 1600:

> Thus, suppose, all authors, in all languages, agree, that, from the first of January 1600, there was a total darkness over the whole earth for eight days: suppose that the tradition of this extraordinary event is still strong and lively among the people: that all travellers, who return from foreign countries, bring us accounts of the same tradition, without the least variation or contradiction: it is evident, that our present philosophers, instead of doubting the fact, ought to receive it as certain, and ought to search for the causes whence it might be derived.[11]

In other words, he proposed the following testimonial data:

- all authors, in all languages, agree that it happened;
- strong tradition remains till Hume's day (just under 150 years later);
- all travellers to foreign countries testify these countries have the same tradition, without variation or contradiction.

He would not want us to assume the possibility that God caused this miracle. So the following data are available for the prior:

- approximately forty-six, eight-day periods, in a year (365/8);

---

10. Hume, *Enquiry*, Section X: Part II:99.
11. Hume, Enquiry, Section X: Part II:99.

- astronomical records going back approximately 2,600 years (since sixth century BCE);
- approximately 119,600 eight-day periods (forty-six multiplied by 2600).

> **BOX 2. BAYES'S RULE**
>
> There are three main components to a Bayesian approach:
>
> - *prior probability*: p(M), the probability of a model being true before we have looked at the evidence;
> - *likelihood function*: p(E|M)[12], the probability of observing the data, if the model is true;
> - *posterior probability*: p(M|E), the probability of the model being true, based on the evidence observed; this is calculated by multiplying the prior probability and the likelihood function.
>
> To help understand Bayes's rule, I will return to Ahmed's analogy (see Introduction).
>
> ## First scenario:
>
> - you estimate the water temperature within a range of 4 to 20 C (the *prior probability*);
> - five thermometers independently provide readings of 10 C (the *likelihood function*);
> - because the prior and likelihood are similar (results from thermometers are identical), there is a *high posterior probability* the water is 10 C.

---

12. The straight line "|" means "given that", so for example p(M|E) means the probability model M is true, given the evidence we have observed.

> **BOX 2. BAYES'S RULE**
>
> Second scenario:
>
> - *prior probability* is a range of 4 to 20 C;
> - all five thermometers read 30 C (86 F) (*likelihood function*);
> - the water should feel warmer yet is not that different from your prior; evidence is strong and consistent, so the *posterior probability* is *moderately high*.
>
> Third scenario:
>
> - *prior probability* (your estimate of the water's temperature) is again a range of 4 to 20 C; but the five thermometer readings are 600 C (*likelihood function*);
> - the *prior probability* that water feels cool, is in a liquid non-boiling state, and 600 C is *close to zero*;
> - though there are five consistent thermometer readings, evidence is insufficient to overcome the prior (*posterior probability*).

1.3.1 Evaluating Hume's Theoretical Miracle

Hume argued there was insufficient evidence for all miracle claims in his day. It is likely he would have concluded the same for the proceeding 250 or so years after his famous chapter, *Of Miracles*. Therefore a prior probability of 1/100,000[13] for eight days of total darkness.

I will also assume the testimonial evidence proposed by Hume is 100% certain. If the miracle happened, we are certain to expect that type of evidence.[14] The probability of observing this evidence is unlikely if an eight-day period of darkness did not happen. How unlikely? One of the

---

13. p(A)=0.00001 although we calculated a prior of 1/119,600 we have used 1/100,000 to be generous to Hume's argument.
14. p(a&A)=1.

benefits of Bayes's rule is that multiple independent testimonies can increase certainty (for a summary of key concepts, see Box 2).

Yet there is an important trade-off. Certainty increases with consistent testimony from many independent witnesses. But unanimity of agreement may increase suspicion. For example, legal scholar Thomas Starkie pointed out we expect minor variations in testimony:

> It so rarely happens that witnesses of the same transaction perfectly and entirely agree in all points connected with it, that an entire and complete coincidence in every particular, so far from strengthening their credit, not unfrequently engenders a suspicion of practice and concert.[15]

Could the absolute consistency in Hume's example give us pause? We cannot rule out the possibility of collusion, but it seems unlikely. Therefore, I propose an extremely low probability of 1/1000.[16] These assumptions will now be pulled together into a probabilistic graphical model called a Bayesian network. They combine the mathematical insights of Bayes's rule and graph theory:

> They [Bayesian networks] are used in speech-recognition software, in spam filters, in weather forecasting . . . If you play video games on a Microsoft Xbox, a Bayesian network ranks your skill. If you own a cell phone, the codes that your phone uses to pick your call out of thousands of others are decoded by belief propagation, an algorithm devised for Bayesian networks.[17]

These graphical models are made up of:

- Nodes: rectangle boxes illustrate factors included in the model (eight days of darkness, unanimous written testimony, consistent tradition, testimony beyond Hume's home country);
- Links: arrows showing the relationship between factors, with probabilities attached.

---

15. Cited in McGrew and McGrew, *Resurrection*, 599.
16. $p(a\&\sim A) = 0.001$.
17. Pearl, *Why*, 95.

What is Extraordinary Evidence?

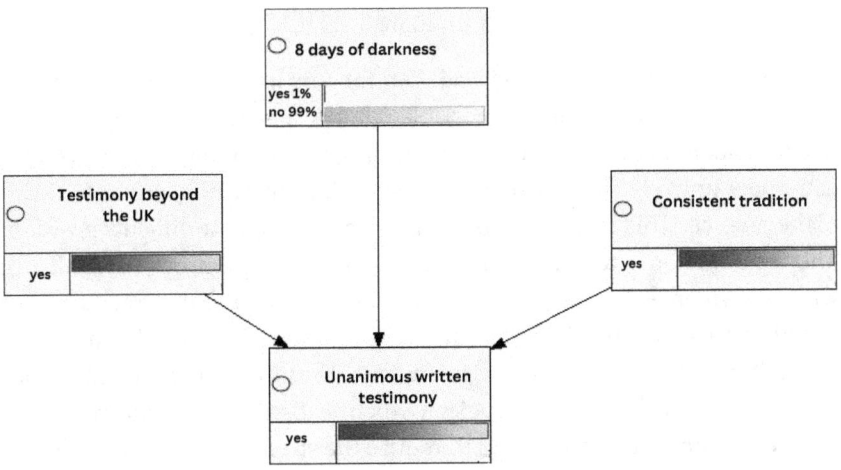

Figure 1. Bayesian network of Hume's theoretical miracle

Given that the prior probability for eight days of total darkness is close to impossible, even if we assume very strong testimonial evidence, this event is still unlikely. The posterior probability of Hume's theoretical miracle is only 0.01 (1/100). Therefore, based on these data, we should not believe it happened (see Figure 1).[18] Where does Hume's example go wrong? The testimonial evidence is strong as can be.[19] It is implausible to posit the chances of collusion any lower than 1/1000. The probability of collusion would need to be a maximum of 1/100,000 for this violation of nature to be judged as likely as not.[20]

1.4 HUME'S RATIONALISM AND IRRATIONALISM

This example illustrates a common dilemma for Hume and his followers:

> every unbelieving system of thought—because it reflects unregenerate hearts—is simultaneously rationalistic and irrationalistic.

---

18. Applying Hume's maxim leads to the same conclusion. The prior probability, p(A)=0.00001, is less than the probability of observing the testimonial evidence if no miracle occurred, p(a&~A)=0.001.

19. It is impossible to increase p(a|A) any further.

20. P(a&~A) is certainly not less than 1/100,000 which would be required for Hume's theoretical miracle to be more likely than not.

Part One: What is Extraordinary Evidence?

While claiming that their reason has ultimate authority (rationalism), unbelievers do not acknowledge anything that connects reason with objective truth (irrationalism).[21]

Hume's argument is empirical. Yet, for this hypothesis to be testable, evidence for miracles must be possible. Unfortunately, his example of sufficient evidence veers into irrationalism. Eight days of darkness in 1600 is extremely unlikely ($p=0.01$ or $1/100$) even after observing strong testimonial evidence. This leaves Hume, and his followers, in a difficult position. They could choose to rule out miracles from the beginning (rationalism), without evidence. However, this contradicts the claim that miracles are rejected because of empirical evidence. Alternatively, they could continue to insist their position is amenable to evidence, but this is incompatible with their prior probability for miracles (which leads to irrationalism). To be coherent, Hume's followers need to reduce the strength of their prior belief, that there is no God.

Hume's approach has benefits. We know that people can lie or be mistaken about miracles. A method for screening out false positives is needed. But this method must also avoid false negatives—denying miracle claims when the event actually happened. Hume's argument relies on an almost certain prior—that God cannot intervene in our universe. In Part Two, I will explore the validity of this type of prior in more detail.

---

21. Frame, *Apologetics*, 192.

Chapter 2

Probability Theory and Theology

2.1 INTRODUCTION

CHRISTIANS AND ATHEISTS DISCUSSING Jesus' resurrection can sometimes resemble young children on a play date. They use the same toys but play *alongside* each other—rather than *with* each other. On the surface, disagreements are about evidence. Christians think there is an abundance, atheists far too little. Yet, as Gary Habermas's minimal facts approach highlights, most scholars (no matter what their belief) agree on many key issues.

Yet we often address subtly different questions. Minimal facts proponents seek to show the resurrection accounts for the data better than all alternatives. Most atheists take a different starting point. They first ask, is a naturalistic explanation possible? If so, any naturalistic option is more probable than a miracle.

> But simply looking at the matter from a historical point of view, any of these views [various naturalistic options] is more plausible than the claim that God raised Jesus physically from the dead.[1]

From this perspective, the strength of evidence for the resurrection is of little consequence—since the prior probability for a miracle is close to impossible. Christians, on the other hand, are often reluctant to discuss prior probabilities—Richard Swinburne is a rare exception. Christians complain that atheists are close-minded to the evidence. Atheists, in contrast,

---

1. Ehrman, *Jesus*, 165.

consider it irrational to treat miraculous and naturalistic explanations on an equal footing.

I will argue a Bayesian approach addresses both concerns. This provides a mathematically rigorous method of integrating the prior probability for Jesus' resurrection (the concern of atheists) with an assessment of which hypothesis best explains the data (the concern of Christians). Of course, we will still disagree! But we are more likely to address the same question.

In this chapter, I will introduce probability theory and consider some of the concerns Christians and atheists may have with these approaches. I will discuss the following issues below:

- regularities and uncertainties in our experience of reality;
- types of probabilities (logical/evidential, subjective, frequentist);
- when it is, and when it is not, appropriate for Christians to apply probability theory to apologetic questions;
- objections to a Bayesian approach applied to historical evidence;
- ways to think about the prior probability of Jesus' resurrection.

2.2 REGULARITY AND UNPREDICTABILITY

Speaking as a theologian and mathematician, Vern Poythress argues that probability theory reflects our ability to understand the world—since God made us in his image. He is the foundation for the regularities that ground probability theory:

> The world of coin flips and dice rolling existed even before investigators like Cardano, Fermat, and Pascal began to formulate a theory of probability. The theory is in a sense a human product. Human beings had to think things through, watch coin flips and die rolls, and write up their arguments and conclusions. But the reality of probabilistic regularity exists in the world already. The regularities do exist.[2]

These regularities enable us to predict patterns. For example, clinical trials help inform how likely patients will benefit from a particular treatment. But physicians must still use their experience to apply these data to their patients. Clinical trials tell us primarily about the benefits (or side

2. Poythress, *Chance*, 163.

effects) averaged over a population.³ Each patient may vary in any number of ways from the average person in a clinical trial.

We may be tempted to emphasize the predictability of clinical trial results. This can lead us to downplay that a medicine, on average beneficial, may not work as well for every patient. Alternatively, we might emphasize that trials cannot tell us *who* will benefit. This can lead to extremes of rationalism ("we just need to follow the science") or irrationalism ("we cannot know if medicines are safe or effective"). These polarised responses ignore the surprising coherence between seemingly contradictory observations. Poythress argues this coherence reflects the Christian view of reality, that unity and plurality are co-ultimate.

> But the remarkable coherence between the unpredictabilities of individual coin flips and the predictabilities about averages and patterns remain unexplained. The unpredictabilities represent chance with a small c, events that we as human beings cannot predict. Why do these unpredictabilities cohere with the predictabilities?[4]

2.3 TYPES OF PROBABILITY

There are further complications. Probability has several distinct, yet complementary, meanings, including:[5]

1. logical/evidential—probability as an objective statement about evidential support: $p(E|H)$ is the extent to which evidence (E) provides support for a hypothesis (H);[6]

2. subjective—probability as a person's degree of confidence in a proposition;[7]

3. frequentist—probability as the frequency of an event.[8]

   3. Technically they sample from a population, in order to make inferences about the population.
   4. Poythress, *Chance*, 164.
   5. For further details, see Hajek, *Probability*, §3.
   6. For example, strong evidence (E) from a clinical trial showing a new cancer medication increases survival after five years would support hypothesis (H) that the new medication is an effective treatment.
   7. For example, if I am unsure if it will rain or not, I could express this uncertainty as $p(R) = 0.5$, 50% probability that it will rain.
   8. For example, if we toss a coin 10 times, we may not observe exactly five heads.

Part One: What is Extraordinary Evidence?

Because of limited knowledge and biases, these concepts of probability can sometimes conflict:

> One of the main difficulties consists in the very multiplicity of concepts. At first concepts 1 and 3 may seem to be the same. But concept 1 locates the foundation for probability in "quasi-logical" relationships, and thus relates it closely to the world of ideas, while concept 3 locates the foundation in the world outside us—how radium atoms behave. Concept 1, as a "quasi-logical" concept, focuses on abstract necessities or their probabilistic analogues, while concept 2 focuses on subjective, personal evaluations and estimations, which may be based on hunches or on information that may be unique to a particular person.[9]

Poythress argues God is the source of unity between the various aspects of probability:[10]

- our rationality is a pale reflection of God's; therefore he is the foundation for logical/evidential probability;
- God is personal and has created us to be personal, relational, and self-reflective; which is the foundation for subjective probability;
- God is the creator of our intelligible world; so we are able to empirically investigate our world using frequentist probability.

Chapter one provides an example of how naturalist assumptions can lead to contradiction between different types of probability. Hume outlined his subjective probability, that the evidence he proposed was sufficient to accept a theoretical miracle. However, when I formally applied Bayes's rule, the posterior probability (logical/evidential) for the theoretical miracle was very low.

2.4 CERTAINTY, PROBABILITY, AND THEOLOGY

As Christians, we are certain about the authority of God's word, and that he wants everyone to know the truth (1 Timothy 2:4). In addition, the Holy Spirit confirms these words with power (1 Corinthians 2:4–5):

But if we repeated the experiment enough times, we would find the coin landed heads half the time, p(heads)=0.5.

9. Poythress, *Chance*, 170.
10. Poythress, *Chance*, 171–78.

> Scripture speaks of the certainty of the evidence that God has given us his truth ... Luke speaks of the "convincing proofs" (Acts 1:3) that Jesus presented to the disciples after his resurrection. The evidence for Christian theism, therefore, is "absolutely certain."[11]

So should Christians avoid making probabilistic arguments? John Frame makes an important distinction between the absolute certainties of Scripture and our fallible attempts to articulate these truths. It might be possible for us to construct an argument replicating the certainties of Scripture. Yet this is an unrealistic standard for many arguments:

> The word *probability* deserves to be rehabilitated in Reformed apologetics. We dare not concede that the evidence for God's existence or the justification for believing in God's existence is merely probable ... But to be honest, we ought to admit that many of our arguments are only probable, if only because there is so much room for error in their formulation.[12]

2.5 OBJECTIONS

2.5.1 "Trying to Prove God with Maths?"

Atheists might also balk at the use of probability theory. For example, in response to a Bayesian argument, Bart Ehrman quipped that William Lane Craig claimed to have mathematical proof for God.[13] Bayes's rule is not trying to prove god with maths. If it were even possible, such a god would have nothing to do with Christianity. Christoph Heilig, an NT scholar, emphasises Bayes's rule is not a replacement for careful historical analysis. It's a helpful method for reducing biases in historical reasoning.[14]

2.5.2 Probabilities Only for Quantifiable Data?

You may feel uncomfortable expressing judgments about evidence for Jesus' resurrection in probabilities. Some Bible scholars, like Dale Allison, share these concerns:

11. Frame, *Apologetics*, 86–87.
12. Frame, *Apologetics*, 92.
13. Craig, *Reasonable Faith*, 280.
14. Heilig, *Bayesian*, §3.

Part One: What is Extraordinary Evidence?

> Maybe attending to the flux that is history with Bayes' theorem is like measuring beauty with a thermometer, or like evaluating education with quantified outcomes assessment: it is a futile attempt to calculate what cannot be calculated.[15]

I both agree and disagree with Allison. I agree that trying to quantify the unquantifiable is silly. But I think he is articulating a common misconception—that probabilities only apply to phenomena we can quantify and empirically evaluate (e.g., data from clinical trials in medicine or from particle accelerators in physics). However, the laws of probability apply equally to objective frequencies as they do to our judgments.[16] Therefore probabilistic models can "reflect the state of knowledge of a particular individual . . . not corresponding to anything that can be measured by a physical experiment,"[17] "physical quantities that can be not only measured but possibly controlled as well,"[18] or both.

Many of the models we work with in the medical sciences include both objective frequencies and various judgments. Take, for example, the benefits and harms of gene therapies. We usually have some quantifiable data, such as how many people receive the treatment. We know how many people survive at different ages, if their symptoms have improved, what side effects they have experienced.

But there are also questions far harder to quantify. Gene therapies are often developed for children with very low life expectancy. How can we quantify what life will look like for these children in future, when no one with this condition has ever survived to adolescence or adulthood before? Often, we may only have three to five years of data, will these children still be healthy in ten, twenty, or thirty years?

How long should we collect data, before giving the intervention to more patients? How many children will die waiting for this potentially life-saving treatment? Alternatively, if we are too hasty, we may end up prescribing a harmful treatment to patients—serious adverse effects may take longer to emerge, so may not yet be observed in studies.

These questions are extremely challenging to investigate empirically. We can use the evidence we have, as well as make logical inferences, and subjective judgments. We can explore the consequences of applying

---

15. Allison, *Resurrection,* 351.
16. Darwiche, *Modeling,*6.
17. Darwiche, *Modeling,*6.
18. Darwiche, *Modeling,*6.

different assumptions, but little more. There are potentially life changing benefits and huge risks. We want to use all the tools available to make the best judgments. Probability theory is one of these tools.

Of course, historical and theological concepts offer very different challenges. But, as we saw above, probabilities do not have to be based on objective frequencies—they can also reflect our judgments. Debates on Jesus' resurrection are informed by a range of subjective and evidential/logical judgments, as well as empirical data. Probability theory has a great track record for integrating complex sources of data.

My atheist readers have further reason for considering probabilistic approaches to Jesus' resurrection. Hume and Sagan's arguments, that all miracle claims fail, are fundamentally probabilistic. Atheists who reject assigning probabilities to historical arguments, will also have to abandon arguments that "extraordinary claims require extraordinary evidence." I think it better to explore the assumptions underlying this argument.

2.5.3 Plantinga and Dwindling Probabilities

Alvin Plantinga is another high-profile critic of Bayesian approaches. He argued probabilistic arguments for God's existence, or Jesus' resurrection, succumb to the problem of dwindling probabilities:

> The conclusion to be drawn, I think, is that K, our background knowledge, historical and otherwise (excluding what we know by way of faith or revelation), isn't anywhere nearly sufficient to support serious belief in G [generic theism]. If K were all we had to go on, the only sensible course would be agnosticism. "I don't know whether G is true or not: all I can say for sure is that it is not terribly unlikely." The main problem for such a historical case, as I see it, is what we can call the principle of dwindling probabilities: the fact that in giving such a historical argument, we can't simply annex the intermediate propositions to K (as I'm afraid many who employ this sort of argument actually do) but must instead multiply the relevant probabilities.[19]

---

19. Plantinga, *Christian Belief*, 280.

Part One: What is Extraordinary Evidence?

2.5.3.1 Points of Agreement

I agree with Plantinga that generic theism is an awkward starting point for a probabilistic argument for Jesus' resurrection (see the next section below). The principle of dwindling probabilities is also true—particularly for independent events. For example, if I assume the following probabilities for these events happening this weekend:

- it will rain ($p=0.6$);
- England will win a football match against Serbia at Euro 2024 ($p=0.6$);
- I will receive an email from a work colleague ($p=0.6$).

To estimate the probability that all three events will happen—we should multiply them. Each event, in isolation, is more likely than not. But it is unlikely they all happen ($p=0.216$).[20]

Plantinga rightly points out, the probability for Jesus' resurrection depends on the following probabilities, that must be multiplied:

- God's existence;
- that God would become human, and want to atone for our sins;
- we would observe this evidence if Jesus was resurrected.

2.5.3.2 Where Plantinga Went Wrong

In Plantinga's view when we multiply these probabilities, Jesus' resurrection must be judged unlikely (a probability somewhere between 0.21 and 0.35). But this argument proves too much:

> For this objection wouldn't undercut merely belief in the resurrection of Jesus; it would make it impossible to believe almost anything in history that was based upon a series of events.[21]

A simple illustration may help. The probability that I am a fan of Arsenal, a Premier League football (soccer) club, is based on several factors:

- I am from North London (let us say, $p=0.02$ or 2%, North London population divided by UK population);

---

20. $0.6 \times 0.6 \times 0.6 = 0.216$.
21. Craig, *Probabilities*, §4.

- my dad was an Arsenal fan; (p=0.1 or 10%, since about 30% of UK residents are football fans and Arsenal is one of the most popular teams);
- my granddad was an Arsenal fan (p=0.1 or 10%, as above).

If we assume these factors are all independent, the probability of me being an Arsenal fan is very low (p=0.0002).[22] But this ignores several dependencies including that the probability of my dad being an Arsenal fan is far higher, given that his father also supported them. Tim and Lydia McGrew point out Plantinga's argument assumed probabilities at each step remain fixed.

> Plantinga's focus on the Theorem on Total Probability is central to the whole strategy of the PDP [problem of dwindling probabilities], which can be applied only when the probabilities of all propositions are fixed. Once one allows for updating on new evidence, all bets are off, as a new set of coherent probabilities will be generated every time one updates, and the initial estimate of the probability of theism on some minimal background evidence will constitute no upper bound on the probability of either theism or Christianity after all updates have taken place and all pertinent evidence is taken into account.[23]

But to his credit, Plantinga later accepted he was mistaken:

> Therefore, Plantinga's objection based upon dwindling probabilities turns out to be misconceived. In all fairness, Plantinga agreed with McGrew's analysis and insisted that he was objecting merely to the way Swinburne had originally formulated his argument, which Plantinga thought was subject to the problem of dwindling probabilities. Swinburne in reply said that his intention was to offer a probability argument along McGrew's lines.[24]

2.6 DISAGREEMENTS ABOUT THE PRIOR

Naturalists and Christians have very different beliefs about the existence of God. In chapter 1, I argued beliefs about God have a substantial impact on the prior and posterior probabilities for miracles; for example, our overall

---

22. 0.02x0.1x0.1=0.0002.
23. McGrew and McGrew, *Resurrection*, 648.
24. Craig, *Probabilities*, §5—6.

Part One: What is Extraordinary Evidence?

judgment on whether evidence supports our hypothesis. If God's existence is close to impossible, then miracles are also close to impossible.

For Christians, who are certain of God's existence, and his ability to perform miracles, the prior probability of miracles happening is higher than assumed by naturalists. This is why people often speak past each other when discussing Jesus' resurrection. One strategy is to set aside these differences to focus on the evidence.

2.6.1 Just the Facts?

The minimal facts argument is the most popular Christian apologetic approach to the resurrection. Gary Habermas developed this almost fifty years ago.[25] William Lane Craig[26] and many other scholars (such as Mike Licona) use similar methods. The aim is to find common ground on key "facts" (e.g., Jesus was buried, his disciples reported seeing him after his death) agreed upon by the vast majority of New Testament scholars (Christians and sceptics alike). We argue from these empirical facts to the resurrection.

Tim and Lydia McGrew proposed a Bayesian solution.[27] They assessed the strength of the evidence, and how low the prior for resurrection would need to be to overturn conclusions. The McGrews argued Jesus' resurrection is close to certain even with a prior belief that resurrection is close to impossible.[28] These approaches attempt to set the prior aside to focus on the evidence in a neutral manner. There are great strengths to the minimal facts approach and the more maximal approach proposed by the McGrews. But, as Hume's example illustrates, if our prior for naturalism is close to certain, evidence is insufficient to conclude a miracle happened.

2.6.2 Theism and the Life of Jesus

Richard Swinburne, like the McGrews, proposed a Bayesian argument for Jesus' resurrection.[29] He partly based his prior on an earlier Bayesian

---

25. For example, Habermas and Licona, *Resurrection*, 43–77.
26. For example, Craig, *Reasonable Faith*, 333–404.
27. McGrew and McGrew, *Resurrection*, 593–662.
28. The prior probability of resurrection, $p(R) = 10^{-40}$.
29. E.g., Swinburne, *Resurrection*, 201–16.

argument, *The Existence of God*,[30] where he concluded theism was more likely than naturalism. However, to be conservative, Swinburne assumed equivalence[31] between these two views in his resurrection argument.

He also argued it was not unlikely God would become a human to rescue humanity and show empathy with their suffering. If so, it is likely God would raise Jesus from the dead—as a super miracle confirming Jesus' identity.

2.6.3 Starting with the Triune God

In terms of priors, Christians have two options. Swinburne and the McGrews start with generic theism. However, several Christians (e.g., Alvin Plantinga and Willian Lane Craig)[32] and atheists (e.g., Michael Martin)[33] have argued it is very difficult to justify priors for a theistic God becoming human and dying for his people.

The approach in this book will be to start with the Triune God of Scripture. I will trace this message of creation, fall, and the promise of redemption in the Hebrew Bible. If naturalism is true, we have better things to do with our time than examine evidence for the resurrection. Of course, Christianity and naturalism are not the only available options—we must also consider additional views. This is the aim of the next chapter.

---

30. Swinburne, *Existence*, 328–42.
31. Assigning prior probabilities of p(naturalism)=0.5 and p(theism)=0.5.
32. Plantinga, *Christian Belief,* 268–80; Craig, *Reasonable Faith*, 359.
33. Martin, *Resurrection*, 68.

Chapter 3

Worldviews

3.1 INTRODUCTION

I HAVE ARGUED THE nature of reality is a key component of the prior probability for Jesus' resurrection (an assessment of how probable before we have seen the evidence). Christians interpret evidence for the resurrection within the Bible's "redemptive-historical setting":[1]

> He [Paul in Acts 17] was not interested in having them endorse the Resurrection as an isolated event. He was, rather, concerned that they accept it as the climax of the work of redemption from sin by Jesus, truly God and truly man . . . [they] should not existentially accept the resurrection unless, in doing so, they received it as part of the entire biblical redemptive framework.[2]

In contrast, as we saw in Chapter 1, Hume and Sagan insist we view evidence for the resurrection from a naturalistic perspective. I sometimes hear atheists compare religion to TV channels. Religious people have various channels to pick from. Naturalists, in contrast, switch the TV off—or cancel their subscription. From this perspective, the prior probability of resurrection is prohibitively low.

However, views on reality rarely fall into binary categories. Does the *denial of a creator God* set apart naturalism from all other worldviews? Most forms of animism, Hinduism, and Buddhism share this denial. For

---

1. Tipton, *Resurrection*, 41.
2. Van Til, *I am*, 8.

Muslims, Rabbinic Jews, and Christians, God is the ultimate foundation for reality. For those who deny a creator, ultimate reality is founded on mind (e.g. Hinduism, Buddhism, animism) or the physical (naturalism).

Is naturalism unique in affirming *ethics* that vary between groups and evolve over time? Most schools of Buddhism and Hinduism also believe in the *conventional nature of morality*. Muslims, Rabbinic Jews, and Christians argue that God is the *objective foundation for morality*. Other naturalists may argue that their morality is as *objective* as any theistic versions.[3]

The nature of reality is a vital contributor to the prior probability of Jesus' resurrection. This chapter will classify naturalist and religious views on the nature of reality into five categories. Part Two will explore in more detail how well these categories account for reality.

- *physical-first*: naturalists believe the foundation for ultimate reality is physical; this category will be divided into i) *the universe is necessary* (i.e., it always existed and could not fail to exist) or ii) *contingent* (i.e. our universe did not have to exist, or it could have turned out very differently);
- *mind-first*: Hindus, Buddhists, and animists believe that ultimate reality is founded on mind;
- *unipersonal theism*: religions, such as Islam and Judaism, believe that ultimate reality is founded on a single person creator God;
- *Christianity*: Christians believe the Triune God created the world to dwell with us in personal relationship; humans are made in God's image and therefore are relational and intelligent.

3.2 CREATION BY THE FATHER, THROUGH THE WORD AND SPIRIT

The Bible does not begin with a generic theistic God: "In the very beginning, God creates by his Word . . . and he does so by sending out his Word by the power of his Spirit or Breath."[4] Psalm 33:6 is a succinct summary of Genesis 1, "By the word of the Lord the heavens were made, their starry host by the breath of his mouth." Charles Spurgeon explains:

---

3. Chapter 7 will also consider the difficulties naturalists have justifying this claim.
4. Reeves, *Good God*, 12.

Part One: What is Extraordinary Evidence?

> The angelic heavens, the sidereal [starry] heavens, and the firmament or terrestrial heavens, were all made to start into existence by a word; what if we say by *the* Word, "For without him was not anything made that is made." It is interesting to note the mention of the Spirit in the next clause, "and all the host of them by the breath of his mouth;" the word "breath" is the same as is elsewhere rendered Spirit. Thus the three persons of the Godhead unite in creating all things.[5]

Irenaeus referred to the Word and the Spirit, as the Father's "hands and feet." Of course, he did not mean that literally. Only that the Father sends the Word and the Spirit to do his will, not only at the creation of the universe, but throughout the Bible. "Therefore it was this Word, Jesus Christ, that had spoken with Adam in the garden, with the patriarchs, the prophets, the faithful in exile in Babylon, and even less salubrious characters such as Balaam."[6]

Some might see this as reading Christian doctrine back onto the Hebrew Bible. But Jewish scholar Daniel Boyarin shows the early Jewish targums (paraphrases of the Hebrew Bible in Aramaic) often referred to the Word (*Memra*) as a personal agent in creation. For example, Targum Neofiti (dated between first to fourth century): "And the Memra of H'[7] said, 'Let there be light' and there was light by his Memra."[8] Targum Neofiti continues to attribute all the creative actions of Genesis 1 to the *Memra*.

His work is not limited to creation. The targums continue to attribute the actions of the Lord (YHWH) to the *Memra* (for example, Targum Jerusalem on the destruction of Sodom in Genesis 19:24).[9] But are these works just borrowing from earlier Christian ideas? Craig Evans, Distinguished Professor of Christian Origins, argues this is unlikely:

> There is little evidence that the early interpretive traditions preserved in the targums and midrashim have been contaminated by Christian ideas. Parallels should normally be viewed as independent and not in terms of later documents (such as targums or

---

5. Spurgeon, *Treasury*, 106.
6. Reeves, *Good God*, 33.
7. H' means *HaShem*—the divine name.
8. Boyarin, *Borderlines*, 119; his translation of Genesis 1:3.
9. Targum Jerusalem, Genesis 19:24. For English translation see Etheridge, *Targums*, 217.

rabbinic writings) borrowing ideas from earlier documents (such as the New Testament).[10]

An important objection to Boyarin's argument is that *Memra* is used to avoid anthropomorphism and use of the divine name. This explains some uses. But not all. Distinctions are made in the targums between the Lord and the *Memra* of the Lord. For example, "My Word [*Memra*] loathed you just as the Lord loathed Sodom and Gomorrah" (Targum of Amos 4:11).[11] He also plays an intermediary role (e.g., Targum of Isaiah 65:1), "I [YHWH] let myself be entreated through my Word [*Memra*] by those who did not inquire of me . . . by a people who do not pray in my name."[12]

3.3 HUMANITY DWELLING WITH GOD

3.3.1 Eden and the Tabernacle

L. Michael Morales argues the goal of creation, and the plot line of the Bible, is for humanity to dwell with God.[13] This is consistent with a Trinitarian creation, where relationship is the foundation of reality. For Morales, and many other Biblical theologians,[14] this theme begins at Eden. The many parallels between Eden and the tabernacle (the prototype for Solomon's later temple) support this view (see Table 1). In addition, Ezekiel 28 calls Eden "the Garden of God", "the holy mountain of God" and "sanctuaries"—expressions used to describe the temple.[15]

Eden	Tabernacle
The Holy Spirit's role in creation (Genesis 1:2)	The Holy Spirit's role in construction (Exodus 31:3, 35:31)
The "lights" or "lamps" in the sky (Genesis 1:14–15)	The Hebrew word translated "lights" in Genesis 1, elsewhere in the Torah refers always to the lamps in the tabernacle.

---

10. Evans, *Word*, 114.
11. Evans, *Word*, 127.
12. Evans, *Word*, 128.
13. Morales, *Ascend*, 39.
14. E.g. Greg Beale.
15. Beale and Kim, *Dwells*, 18.

Eden	Tabernacle
Creation is described as like a tabernacle: e.g. "he stretches out the heavens like a tent" (Psalm 104:2, NIV)	The tabernacle literally was a tent
The presence of God: God walking in the Garden (Genesis 3:8)	God's presence described in similar ways in the tabernacle (Leviticus 26:12, Deuteronomy 23:15) and temple (2 Samuel 7:6–7)
Adam's work in Genesis 2:15, in Hebrew literally means "worship and obey," the language of a priest.	Elsewhere in the Torah, "worship and obey" is only used to describe the Levites work at the tabernacle (Numbers 3:7–8, 8:26)
Cherubim guard the way to the tree of life, after Adam and Eve are driven out of God's presence (Genesis 3:24)	Veil of the tabernacle's holy of holies embroidered with cherubim (Exodus 26:1)

Table 1. Comparing Eden and the Tabernacle/Temple

3.3.2 Humanity in the image of God and the image of Christ

A common theme in Genesis, and the rest of the Bible, is that God created humanity in his image. A comprehensive discussion of the image of God is beyond the scope of this current work.[16] I will focus on Irenaeus's perspective on the image of Christ:

> For in times long past, it was said that man was created after the image of God, but it was not [actually] shown; for the Word was as yet invisible, after whose image man was created, Wherefore also he did easily lose the similitude. When, however, the Word of God became flesh, He confirmed both these: for He both showed forth the image truly, since He became Himself what was His image; and He re-established the similitude after a sure manner, by assimilating man to the invisible Father through means of the visible Word.[17]

This likely has origins in Paul's letters, where he describes Christ as the image of God (Second Corinthians 4:4; Colossians 1:15). This is also consistent with Targum Jerusalem's paraphrase: "And the Word of the Lord [*Memra*] created man in His likeness, in the likeness of the presence of

---

16. For a more detailed summary see Cortez, *Anthropology*, 14–40.
17. Cited in Reeves, *Good God*, 20.

the Lord He created him, the male and his yoke-fellow He created them."[18] As theologian Edmund Clowney noted, even before the Fall, this points forward to Jesus, the second Adam:

> Adam, the representative man, prepares us for Christ. Christ is more than a substitute for Adam, a stand-in, as it were, to succeed where Adam failed. Christ, who is the Omega, the goal of human history and of created humanity, is also the Alpha, the true Adam, Head of the new and true humanity.[19]

Therefore, Christ's incarnation fulfilled humanity's task of bearing the image of God: "Thus it was only with the visible appearance of the true Image in the incarnation that Adam, created to be like Christ, could be perfected after the Image and Likeness."[20]

3.4 ALTERNATIVE VIEWS OF REALITY

Christianity centres on the Triune God, personal and active in creation. The universe is contingent, dependent on God for its existence. There are potentially thousands of alternative worldviews.[21] Yet most of these can be divided into four categories summarised in Table 2.

	Physical-first: necessary	Physical-first: contingent	Mind-first	Unipersonal theism	Triune theism
Worldview examples	Naturalism	Naturalism	Animism (e.g., Shintoism) Buddhism Hinduism Pantheism Panpsychism	Islam Judaism	Christianity
Existence	Necessary	Contingent	Necessary	Contingent	Contingent
Science and knowledge	Bottomless	Bottomless	Bottomless	Foundationalist	Foundationalist

18. Etheridge, *Targums*, 160.
19. Clowney, *Christ*, 22.
20. Reeves, *Glory*, 20.
21. Barrett, *Encyclopedia*, 1–12.

	Physical-first: necessary	Physical-first: contingent	Mind-first	Unipersonal theism	Triune theism
Suffering	Indifference	Indifference	Indifference or illusion	Semi-personal loving God	Personal loving God
Good and Evil	Bottomless morality	Bottomless morality	Bottomless morality	Foundationalist morality	Foundationalist morality

Table 2 Comparison between four worldview categories and Christianity

3.4.1 Physical-First

According to naturalists, there is no creator God. The universe is founded on matter and/or energy. For example, naturalists "suppose that the fundamental external relation is spatiotemporal."[22] Reductive physicalism, is a common form of naturalism which posits all reality reduces to the physical. Non-reductive physicalists distinguish between the physical and mental—yet the physical is fundamental.

Philosopher Graham Oppy proposed a further distinction among physical-first views (see Box 3)—that our universe is necessary (it is eternal or that there were eternal initial states[23]) or contingent.[24]

> **BOX 3. GRAHAM OPPY'S NATURALIST OPTIONS FOR CAUSAL REALITY**
>
> Regress
>
> "Causal reality does not have an initial maximal part."[25] In other words, our universe exists necessarily.

---

22. Oppy, *Naturalistic*, 2.

23. This means there are initial states (such as the law of gravity) which necessarily lead to the development of our universe.

24. Oppy, *Naturalistic*, 10.

25. Oppy, *Naturalistic*, 3.

> **BOX 3. GRAHAM OPPY'S NATURALIST OPTIONS FOR CAUSAL REALITY**
>
> ### Necessary Initial Part
>
> "Causal reality has an initial maximal part, and it is not possible that causal reality had any other initial maximal part."[26] This option only requires that the initial part of our universe is necessary. The rest of the universe is not fully determined.
>
> ### Contingent Initial Part
>
> "Causal reality has an initial maximal part, but it is possible that causal reality had some other initial maximal part."[27] Neither the universe, nor initial parts, are necessary.

3.4.2 Mind-First

The Hindu *Advaita Vedanta* school posits that mind is the foundation for ultimate reality: "the truth which underlies everything and is its essence is also identical with [our] own self (atman). This truth or self is the life force (brahman) within both the world and humanity."[28] For the famous Vendantin philosopher Shankar, "atman [self] was really none other than brahman [God]. There was no plurality of consciousness or being. It was all one."[29] In contrast, the *Dvaita Vedanta* school of Hinduism (founded by Madhva), distinguishes between Vishnu, the universe, and other gods:

> Brahman and atman were not identical. What is more, he [Madhva] saw the selves as different from one another, and from the world. Even within the world, he understood phenomena to be

---

26. Oppy, *Naturalistic*, 3.
27. Oppy, *Naturalistic*, 3.
28. Knott, *Hinduism*, 25.
29. Knott, *Hinduism*, 28.

distinct. Everything existed within the will of the supreme Lord while maintaining its own particularity.[30]

Shintoism considers finite gods to be the foundation for ultimate reality. There is no absolute creator God—but many finite gods, "The creative function of the world is realized through the harmonious cooperation of the kami [gods]."[31] Humans, although dependent on kami, are also kami[32] along with many other aspects of nature like trees, rivers, and mountains.[33] The movies of Hayao Miyazaki (Studio Ghibli) offer an immersive experience of such a world.

> Perhaps the most illuminative representation of this agency is the kodama, the numerous spirit-like beings that appear in Princess Mononoke. They express "something unseen" that exists in the forest, symbolising the spiritual-world in nature . . . By "something unseen", Miyazaki is not referring to so-called supernatural phenomena but to life itself in nature. To perceive in nature not only the spiritual world but also usually unseen life is at the core of the definition of animism.[34]

Similarly, Mahayana Buddhism, "accepts the existence of many heavenly Buddhas, spread throughout the worlds of the vast universe. None of these is seen to have created the universe."[35]

3.4.3 Unipersonal Theism

Another category of worldview is belief in a single person creator God as the foundation for ultimate reality. Common examples include Judaism and Islam. Unipersonal theists often exhibit an ambivalence between personal and impersonal perspectives on God. For example, medieval Jewish scholar Maimonides (Rambam) asserted: "How, then, could there be any relation between God and His creatures, considering the important difference between them in respect to true existence, the greatest of all differences."[36]

30. Knott, *Hinduism*, 30.
31. Ono, *Shinto*, 8.
32. Although this title is usually reserved for when they die.
33. Ono, *Shinto*, 103.
34. Yoneyama, *Miyazaki Animism*, 253.
35. Harvey, *Buddhism*, 4.
36. Maimonides, *Perplexed*, 72.

Although God is loving in Islam and Judaism, he is not fundamentally relational since there was a time when there was no other beings. As theologian Mike Reeves points out, love requires another person. It is possible to love oneself. But love is ultimately expressed in relationship: "But how could Allah be loving in eternity? Before he created there was nothing else in existence that he could love (and the title does not refer to self-centred love but love of others)."[37] Allah shows his love by his care for his people. However, this leads to a problem. He potentially becomes dependent on creation to be who he is.

3.5 CONCLUSION

The nature of reality is a key determinant of the prior probability (i.e., the plausibility before assessing the evidence) for Jesus' resurrection. This chapter has introduced five views on the nature of reality:

- physical-first (necessary);
- physical-first (contingent);
- unipersonal theism;
- Christianity;
- mind-first.

Part Two will compare how these worldviews account for our universe's existence, the success of science, suffering, and evil.

---

37. Reeves, *Good God*, 22.

PART TWO

The Nature of Reality

RECAP FROM PART ONE

"EXTRAORDINARY CLAIMS REQUIRE EXTRAORDINARY *evidence*" *is a phrase frequently heard in discussions between Christians and naturalists on the resurrection. But what does it really mean? David Hume's approach to miracles likely inspired this famous slogan. His basic criteria are reasonable, but his conclusions depend on the assumption that the laws of nature cannot be impacted by anything external to the universe (i.e., naturalism). In other words, the validity of Hume's denial of miracles depends on whether naturalism is true. Therefore, the nature of reality is a key determinant of the prior for miracles. This is the focus of Part Two. Part One proposed five worldview categories:*

- *physical-first (necessary): ultimate reality is founded on the physical which has always existed and cannot fail to exist; a common example is naturalism (e.g., reductive and non-reductive physicalism)*
- *physical-first (contingent): as above, but this view considers our universe's existence was not inevitable;*
- *unipersonal theism: there is a single person God that created our universe; examples include Islam and Judaism;*
- *Christianity: the Triune God (Father, Son, and Holy Spirit) created our universe; we are relational beings created by an eternally relational God;*
- *mind-first: there is no creator God, but many finite gods (e.g., Hinduism, Buddhism, animism).*

Part Two: The Nature of Reality

INTRODUCTION TO PART TWO

The goal of Part Two is to assess how well each worldview accounts for the nature of reality—a key determinant of the prior probability for Jesus' resurrection (see Box 4). I will compare the internal coherence of the five worldviews discussed in Part One and how well they account for the existence of the universe, success of science, evil, and suffering.

BOX 4. SUMMARY OF PART TWO

Chapter 4. The existence of the universe. The likelihood that the universe had a beginning or is past eternal; probability of the universe emerging from nothing.

Chapter 5. Intelligibility and the success of science. Naturalism and subtraction stories; Draper's argument for naturalism from the success of science; Christianity and the history of science; bottomless nature of reasoning in physical-first and mind-first worldviews.

Chapter 6. Suffering and Evil I. Christianity: how the fall accounts for suffering and evil, the hope of a redeemer; unipersonal theism: suffering and evil; naturalism: Draper's evidential argument for naturalism from suffering, logical problem of evil; Buddhism and Hinduism: views on suffering.

Chapter 7. Suffering and Evil II. physical-first, mind-first views, and evil; unipersonal theism and evil; Christianity and evil.

Chapter 8. Conclusion. Comparing internal coherence and how well each worldview is consistent with our reality. This is an important driver for the prior probability of Jesus' resurrection.

Chapter 4

Existence of the Universe

4.1 INTRODUCTION

THE PURPOSE OF THIS chapter is not to prove God's existence, or to prove that he created the universe. I do not think we can prove this empirically or mathematically. It is equally impossible to demonstrate the universe has always existed, or that there were eternal initial conditions. Yet it is possible to compare how well these competing models are consistent with current data.

As I argued in chapter 3, views on the existence of the universe do not separate into simple binary categories. Naturalists, Buddhists, Hindus, and animists all reject the distinction between creature and creator. For example, sociologist Shoko Yoneyama cites a scene from Miyazaki's *Nausicaa* challenging the idea of a creator God. Nausicaa confronts a monotheistic God-like figure:

> 'A life is a life, regardless of how it comes into being . . . Every life form, no matter how small, contains the outside universe within its internal universe' . . . These lines crystallize Miyazaki's animism based on the oneness of life, nature, and spirit/soul (*tamashii*).[1]

Bill Bryson makes a similar argument about the oneness of life from the perspective of naturalism:

> Every atom you possess has almost certainly passed through several stars and been part of millions of organisms on its way to

---

1. Yoneyama, *Miyazaki Animism*, 253.

becoming you. We are each so atomically numerous and so vigorously recycled at death that a significant number of our atoms—up to a billion for each of us, it has been suggested—probably once belonged to Shakespeare. A billion more each came from Buddha and Genghis Khan and Beethoven, and any other historical figure you care to name.[2]

Most physical-first and mind-first views posit that our universe exists necessarily. They are also compatible with belief in the cyclical nature of life. This chapter will consider two main questions:

- Is the past more likely to be finite or eternal?
- Is there evidence the universe can emerge from nothing?

You may be wondering what these questions have to do with Jesus' resurrection? It comes back to prior probabilities. If our universe has always existed, or emerged from nothing, then God did not create the universe. If so, the prior probability (i.e., before we look at the evidence) for Jesus' resurrection is prohibitively low.

4.2 EVIDENCE FOR A FINITE PAST

George Ellis, a cosmologist, has shown an eternal universe is mathematically possible.[3] However, he conceded these are toy models, not intended to reflect reality. In addition, they do not imply an eternal universe is testable or plausible:

> In any case it is not possible to prove that the universe as a whole, or even the part of the universe in which we live, is past infinite; observations cannot do so, and the physics required to guarantee this would happen (if initial conditions were right) is untestable.[4]

There is good reason to think an eternal universe is unlikely. First, the expanding nature of the universe has often been interpreted as evidence for a past finite universe. Various models including the Penrose-Hawking Singularity Theorem and Borde-Guth-Vilenkin Theorem suggest the universe began from an initial singularity:

---

2. Bryson, *Everything*, 304.
3. Ellis, *Cosmology*, § 2.7.1.
4. Ellis, *Cosmology*, § 9.3.2

if the average expansion rate is positive along a given world line, or geodesic, then this geodesic must terminate after a finite amount of time... The volume of the universe increases with time. Inflation cannot be eternal and must have some sort of a beginning.[5]

Cosmic background radiation is also consistent with the universe beginning from a very dense state and expanding to its current size. The singularity suggested by the standard model of the Big Bang has troubled many physicists. It seems to rule out an impersonal explanation, it is too suggestive of an external cause. Is there a way around this—a universe out of nothing? Physicists have proposed several options without a singularity. I will focus here on the Hartle-Hawking (HH) model (see Box 5). But most criticisms will apply to other options.

BOX 5. SUMMARY OF THE HARTLE-HAWKING MODEL[6]

Basic assumptions:

- particles (e.g., electrons) do not take a single path from one point to another in space-time—they take all possible paths connecting these points; this is consistent with quantum mechanics;
- many possible universes—a wave function summing across "histories" of all possible universes estimating the probability of our universe;
- A state (S) when (or shortly after) the universe switches over from the quantum scale to the expanding state predicted by the standard big bang model and general relativity (GR).

---

5. Vilenken, *Beginning*, §4
6. For further details see Hutchings, *Hawking*, 129–36.

> **BOX 5. SUMMARY OF THE HARTLE-HAWKING MODEL**[6]
>
> The HH model successfully meets its aims:
>
> - a gravitational field consistent with GR;
> - the wave function for the universe (although a simplified version) does not collapse;
> - the universe reaches the point S where it begins to expand without the need for a singularity.

4.3 HARTLE-HAWKING (HH) MODEL

4.3.1 Not a Universe from Nothing

Neither the HH, nor any other model, has shown the universe came from nothing. Unless we redefine the meaning of nothing. For example, the HH, and other quantum gravity models, assume the laws of physics were operating before inflation began. George Ellis's critique of Laurence Krauss's book *A Universe From Nothing* applies to most attempts to remove the initial singularity:

> And above all Krauss does not address why the laws of physics exist, why they have the form they have, or in what kind of manifestation they existed before the universe existed (which he must believe if he believes they brought the universe into existence). Who or what dreamt up symmetry principles, Lagrangians, specific symmetry groups, gauge theories, and so on? He does not begin to answer these questions.[7]

4.3.2 Further Problems

The HH, and other quantum gravity models, use imaginary time (or imaginary numbers) to cancel out infinities predicted by GR. The transformation makes the singularity disappear. A pragmatic solution, but this comes at a

---

7. Horgan, *George Ellis*, lines 84–89.

cost.[8] The HH model no longer reflects Einstein's theory. Back transforming to reflect our universe[9] leads to the reappearance of the singularity.[10]

Leonard Susskind, professor of theoretical physics at Stanford, identified a further problem. The HH model predicts a near empty universe:

> the cosmological constant or quintessence or dark energy that is the source of the present observations of the cosmic acceleration would give a large Euclidean 4-hemisphere as an extremum of the Hartle–Hawking path integral that would apparently swamp the extremum from rapid early inflation. Therefore, to very high probability, the present universe should be very nearly empty de Sitter spacetime, which is certainly not what we observe.[11]

The HH model works well in simplified "toy universe" scenarios. However, in more realistic situations it is inconsistent with empirical data.[12] According to Graham Oppy, "there is no reason at all to think that "the Hartle-Hawking cosmology" has dramatic consequences for classical theism (or for any other kind of religious belief)."[13]

4.4 A FINITE PAST, FINE-TUNING, AND AN EXTERNAL CAUSE

Current data suggests (although not definitively) a finite past is likely. Therefore, even atheist philosopher, Paul Draper, concedes this makes an external cause more plausible.[14] Recent research has shown the standard models of particle physics and cosmology contain thirty-one fundamental constants that mean a life-permitting universe is only possible within a very narrow range of values:

> if gravity were repulsive, matter wouldn't clump into complex structures. In a universe of Newtonian gravitating masses (with no other forces), unless the initial conditions are exquisitely fine-tuned, collections of particles either exhibit boring periodic

---

8. Using imaginary time, transforms the model from Lorentzian spacetime (reflective of our universe) to Euclidean space (not reflective of our universe).
9. Lorentzian spacetime.
10. Hutchings, *Hawking*, 134.
11. Page, *Susskind*, 2.
12. Hutchings and Wilkinson, *Hawking*, 168–71.
13. Oppy, *Gods*, 167.
14. Draper, *Confessions*, 200.

motion or unstable chaotic motion, but not the kind of complexity of arrangement required by life.[15]

Cosmologist Luke Barnes's Bayesian model estimates the probability of a life permitting universe, given naturalism, to be close to impossible (1 in 10–136). Of course, naturalists have not yet conceded! The anthropic principle (or the puddle argument) is a popular response.[16] Douglas Adams, a science fiction writer, provided a nice illustration:

> If you imagine a puddle waking up one morning and thinking, "This is an interesting world I find myself in—an interesting hole I find myself in—fits me rather neatly, doesn't it? In fact it fits me staggeringly well, must have been made to have me in it!"[17]

The only evidence of a life-permitting universe is that we exist. So there is a selection effect. We would not be alive to observe another kind of universe. However, this criticism misunderstands fine-tuning. The aim of the argument is not to confirm that we exist—we all know that! The point is that life is possible only within a narrow range of values for fundamental physical constants. Therefore, given these narrow constants, the probability of a life-permitting universe emerging by chance is extremely low.[18]

But what if there was a multiverse? Our universe would be just one of innumerable universes. Life-permitting universes are less surprising. Arguments for the multiverse are often exposited in the language of modern physics and mathematics. Yet they go back to at least ancient Greece (fifth

---

15. Barnes, *Fine Tuning*, 1231.

16. There are, of course, many other objections to fine-tuning arguments. For in depth responses to these objections see for example Barnes, *Fine Tuning*, 4:2; Isaacs, *Fine Tuning*, 136–68.

17. Adams, *Doubt*, 131.

18. For the mathematically minded I am talking about two distinct conditional probabilities:
 a) The probability of narrow physical constants given our life-permitting universe: $p(NC|LP)$—since we and our universe exist, and we observe evidence of narrow physical constants, the probability is close to certain. This is the puddle argument.
 b) The probability of a life permitting universe given narrow physical constants: $p(LP|NC)$—since life is only possible within a very narrow range of physical constants, life permitting universes are only a very small subset of possible universes, therefore the probability of a life permitting universe emerging by chance is extremely low. This is fine tuning.

century BCE). Despite the passage of time, these theories remain impossible to test empirically.[19]

Our atheist friends may counter that fine tuning implies a multiverse. However, this may be an instance of the inverse gambler's fallacy.[20] An example of a rare event—I have seen a black swan—may help illustrate. In the UK (where I live), there are perhaps only nine or ten breeding pairs. As Nassim Taleb points out, "Before the discovery of Australia, people in the Old World were convinced that *all* swans were white, an unassailable belief."[21] You may argue, this rare observation is evidence that I have seen many thousands of swans. You may hypothesise that I travel the world searching for them. If so, you would be wrong.

The fact I have witnessed a black swan does not inform how many other swans I have observed. To suppose so is to commit the inverse gambler's fallacy. I withheld an important piece of information. I used to work at the University of York (in the UK)—where a male black swan was a famous resident!

4.5 SUMMARY AND CONCLUSIONS

The most plausible physical-first and mind-first explanations for the universe require assumptions about its necessity. In one sense, this leads to irrationalism.[22] Since this an assumption held despite, rather than because of, current data. In another sense, physical-first and mind-first explanations of the universe are rationalistic. For example, methodological naturalists insist science requires we act as if there is nothing but the physical, even if we do not know whether that reflects reality. To defend the eternality of the universe, or initial states, is not only to defend a theory but the integrity of science.

In summary, it is plausible that our universe had a beginning (i.e., the past does not extend into infinity). It is more likely to have had an external cause, therefore Christianity and unipersonal theism are the most likely explanations for the existence of the universe. The scientific argument is far from settled, yet evidence supporting a past eternal universe is currently lacking. In other words, there are reasons to consider physical-first

19. Ellis, *Multiverse*, §3.
20. For further details, see Goff, *Multiverse*, 1–22.
21. Taleb, *Black Swans*, xxi.
22. Frame, *Apologetics*, 192.

Part Two: The Nature of Reality

(necessary) and mind-first views as implausible accounts of our universe. If the universe is contingent, an external cause is far more plausible. Evidence of fine tuning makes the existence of our universe close to impossible if physical-first or mind-first views are true.

The next chapter will consider the intelligibility of the universe. The success of science suggests we can have genuine, if limited, knowledge about the world. What does this suggest about the nature of reality?

Chapter 5

Intelligibility and the Success of Science

5.1 INTRODUCTION

ACCORDING TO SUBTRACTION STORIES, the success of science is evidence for naturalism. As we began to study our universe, supernatural explanations were increasingly replaced by scientific theories:

> Once upon a time, as these subtraction stories rehearse it, we believed in spirits and fairies and gods and demons. But as we become rational, and especially as we marshaled naturalist explanations for what we used to attribute to spirits and forces, the world became progressively disenchanted. Religion and belief withered with scientific exorcism of superstition.[1]

In contrast, for centuries many have considered the success of science evidence for Christianity, others support for unipersonal theism. The intelligibility of the universe is consistent with a rational God, who created an ordered universe. It is expected that his image bearers can explore reality using scientific methods.

The success of science is so extensive, most of us take for granted that knowledge is possible. Yet, as Albert Einstein pointed out: "the world of our sense experience is comprehensible. The fact that it is comprehensible is a miracle."[2] Another Nobel prize-winning physicist, Eugene Wigner, spoke

---

1. Smith, *Secular*, 24.
2. Einstein, *Physics*, 351.

of the "unreasonable effectiveness of mathematics." The laws of nature are written in the language of mathematics:

> However, it is important to point out that the mathematical formulation of the physicist's often crude experience leads in an uncanny number of cases to an amazingly accurate description of a large class of phenomena. This shows that the mathematical language has more to commend it than being the only language which we can speak; it shows that it is, in a very real sense, the correct language.[3]

I will compare how well each of the five worldview categories account for an intelligible universe. This chapter will consider the following topics:

- Draper's argument for naturalism from the success of science;
- naturalism and the validity of reasoning;
- Christian theological assumptions and the scientific method;
- mind-first views and knowledge.

5.2 DRAPER'S ARGUMENT: PART ONE

Draper's argument retains key elements of the subtraction narrative—but is more nuanced. First, he assumed theistic religions (such as Christianity), and the laws of nature, are competing explanations:

> Thus, because the natural sciences have established that the nomic regularities we call the laws of nature operate, not just here and now, but everywhere and always, it follows that the claim that God acts in the world, though not absolutely ruled out by science since it is possible that violations of laws of nature occur undetected by science, is nevertheless strongly disconfirmed.[4]

However, this argument conflicts with the history of science. For example, Harrison points out arguments like Draper's assume: "an unproblematic distinction can be drawn between "natural" and "supernatural", and that this distinction was routinely operative in the history of science. This turns out to be mistaken."[5] Draper seems to compare naturalism with

3. Wigner, *Mathematics*, 5.
4. Draper, *Science*, 281.
5. Harrison, *Naturalism*, 275.

a "god-of-the-gaps." Where god explains parts of the universe we cannot understand. As our scientific knowledge progresses, and these gaps narrow, the need for god disappears:

> given that natural phenomena typically do have explanations—the fact that so much in nature is known to have a naturalistic explanation (and no part of nature that could have a naturalistic explanation is known not to have one) strongly supports metaphysical naturalism over theism.[6]

However, Christians do not believe in a god-of-the-gaps. Therefore, this argument is uncompelling to us.

5.2.1 History of Science Challenges the Subtraction Story

Before moving onto the next stage of Draper's argument, we will pause to reflect further on how the history of science challenges the first part of his thesis. If Christian and scientific explanations are competing accounts, it is surprising that modern science emerged in Western Europe—a culture immersed in over 1500 years of Christian thought. "Although science has a long history with roots in ancient Egypt and Mesopotamia, it is indisputable that modern science emerged in the seventeenth century in Western Europe and nowhere else."[7]

Some have tried to argue the rise of science was an inevitability—it just happened to occur in Western Europe. However, Edward Grant, a leading historian on the origins of science, argued Christianity was a key factor—along with the discovery of Aristotle's works, and the rise of medieval universities. Latin Christianity provided:

> a sympathetic environment for the sustenance and advance of natural philosophy and science. It posed few obstacles to their practice and development. In fact, by allowing natural philosophy to form the graduate curriculum in the medieval universities, medieval Christianity showed that it was prepared to do more than merely tolerate its existence. It actively promoted natural philosophy in an open and public way.[8]

---

6. Draper, *Science*, 299–300.
7. Grant, *Science*, 168.
8. Grant, *Science*, 184.

Islamic centres of learning preserved and translated Aristotle's texts. They were also responsible for significant advances in mathematics. But it was only in Western Europe that science flourished. Grant argued this is partly explained by the uneasy relationship between "natural philosophers" and theologians in Islamic societies.[9] Harrison points out Christianity's unique balance of scepticism and optimism about knowledge was key to the development of modern science:

> [an] apparently pessimistic assessment was combined with a remarkable optimism about what could be achieved if limited human capabilities were acknowledged . . . It is thus the recognition of the radically circumscribed nature of human knowledge that has made possible the advances of modern science.[10]

5.3 DRAPER'S ARGUMENT: PART TWO

Draper's "methodological" argument is also problematic. He argued naturalism has an advantage over supernaturalism because of its testability. Since supernatural explanations are untestable, they are unjustifiable.[11] This argument uses several technical words, summarised in Box 6.

BOX 6. KEY DEFINITIONS USED IN DRAPER'S ARGUMENT FROM THE SUCCESS OF SCIENCE

- supernatural: "x is not a part of nature but can effect nature"[12]
- methodological naturalism: "scientists should not appeal to supernatural entities when they explain natural phenomena."[13]
- metaphysical naturalism: "supernatural entities do not exist."[14]

---

9. Grant, *Science*, 176–86.
10. Harrison, *Science*, 249.
11. Draper, *Science*, 292.
12. Draper, Science, 277.
13. Draper, *Science*, 279.
14. Draper, *Science*, 279.

I agree with Draper that we cannot test, at least directly, supernatural explanations. But he offered no justification that naturalism is testable. Similarly, proponents of methodological naturalism assume it is straightforward to distinguish between "natural" and "supernatural". As we observed above, these distinctions depend on beliefs about the nature of reality. Draper appears to conflate methodological naturalism with the "procedures of science."[15]

> the success of science in providing naturalistic explanations of natural phenomena strengthens the presumption of naturalism and so helps to support a modest methodological naturalism. More important, though, it strongly supports metaphysical naturalism over both supernaturalism in general and theism in particular.[16]

Peter Harrison, professor of the history and philosophy of science, wryly observed that arguments for naturalism from the success of science lack historical reflection: "The twentieth century witnessed the final stages of the secularisation of scientific knowledge, along with the development of a degree of historical amnesia about the role of religion in its early modern origins."[17] The scientific method involves the use of empirical data to test hypotheses using logic and maths. The success of these methods is evidence for the success of the procedures of science. It does not provide evidence for either the validity or testability of methodological naturalism.

5.4 FURTHER PROBLEMS FOR DRAPER'S ARGUMENT

Draper argues the success of science (SS) is more likely given naturalism (N) than for the success of science given Christianity (C).[18] However, there is a complication. His argument assumes intelligibility (I)[19] as background knowledge.[20] On one hand, this is understandable, because our experience supports that the universe is intelligible. However, this can lead to

---

15. Dawes, *Naturalism*, 7.
16. Draper, *Science*, 299.
17. Harrison, *Science*, 245.
18. $p(SS|N) > p(SS|C)$.
19. Lowder, *Science*, §3.
20. Therefore his argument is actually: $p(SS|N\&I) > p(SS|C\&I)$. That is, the probability of the success of science, assuming naturalism is true, and that the universe is intelligible, is greater than the probability of the success of science assuming Christianity is true, and that the universe is intelligible.

a problem called confounding (see Figure 2).[21] If the intelligibility of the universe is more likely, given Christianity, failing to consider these differences leads to a bias that favors naturalism. This is a significant limitation, since intelligibility of the universe is a key factor in the success of science.

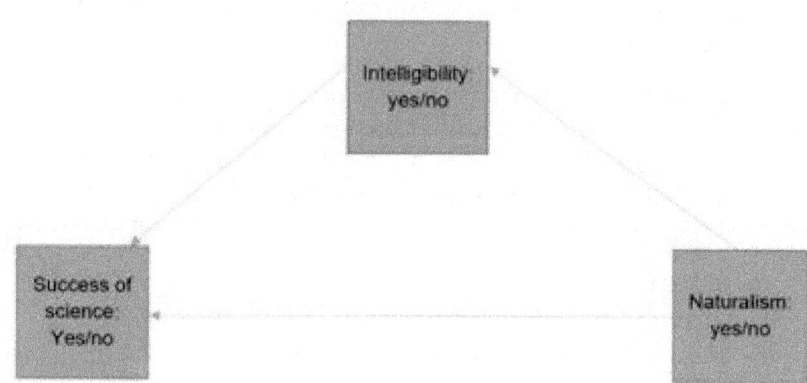

Figure 2. Intelligibility as a confounder of the association between naturalism and the success of science

5.5 WORLDVIEW AND SCIENCE

As we have seen, both naturalists and Christians claim the success of science is support for their views. This section explores the extent to which various worldviews are consistent with the assumptions of the scientific method.

5.5.1 Naturalism and Reason

One of the foundational assumptions of the scientific method is the objective validity of reason.[22] We distinguish truth from opinion by empirical methods—the testing of our hypotheses, or models, with data from our

---

21. Confounding is where the association between two factors (here, success of science and naturalism) is distorted by a third factor (here, intelligibility)—which is associated with both factors. Confounding can have a profound impact on conclusions, so cannot be ignored.

22. For example, if your argument includes a logical contradiction it does not matter whether the rest of the world is persuaded by this argument. It is simply wrong.

world. If scientists disagree on how to interpret the data, reason is the final arbiter. Thomas Nagel, an atheist professor of philosophy, identified a key challenge for naturalistic accounts of reasoning:

> It is not enough to be able to think that if there are logical truths, natural selection might very well have given me the capacity to recognize them. That cannot be my ground for trusting my reason, because even that thought implicitly relies on reason in a prior way . . . Therefore any evolutionary account of the place of reason presupposes reason's validity and cannot confirm it without circularity.[23]

Nagel pointed out that the validity of our reasoning requires important assumptions:

- there are objective truths (such as scientific laws, necessary truths of logic and maths);
- we can use reason to develop justified beliefs about some of these objective truths.

However, there are currently no viable naturalistic theories to justify these assumptions:

> Such an explanation would complete the pursuit of intelligibility by showing how the natural order is disposed to generate beings capable of comprehending it. But the obstacles seem enormous. In light of the remarkable character of reason, it is hard to imagine what a naturalistic explanation of it, either constitutive or historical, could look like.[24]

Nagel is hopeful that a viable naturalistic account of reasoning will be developed in the future. Antonio Ramos Diaz, a Christian philosopher, is less optimistic. His adaptation of the Kripke-Ross argument (KRA), suggests a naturalistic account of formal logic and mathematics is impossible.[25]

---

23. Nagel, *Mind*, 80–81.
24. Nagel, *Mind*, 86.
25. Ramos Diaz, *Understanding*, i.

5.5.2 Christianity, Unipersonal Theism, and the Intelligibility of the Universe

If the Triune God is our creator, we expect the universe to display order and regularity. "It is, therefore, not surprising when the mathematical theories spun by human minds created in the image of God's Mind, find ready application in a universe whose architect was that same creative Mind."[26] According to James Anderson, the possibility of human knowledge is grounded in God's perfect knowledge:

> if God exists, then presumably he is able to so arrange things that the noetic faculties of human beings function in such a way as to implicitly take into account all that God alone knows. The idea is not that each one of us has an exhaustive knowledge of the universe tacitly built, as it were, into our cognitive apparatus. Rather, it is that—to use a motoring metaphor—we have been given reliable vehicles and set off in the right direction on accurately signposted, well-constructed and well-connected roads.[27]

Alvin Plantinga, Professor Emeritus of Philosophy, ties this argument to our creation in the image of God.[28] Christian theology provides a unique combination of scepticism and optimism about human knowledge.[29] Peter Harrison showed Christian theological assumptions were key to the development of experimental science. Ian Shaw, in a review of Harrison's book, summarises the argument:

> For him [Francis Bacon—a pioneer of modern science] "by far the greatest hindrances and aberration of the human mind proceeds from the dullness, incompetency, and deceptions of the senses." They fail in two ways in that "sometimes they provide no information, sometimes they provide false information." He saw the answer as lying in "experimentation", "For the subtlety of experiments is far greater than that of the sense itself."[30]

These arguments also partly apply to unipersonal theism. If Judaism or Islam are true, we would also expect a rational ordered creation—that is intelligible.

26. Lennox, *Science*, 62
27. Anderson, *Knowledge*, 20.
28. Plantinga, *Conflict*, 268.
29. Harrison, *Science*, 184.
30. Harrison, Review of *Science*, lines 59–63.

5.5.3 Mind-First Views and Knowledge

Objective knowledge consists of facts about the world we discover, rather than invent. If such knowledge exists, its validity is independent from the opinions of you or me. Mind-first views often lead to scepticism about objective knowledge. Buddhism's concept of two truths (conventional and ultimate truth) is a good example.

Buddhists often use the analogy of a mirage.[31] Refraction patterns of light rays can give the impression of seeing water or sky. But these perceptions are ultimately deceptive—there is no water or sky. The mirage represents conventional truth—how we perceive reality. Our perceptions feel real to us and hence, for Buddhists, are a source of truth. But these "truths" are ultimately deceptive—like the mirage—they are empty. Ultimate truth is emptiness, "To be empty of inherent existence is to exist only conventionally, only as the object of conventional truth."[32] Conventional truth—in all its deceptiveness is all we have—which is the ultimate truth.

As we saw above (section 3.4.2), the Hindu *Advaita Vedanta* school posits a similar distinction between ultimate reality (*brahman*) and the reality we often perceive. For example, it appears to me that I am a distinct person, among billions of other humans on this planet. However, this experience is viewed as ultimately illusory. True wisdom is understanding that all reality is oneness—*atman* (self) is *brahman* (God).[33]

5.6 CONCLUSION

Christianity and unipersonal theism are consistent with an intelligible universe, and therefore the success of science. However, if naturalism is true, there are important reasons to doubt if the universe would be intelligible. Both physical-first and mind-first views have difficulty accounting for objective knowledge.

---

31. Garfield, *Buddhism*, 240.
32. Garfield, *Buddhism*, 240.
33. Knott, *Hinduism*, 28.

Chapter 6

Suffering and Evil I

6.1 INTRODUCTION

NATURALISTS BELIEVE THERE IS no benevolent creator.[1] We are alone, in an unforgiving and impersonal world.

> The real world is utterly indifferent to us, and even to a certain degree dangerous, threatening. As children, we have to see ourselves as surrounded by love and concern, or we shrivel up. But in growing up, we have to learn to face the fact that this environment of concern can't extend beyond the human sphere, and mostly doesn't extend very far within it . . . religion emanates from a childish lack of courage. We need to stand up like men, and face reality.[2]

Suffering and evil challenge theistic worldviews. In our desire to vindicate God, we can become defensive. We sometimes unwittingly deny the reality of suffering, or shame the hurting:

> A too benign picture of the human condition leaves something crucial out, something that matters to us. There is a dark side to creation . . . along with joy, there is massive innocent suffering; and then on top of this, the suffering is denied, the story of the victims is distorted, eventually forgotten, never rectified or compensated.[3]

---

1. To be more precise, metaphysical naturalists believe there is no benevolent creator. Methodological naturalists act as if there is no benevolent creator, until "proved" otherwise.
2. Taylor, *Secular*, 561.
3. Taylor, *Secular*, 319.

Jesus sweating blood and tears at Gethsemane, his cry of dereliction on the cross, his gentleness to sufferers, suggests a different narrative. God does not need us to vindicate him. Although Jesus had the riches of heaven "yet for your sake, he became poor, so that you through his poverty might become rich" (Second Corinthians 8:9).

Hindus and Buddhists find other solutions to the problem of suffering as we will see later. As with the existence of the universe (chapter 4), and success of science (chapter 5), the aim is for us to explore the prior probability of Jesus' resurrection. This chapter will assess:

- Christian perspectives on suffering;
- unipersonal theist perspectives on suffering;
- the logical argument from suffering;
- Draper's evidential argument for naturalism;
- Hindu and Buddhist perspectives on suffering.

6.2 CHRISTIAN PERSPECTIVES ON SUFFERING

6.2.1 The Fall and the Hiddenness of God

Many arguments from suffering or evil target generic theism. However, as philosopher Eleonore Stump points out, most people do not identify as generic theists. It is important to understand suffering and evil within the context of a more complete set of Christian beliefs: "because what appears inconsistent if we take a partial sampling of beliefs may in fact look consistent when set in the context of a more complete set of beliefs."[4]

Genesis begins at the heights of Eden. Perfect relationship within the Trinity overflows into creation. People are made for relationship with God in a good world. Yet, the rest of the book is a downward trajectory into exile and death: "Broadly, Genesis moves from the life-giving Presence of God in Eden (Gen. 2–3) to the death and burial of Joseph in Egypt (Gen. 50:26)—that is, from the heights of Eden upon the mountain of God down to Sheol, the grave."[5]

Genesis 1–2 defines good in the context of relationship with a faithful and generous God (Genesis 1:31). Love, relationship, and beauty are good

---

4. Stump, *Evil*, 399–400.
5. Morales, *Ascend*, 49.

because they reflect the goodness of God: "Not only is the man who is an island—Descartes' isolated cogito—ruled out from creation itself, but this particular differentiation is integral to our correspondence with God and so the very existence of creation."[6]

God gives Adam and Eve the responsibility to choose between good (to trust and obey God's word) and evil (to go their own way): "Whilst it is good to obey God, and evil not to obey God, Adam chose, in disobedience to God, to obtain his own, immediate knowledge of good and evil."[7] Genesis 3 places the origin of suffering and evil[8] in human rebellion. "Movement away from God is therefore understood as the descent away from life (creation) toward death (chaos); and conversely, movement toward God is expressed as ascent from death to life."[9] This pattern of humanity driven from the presence of God is repeated within Genesis. Chapters 2–11 move from Eden to Noah's flood, then to scattering after the tower of Babylon. Chapters 12–50 move from the land of Canaan promised to Abraham to exile in Egypt.[10]

6.2.2 The Limits of our Understanding

The doctrine of the fall explains how suffering and evil fits into the Christian story. Yet questions remain, "Cannot God display his power without contradicting his goodness? Cannot God display his name without making little babies suffer pain? . . . Does the God displayed, then, become less than our God of love?"[11] We do not have complete answers to these and many other questions:

> given the limitlessness of God's intellect and the finitude of ours, the mysteriousness of evil in our world is just what we might expect; it is reasonable to suppose that we cannot understand why an omniscient and omnipotent entity does what he does.[12]

---

6. Reeves, *Glory*, 139.

7. Reeves, *Glory*, 19.

8. Of course, there remains an important distinction between "natural evil" (like earthquakes or tsunamis a consequence of the "fall") and "moral evil" (such as the violence and abuse common throughout our bloody history).

9. Morales, *Ascend*, 46.

10. Morales, *Ascend*, 51.

11. Frame, *Apologetics*,158.

12. Stump, *Evil*, 396.

Yet, the Bible writers do not hide the doubts we all experience. Approximately a third of all psalms are complaints addressed to God,[13] full of questions about the why and how of suffering. Why does God often appear absent? Why do the wicked prosper?

6.2.3 God's Response to Suffering and Evil

Chapter 4 has already considered parallels between Eden and the tabernacle, which later became the temple. As cherubim guarded the way to the Garden of Eden (Genesis 3:24), they were sown onto the curtain of the holy of holies, the area representing the presence of God (Exodus 26:1). The tabernacle/temple became a symbol of hope that humanity may again dwell in God's presence. The Psalms often reflect this anticipation, "When I tried to understand all this, it troubled me deeply till I entered the sanctuary of God; then I understood their final destiny" (Psalm 73:16–17). God's presence in the temple comforted the psalmist:

> the sanctuary of God could refer to the tabernacle or temple, where God made his holy presence known among his people. In other words, the psalmist's experience of the presence of God calibrated his perspective. He now realized that present realities are not ultimate realities.[14]

He is also comforted by God's promise to defeat evil (Psalm 73:17). War and violence will end. "He will judge between the nations and will settle disputes for many peoples. They will beat their swords into plowshares and their spears into pruning hooks. Nation will not take up sword against nation, nor will they train for war anymore" (Isaiah 2:4). The reformer Martin Luther saw these promises of the defeat of evil and the hope of the new heavens and new earth, fulfilled in Jesus:

> Divine power is revealed in the weakness of the cross, for it is in his apparent defeat at the hands of evil powers and corrupt earthly authorities that Jesus shows his divine power in the conquest of death and of all the powers of evil. So when a Christian talks about divine power, or even about church or Christian power, it is to be conceived of in terms of the cross—power hidden in the form of weakness.[15]

13. Vroegop, *Dark Clouds*, 29–30.
14. Longman, *Psalms*, 276.
15. Trueman, *Luther*, §4.

6.3 UNIPERSONAL THEISM

There is overlap among how different forms of theism account for the coexistence of evil and a loving God. Theists generally agree we have insufficient information to judge whether an omniscient (all wise) God has good reason for the suffering and evil we observe. However, in contrast to Christianity, unipersonal theism lacks a clear account of why evil and a loving God coexist. Unipersonal theism lacks the incarnation, that God through his Son came to live in our world. There is no equivalent to Jesus' sacrificial death and the defeat of evil through his resurrection and ascension. God does not enter our suffering.

Atonement also plays a less prominent role in Judaism. For example, Rabbi Singer argues sacrifice is the least important method in the Hebrew Bible for dealing with sin.[16] Islam is closer to Judaism in its account of sin and atonement. The Qur'an has a version of the garden of Eden story, it also has some examples of atonement but, like Rabbinic Judaism, denies the current need for substitutionary atonement.

6.4 NATURALISM AND SUFFERING

The problem of evil is essentially an argument that our universe is indifferent to love, integrity, relationships, and justice. We value these relational concepts in courageous rebellion against our impersonal and pitiless reality. Arguments from suffering and evil can be divided into two main types:

- logical problem of evil—the existence of God and suffering are logically inconsistent;
- evidential problem of evil—suffering is evidence against the existence of God.

6.4.1 Logical Problem of Evil

The logical problem of evil can be traced back to Epicurus (third century BCE):

1. if an all-powerful, all-good, and all-knowing God exists then evil does not;

---

16. Singer, *Biblical*, 68–87.

2. evil exists;

3. therefore an all-powerful, all-good, and all-knowing God does not exist.

However, this argument requires an additional assumption: "There is no morally sufficient reason for God to allow instances of evil."[17] Since we are not omniscient, it is a high burden to demonstrate God could not have a sufficient reason. Therefore, most philosophers consider this argument unsuccessful. For example, Graham Oppy, a leading atheist philosopher, concludes: "I think that it is quite clear that no one has yet produced an argument which shows that our current best partially articulated theistic worldviews are rendered inconsistent by claims about the distribution of evil in our universe."[18] Atheist philosophers have not abandoned the logical argument but often favour evidential arguments for evil.

6.4.2 Evidential Argument from Suffering

Paul Draper argues suffering is evidence for the hypothesis of indifference (HI): "neither the nature nor the condition of sentient beings on earth is the result of benevolent or malevolent actions performed by non-human persons."[19] His three main arguments to support HI are:

- biologically useful pain (O1);
- biologically gratuitous pain (O2);
- biologically useful pain experienced by sentient non-human animals (O3).

Draper defined biologically useful pain as suffering that contributes to the biological goals of organic systems, mainly survival and reproductive success (O1).[20] For example, if I spill boiling water on my foot, I reflexively jump out the way. The pain indicates danger and helps me avoid further harm. He argued O1 is less likely if theism (or Christianity) is true:

> Thus, since a morally perfect being would try to accomplish its goals with as little pain as possible, the value of organic systems gives us no reason on theism to expect pain to have biological

17. Stump, *Evil*, 395.
18. Oppy, *Evil*, 75.
19. Draper, *Pain*, 555.
20. Draper, *Pain*, 557.

functions. And since pleasure has intrinsic value and so is worth producing whether or not it furthers some other goal, the value of organic systems gives us very little reason on theism to expect pleasure to have biological functions.[21]

For Christians, suffering can sometimes lead to maturity of faith, perseverance, and character (e.g., Romans 5:3–5). However, if we assume only humans are moral agents, non-human animals will not experience these benefits. Yet, many sentient non-human animals still experience pain (O2):

> since the subjects of it [pain] are not moral agents . . . it gives us some reason on theism & O1 to expect that the good moral reasons God has for permitting moral agents to experience pain do not apply to animals that are not moral agents, and hence some reason to believe that God will not permit such beings to experience pain.[22]

Another set of data, according to Draper, are instances of biologically gratuitous pain (O3).[23] For example, the pain experienced before burning to death serves *no biological value*. If I cannot escape, and will lose my life anyway, the pain is *gratuitous*. Yet it is *biologically appropriate* since the ability to feel pain is useful. In addition, pain can be pathological, when the organic system fails to function properly. For example, through illness, or the sadistic acts of others. Draper argues HI accounts for O1-O3 much better than theism. Therefore evidence of pain and suffering favors naturalism. However, most Christians disagree that O1 better reflects naturalism. In addition, O2 and O3 are consistent with a Christian account of the fall.

6.5 MIND-FIRST VIEWS AND SUFFERING

Buddhists and Hindus believe in a mind-first reality. Although there are important differences in their approach to suffering, there is also significant overlap. For Buddhists, the cycle of suffering has no beginning (although there is a potential end):

> The Buddhist view, in fact, is that there is no known beginning to the cycle of rebirths or to the world: "Inconceivable is any beginning of this wandering on [from rebirth to rebirth;] an earliest

21. Draper, *Pain*, 560.
22. Draper, *Pain*, 560.
23. Draper, *Pain*, 561–62.

point is not discerned of beings who, obstructed by spiritual ignorance and fettered by craving, run and wander on" (S.II.178 (BW. 37–40)).[24]

Similar teaching on the past eternal nature of suffering is found in Hinduism:

> Like the Vedanta-sūtras, the Bhāgavata strongly relies upon the doctrine of beginningless karma in its explanation of suffering. Both God and the jīvas (individual selves) are eternal, and karma (activity) is their everlasting characteristic. The Bhāgavata's Purañjana allegory, for example, strongly indicates that the individual selves were originally with God in the absolute realm, but then fell from that status into the realm of birth and death due to the wrong exercise of their free will.[25]

In Hinduism and Buddhism alike, the problem of suffering lies in our entanglement with matter. For many Hindus, escape from the cycle of suffering is found through knowledge that we are inseparable from Brahma (God):

> The Bhāgavata argues that the self's association with māyā [illusion that we can be separate from God] is a necessary step in their spiritual evolution—and thus is permitted, although not desired, by God . . . When the individual self remembers its eternal relationship with the Lord, and takes refuge in him, it gains the greatest freedom, even in suffering, and after death returns to its original home beyond matter.[26]

For Buddhists, the solution to the problem of suffering is overcoming our selfish desires: "'Nirvana' literally means 'quenching' or 'blowing out', in the way that the flame of a candle is blown out . . . What is extinguished, in fact, is the triple fire of greed, hatred, and delusion which leads to rebirth."[27]

---

24. Harvey, *Buddhism*, 7.
25. Gupta, *Maya*, 141.
26. Gupta, *Maya*, 150.
27. Keown, *Buddhism*, 56–57.

Chapter 7

Suffering and Evil II

7.1 INTRODUCTION

SUFFERING IS CONSISTENT WITH an indifferent universe. Yet, our human capacity for evil and self-destruction are more difficult for physical-first (like Oppy's and Draper's) and mind-first (e.g., Buddhists and animists) views to account for. The holocaust, or the history of the transatlantic slave trade, are paradigmatic examples. We agree these events resulted in terrible suffering. But it is more than that:

> what is genuinely appalling, in other words, is not really human suffering as such so much as human wickedness. This wickedness strikes us as deeply perverse, wholly wrong, warranting not just quarantine and the attempt to overcome it, but blame and punishment. But could there really be any such thing as horrifying wickedness if naturalism were true? I don't see how. A naturalistic way of looking at the world, so it seems to me, has no place for genuine moral obligation of any sort; a fortiori, then, it has no place for such a category as horrifying wickedness.[1]

As discussed in the previous chapter, many naturalists have argued suffering provides strong reasons to doubt the existence of a personal creator God. However, evil raises a distinct challenge, not only for Christianity, but for all worldviews. This chapter will consider:

---

1. Plantinga, *Christian Life*, 72–73.

- how physical-first and mind-first views account for evil;
- do Christianity and unipersonal theism experience similar difficulties?

7.2 NATURALISM AND MORALITY

Naturalists face a difficult dilemma about evil. Some deny the existence of moral facts (anti-realism)—in other words good and evil are just conventions, or subjective judgments that we make. Yet for many, this view lacks plausibility. We instinctively consider some actions to be evil, for example, up to two million deaths under the Khmer Rouge (25% of the Cambodian population); over 500,000 Tutsi deaths in just three months in Rwanda; more than 8,000 Bosniaks killed in Srebrenica. For religious people, and atheists alike, evil was the word that best captured what we saw on our screens. This seemed more than an opinion or preference. Otherwise, we would find ourselves in ethical absurdity:

> we would be committed to thinking that if an individual or group of individuals valued genocide, then it would for that very reason be moral. Surely this is wrong-headed. Genocide is wrong for everyone, not just for us and people who share our preferences and attitudes.[2]

Most ethicists are persuaded by moral realism (that there are moral facts—good and evil).[3] Yet, according to data from a survey of professional philosophers, atheists are 30% less likely than theists to hold this view.[4] This is understandable because most atheists are naturalists—from this perspective, justifying the objectivity of these moral facts is a major challenge.[5] The difficulty, if moral facts exist (realism), is how to ground them objectively:

2. Murray, *Philosophy*, 231.
3. Metcalf, *Realism*. §1.
4. Bourget and Chalmers, *Survey*. The figure cited above is based on my re-analysis of data from this study—freely available online. For the mathematically minded this is a risk ratio of 0.70 (95% confidence interval 0.66 to 0.74). This compares the number of academic philosophers identifying as moral realists and denied theism with the number of academic philosophers identifying as moral realists and affirmed theism. In my view risk ratios are a more intuitive way to compare these groups.
5. Here I define objective as a truth about the world we discover, rather than invent. The objective validity of moral facts are independent from whether you or I agree with them.

If the notions of suffering and flourishing presuppose objective moral values, then if we accept the foregoing theistic argument from evil, the existence of suffering and flourishing would be highly surprising in a naturalistic worldview—in fact, their existence would be rationally inexplicable.[6]

One strategy is to argue for the minimisation of harm to us, and others, as a possible foundation. However, as Hume noted such explanations run into the is/ought fallacy:

> "X brings good consequences" does not logically imply that "X is morally good." Statements about facts (without presupposed principles of moral evaluation) cannot entail any conclusions about morality. Valueless facts do not imply values. *Is* does not imply *ought*.[7]

7.3 MIND-FIRST VIEWS AND MORALITY

Many mind-first views consider that ultimate reality is neither good nor evil.[8] Miyazaki's *Nausicaa* offers a vivid depiction of this belief:

> His negation of dualism [of good and evil] confronts readers most powerfully at the end of the story when Nausicaa" notices that the "blue blood" of the Ohmu, a giant insect which, until that point, appears to represent the "ultimate good", is actually shared by the Crypt of Shuwa, the "ultimate evil".[9]

Most Hindus, Buddhists, and animists prefer to speak of the problem of suffering rather than evil.[10] Just as there are only conventional truths about reality, there are only moral conventions on right and wrong. For example, in Hinduism, "there is no universal morality equally applicable to all human groups."[11] Moral obligation depends on caste membership:

> Caste morality is based on the assumption that what others call "humanity" is really composed of groups of different natures (*guna*) who thus inhabit different locations in ritual space. Moral conduct permissible for members of one caste can be wrong for

---

6. Tratzakis, *Reply*, 87.
7. Frame, *Apologetics*, 99.
8. Harvey, *Buddhism*, 31.
9. Yoneyama, *Miyazaki Animism*, 254.
10. Gupta, *Maya*, 138.
11. Ramachandra, *Faiths*, 68.

those of another . . . This acceptance of contextual relativity of moral ideas, however, is nothing like its counterparts in the postmodern West. For it goes hand in hand with a denial of any freedom of choice on the part of the individual or group which he or she belongs. As no-one can choose the caste in which one belongs, there is also no possibility of preferring one or another set of caste rules for one's personal conduct.[12]

7.4 SIMILAR ISSUE FOR CHRISTIANITY AND UNIPERSONAL THEISM?

John Frame argues that the impersonal standards proposed by naturalists do not generate obligations. Our obligations are to people. For example, as a husband and father, I have a responsibility to take care of my wife and children. Neglecting their needs—whether I feel obligated or not—is wrong.

> If moral obligations arise from personal relationships, then absolute obligations arise from absolute personality . . . Moral standards, therefore, presuppose absolute moral standards, which in turn presupposes the existence of an absolute personality.[13]

The most common response from atheist philosophers, like Graham Oppy, is to argue the grounding of morality is also arbitrary if theism is true.[14] This argument goes back to Plato's Euthyphro dilemma:

- Is good "whatever God says is good?" Some argue, if we take this option, God could say lying or robbing our friends is good. Morality becomes arbitrary.

- Or does "God love the good, because it is good?" If so, then God is unnecessary.

The most common response from Christians is to argue these two questions are complementary. Morality is grounded in God's goodness:

- Father, Son, and Spirit have eternally existed in love, faithfulness, humility, and personal relationship; therefore, as his image bearers, we reflect his goodness in acting likewise;

---

12. Ramachandra, *Faiths*, 68–69.
13. Frame, *Apologetics*, 103.
14. Oppy, *Evil*, 92.

- God cannot sanction lying, robbery, or any kind of evil because this contradicts his nature (e.g., Hebrews 6:18).

Unipersonal theists make similar arguments, that God provides an objective foundation for morality.

7.5 SUMMARY

None of the five worldviews provide complete answers to the problem of evil. I think Christianity and unipersonal theism have an advantage over physical-first and mind-first views:

- physical-first (e.g., naturalism) and mind-first (e.g., Hinduism, Buddhism) views struggle to account for the reality of evil;
- Christians and unipersonal theists have deeper resources for an objective explanation for evil; however, both views are left with questions without full answers; finite beings are unable to discern the judgments of an all-wise being.

Yet Christianity has explanatory advantages over unipersonal theism. God became one of us, through Christ, and walked with us in this suffering and evil world.

> For we do not have a high priest who is unable to empathize with our weaknesses, but we have one who has been tempted in every way, just as we are—yet he did not sin. Let us then approach God's throne of grace with confidence, so that we may receive mercy and find grace to help us in our time of need" (Hebrews 4:15–16).

Chapter 8

Summary of Evidence on the Nature of Reality

8.1 INTRODUCTION

IN PART ONE, I argued Hume's approach to miracles remains the most common response to Jesus' resurrection. However, there are significant limitations. Methodological and metaphysical naturalist assumptions weight the prior probability heavily against accepting miracle claims. This makes their beliefs unamenable to evidence (see chapter 1 for further discussion).

Perspectives on the nature of reality are a key determinant of the prior probability of Jesus' resurrection. In chapter 3, I looked at alternative views to Christianity: physical-first (necessary), physical-first (contingent), mind-first, and unipersonal theism. Hume's approach is consistent with a physical-first view. Hinduism, Buddhism, and animism are prominent examples of mind-first views. Islam and Judaism are examples of unipersonal theism. To help inform the prior probability of Jesus' resurrection, this chapter will compare how well these perspectives compare with Christianity in accounting for:

- the existence of our universe;
- the success of science;
- the presence of suffering and evil.

Part Two: The Nature of Reality

8.1.1 Methods of Comparison

Oppy suggests we compare worldviews based on the following criteria:

- simplicity: if all else is equal, we should choose the simpler option;[1]
- internal coherence: "the determination of which worldviews fail on their own terms";[2]
- comparative evaluation: "which worldview scores best on an appropriate weighting of theoretical commitments . . . explanation of data, predictive accuracy, fit with well-established knowledge . . ."[3]

8.2 SIMPLICITY

Richard Swinburne defines simplicity as:

> postulating few (logically independent) entities, few properties of entities, few kinds of entities, few kinds of properties, properties more readily observable, few separate laws with few terms relating few variables, the simplest formulation of each law being mathematically simple.[4]

The most straightforward way to penalise models with greater complexity is through the prior. Simpler models should have a higher prior probability. Yet we should not weight simplicity more than internal coherence or comparative evaluation. Simplicity should only distinguish between otherwise similar fitting models.

8.2.1 Simplicity of Naturalism

Oppy works from a slightly different understanding of complexity. For him, a necessary universe is the simplest option, since no explanation is required, the universe has always existed (option 1), or always had initial conditions that inevitably lead to our universe (option 2). A contingent universe (option 3) is more complex as it requires an explanation for why

---

1. Oppy, *Evil*, 73.
2. Oppy, *Evil*, 70.
3. Oppy, *Evil*, 71.
4. Swinburne, *Existence*, 53.

the universe exists. Oppy argues physical-first views are simplest because of their emphasis on oneness:

> naturalism is committed to one kind of entity (the natural), one kind of external relation (the spatiotemporal), one kind of causation (the natural), one kind of non-topic-neutral property (the natural) and so forth, whereas theism is committed to two kinds of entities (the natural and the supernatural).[5]

In contrast, Swinburne points out several factors that make naturalism a complex hypothesis:[6]

- to posit something rather than nothing (i.e., before the universe existed) is the more complex hypothesis;
- Oppy's option 1 posits an eternal universe with the complex set of physical laws that we observe today;
- Oppy's option 2 must account for the necessity and eternality of the initial conditions from which our universe developed—such as quantum tunnelling, or the ensemble of universes in the HH model.

8.2.2 Simplicity of Christianity

Swinburne's *Existence of God* provides several arguments for why theism is simpler than naturalism. These arguments are relevant to both Christianity and unipersonal theism. A theistic explanation, according to Swinburne, is also a personal explanation. "Theism postulates God as a person with intentions, beliefs, and basic powers, but ones of a very simple kind, so simple that it postulates the simplest kind of person that there could be."[7] The simplicity of Christian personal explanations are due to the freedom of God. No one can prevent an omnipotent God from carrying out his intentions (Daniel 4:35). He does as he pleases (Psalm 115:3). An omniscient God requires no advisors (Isaiah 40:13–14). Swinburne argues omnipotence is a simpler hypothesis because:

> A finite limitation cries out for an explanation of why there is just that particular limit, in a way that limitlessness does not . . . So in

---

5. Oppy, *Naturalistic*, 7.
6. Which lowers naturalism's prior probability.
7. Swinburne, *Existence*, 97.

postulating a person with infinite power the theist is postulating a person with the simplest kind of power possible.[8]

Similarly, he argues perfect freedom is simpler than determinism. It is more complex to explain the necessity of an eternal universe or eternal initial conditions. It is simpler to explain the actions of a perfectly free person—an uncaused choice.

8.2.3 Simplicity/Complexity of Mind-First Views

Forms of Hinduism that consider everything Bhrama equally meet Oppy's criteria of oneness. Dualist forms of Hinduism, Buddhism, and animism are more complex. Mind-first views must also account for how multiple finite gods cooperate to produce and uphold the regularities we perceive in the world. These regularities are unexpected if mind-first views are true.

8.2.4 Naturalism, Unipersonal Theism, or Christianity?

Unipersonal theism is simpler than Christianity. Although Christianity is a form of monotheism, it posits that plurality and unity are co-ultimate. This is more complex than assuming only unity is ultimate. Whether physical-first views are simpler than unipersonal theism, or Christianity, is debatable. It depends on how simplicity is judged.

Oppy appears to characterise the comparison as primarily naturalism alone vs naturalism + belief in God. He suggests theism must account for two brute facts: the spatiotemporal universe and God, while naturalism must only account for one—the spatiotemporal universe.[9] However, for Christians and unipersonal theists, the creator God explains the universe, it is not an unexplained fact. We agree there is a spatiotemporal universe. But Oppy seems to conflate this common belief with naturalism.

A better way to state the comparison, in my view, is that we account for the existence of our spatiotemporal universe with two competing brute (unexplained) facts—the universe or God. Swinburne argues the theistic model is simpler than the naturalist model. Although, Christianity is more complex than unipersonal theism, it includes all the virtues Swinburne identifies. Therefore, the greater simplicity of naturalism is far from

8. Swinburne, *Existence*, 97.
9. Oppy, *Evil*, 73

Summary of Evidence on the Nature of Reality

obvious. I will argue below Christianity and unipersonal theism have an advantage in terms of internal coherence and comparative evaluation.

8.3 INTERNAL COHERENCE

Physical-first views provide a coherent explanation for suffering, such as, Draper's hypothesis of indifference. However, both physical-first and mind-first accounts for the intelligibility of our universe and the success of science are more problematic. They face an important dilemma. They may assert the objective validity of scientific knowledge (rationalism) yet lack an adequate account of how to justify this knowledge.[10] They could deny the validity of knowledge, but this entails denial of the obvious success of science (irrationalism).

Physical-first and mind-first approaches face similar difficulties when accounting for evil. They may want to argue for the objective validity of certain moral values (rationalism) but lack an adequate foundation for these beliefs (irrationalism). Alternatively, they may posit that morality is based on convention. Yet this leads to the uncomfortable position (irrationalism) of having to justify, "that if an individual or group of individuals valued genocide, then it would for that very reason be moral."[11]

Unipersonal theism provides a coherent account of the existence of the universe and intelligibility. God can make a rational universe: "because he himself is rational and his plan for creation and providence is therefore rational."[12] Our rationality is derivative from God. For Christians, because we are made in the image of God, our knowledge is a pale reflection of God's perfect knowledge. It is a little like a visit to Tokyo with my Japanese wife. When I am with her, Tokyo seems a simple and rational place, getting around is straightforward. I understand a fair bit of Japanese, but she can always explain when I am out of my depth or apologise for my cultural faux pas. But when I venture into the city on my own, it appears a very different place. I understand far less than I thought. The city is bigger than it seemed, the metro more complicated than I realised.

There is an obvious tension in unipersonal theism and Christianity—between a loving God and evil or suffering. But we have insufficient

---

10. Anderson, *Knowledge*, 17.
11. Murray, *Philosophy*, 231.
12. Frame, *Apologetics*, 110. Frame's argument is for Christianity but, at least on this point, can also be used by other forms of theism.

knowledge to judge an omniscient being. Mind-first views are often coherent in their denial of the objectivity of knowledge and morality. Expectation of suffering is also coherent with this view.

8.4 COMPARATIVE EVALUATION

8.4.1 Christianity and Unipersonal Theism vs Physical-First and Mind-First Views

Christianity and unipersonal theism appear to have the advantage in comparative evaluation:

Existence of the universe

- evidence that the universe may have a beginning is more consistent with unipersonal theism and Christianity, than physical-first (necessary) and mind-first views but consistent with physical-first (contingent); we will explore an alternative assumption in chapter 26, that the existence of our universe is evidence of its necessity (favoring physical-first (necessary) and mind-first approaches);

Intelligibility and the success of science

- naturalists argue, as science progresses, the probability of Christianity and unipersonal theism becomes vanishingly small; however, this assumes the intelligibility of the universe, an unexplainable fact, is equally likely whether naturalism or Christianity is true;
- intelligibility is more likely given Christianity or unipersonal theism since there is a rational creator; physical-first and mind-first views are unable to account for the objective validity of our reasoning;

Suffering

- suffering is more likely if physical-first or mind-first views are true, compared with Christianity or unipersonal theism;

Summary of Evidence on the Nature of Reality

Evil

- objectivity of good and evil[13] are more likely given Christianity and unipersonal theism;
- our moral intuitions about evil are generally in conflict with physical-first and mind-first accounts of evil. Christianity and unipersonal theism have the advantage.

8.4.2 Christianity vs Unipersonal Theism

Existence of Universe

- the existence of the universe is more likely if Christianity is true; although all forms of theism posit that God has the power to create, it is only Christianity that claims relationship is foundational to reality;

Intelligibility and success of science

- unipersonal theists and Christians are justified in expecting the universe to be intelligible;

Suffering

- unipersonal theists and Christians are justified in their assumption that humans are limited in their attempts to judge an omniscient being;
- Christianity has significant additional resources available (Jesus' incarnation, his willingness to suffer for us) to account for the goodness of God in a suffering world;

---

13. Obviously, this assumes the objectivity of good and evil (as defined in chapter 7). There are alternative problems for those who deny the objectivity of good and evil, in other words, what gains physical-first views may gain in internal coherence are lost to challenges in accounting for the reality of evil.

Evil

- unipersonal theism and Christianity both provide an objective foundation for good and evil.

8.5 CONCLUSION

In *Part One*, I discussed Hume's dismissal of miracles. Ahmed's water analogy, following Hume, intends to illustrate evidence for Jesus' resurrection is "not worth a second look." They wave away first century miracle accounts as inherently improbable. But John Frame counters: "Why should one prefer the hypothesis of ultimate impersonality, when that creates such an enormous gap between the creator (nonrational) and the nature of the universe, including human beings (rational)."[14]

Part Two has compared how the five worldview categories account for reality. I have argued that Christianity and unipersonal theism best account for the existence of the universe, success of science, suffering, and evil. Physical-first and mind-first worldviews have difficulty accounting for the existence of the universe, the objectivity of reasoning, and the objectivity of morality.

Part Three will move from the biblical narrative of creation and fall to promised redemption. I will consider whether Jesus' resurrection is consistent with the message of the Hebrew Bible.

---

14. Frame, *Apologetics*, 111.

PART THREE

Hebrew Bible and the Messiah

RECAP OF PART TWO

- *Part Two assessed data on the nature of reality: the existence of the universe; the intelligibility of the universe; the success of science; evil and suffering;*
- *five worldview categories (physical-first (necessary), physical-first (contingent), unipersonal theism, Christianity, mind-first) were compared for internal coherence and their ability to account for our reality (see Figure 3);*
- *existence of the universe: physical-first and mind-first worldviews are potentially inconsistent with evidence that the universe may have a beginning; unipersonal theism and Christianity are more consistent with these data;*
- *success of science: physical-first and mind-first worldviews have difficulty accounting for the intelligibility of our universe, since there is no obvious foundation for the validity of our logical inferences; in contrast, unipersonal theism and Christianity provide an objective foundation for the scientific method;*
- *suffering: an inherent expectation within physical-first and mind-first worldviews; but less expected if unipersonal theism or Christianity are true, however our limited perspective means we cannot fully judge whether God is justified in allowing suffering;*

PART THREE: HEBREW BIBLE AND THE MESSIAH

- **evil:** *physical-first and mind-first worldviews have difficulty accounting for good and evil beyond the conventional; unipersonal theism and Christianity provide an objective foundation for morality.*

THESE DATA ARE KEY *drivers for the prior probability of Jesus resurrection. If there is no creator God, it is close to impossible that he was raised from the dead. All we need to know is these events occurred among "ignorant and barbarous peoples" (in the words of Hume).*[1] *But it is not only naturalists who consider the prior probability of Jesus' resurrection to be close to impossible. Unipersonal theists (e.g., Rabbinic Jews, Muslims), and people with mind-first views (e.g., Hindus, Buddhists, or animists) also consider Jesus' resurrection close to impossible.*

However, if the Triune God exists, the historical context is vital. Part Three assesses the promises of a Messiah in the Hebrew Bible. These expectations are key to evaluation of the prior probability of Jesus' resurrection, given New Testament claims that he was the Messiah.

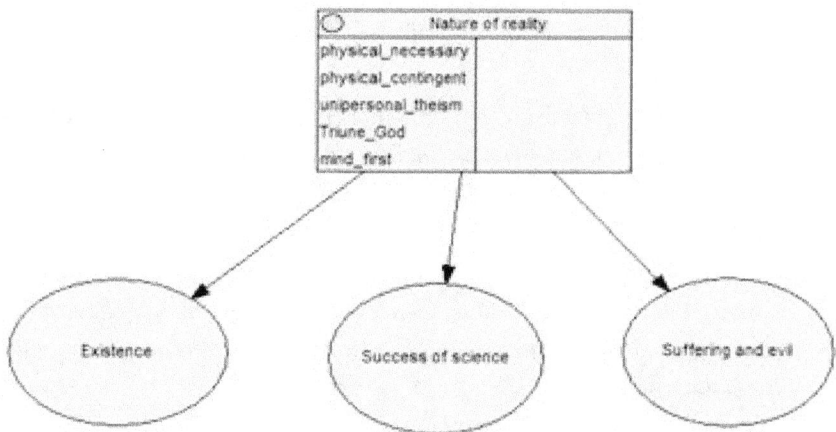

Figure 3 Network diagram summarizing Part Two

INTRODUCTION TO PART THREE

Part Two considered the probability of the Triune God's existence. If he exists, it is probable the Father will send the Messiah—as promised in the

---

1. Hume, *Enquiry*, Section X: Part II:94.

Part Three: Hebrew Bible and the Messiah

Hebrew Bible and New Testament. Part Three surveys some major themes on the promised Messiah—and how Jesus fulfils these criteria. Of course, many readers may be thinking, the Messiah according to whom? Many of the Messianic prophecies claimed by Christians are rejected by modern Rabbinic Jews. Michael Brown, a Messianic Jew, points to a helpful point of contact in the Talmud. This passage offers many possibilities about the Messianic era, I will focus on one of these:

> Rabbi Ḥiyya bar Abba says that Rabbi Yoḥanan says: In their prophecies with regard to redemption and the end of days, all the prophets prophesied only about the messianic era (b. Sanhedrin 99a).

Some Christians can be accused of taking a "gold rush" approach to the Hebrew Bible. We must sift through the esoteric mud of ancient Israelite custom to find nuggets about Jesus. However, Brown points out, there is important agreement between many Rabbinic Jews and Christians, "on the pervasive nature of the Messianic hope in the Hebrew Scriptures."[2] For example, the apostle Paul argued:

> I am saying nothing beyond what the prophets and Moses said would happen—that the Messiah would suffer and, as the first to rise from the dead, would bring the message of light to his own people and to the Gentiles (Acts 26:22–23)

We will see in Part Four, that Jesus made a similar statement in Luke 24 (v25–27 and 44—49). Moses Maimonides, a famous Jewish scholar, diverged from Paul and Jesus on numerous matters. But he agreed with them on the centrality of the Messiah's mission: "this belief in the Messiah is in accordance with the prophecies concerning him, by all the prophets, from our master Moses until Malachi, peace be unto them."[3]

There are two main implications for taking this approach. First, we must avoid simplistic proof-texting. This is not to deny there are explicit prophecies about the Messiah. But we must be attentive to the message of the Hebrew Bible as a whole (see Box 7 for themes considered in Part Three). Second, we must apply sound exegetical principles when interpreting the Hebrew Bible and its fulfilment in Jesus. This includes asking:[4]

---

2. Brown, *Jewish*, 153.

3. Cited in Brown, *Jewish*, 153.

4. These principles are based on Beale and Carson, *Introduction*, xxiii—xxviii. For further details see their chapter.

PART THREE: HEBREW BIBLE AND THE MESSIAH

- What is the context of the passage in the Hebrew Bible?
- How is this passage interpreted in Second Temple Judaism or early Judaism?
- How does the New Testament connect these verses or themes, in the Hebrew Bible, to the life and mission of Jesus?

BOX 7. SUMMARY OF PART THREE

Chapter 9: The Memra (the Word) Made Flesh. Modern Judaism no longer has place for the Memra, the mediator between God and humanity; yet he was a key figure in the Hebrew Bible and early Judaism. This historical context is consistent with the New Testament's account of Jesus' Messianic mission.

Chapter 10: The Tabernacle and Temple. The tabernacle and temple is at the heart of the Hebrew Bible's theology of reality. Atonement and purification for humanity's sins is necessary before God will return to his people. The New Testament depicts Jesus' death, resurrection, and ascension as fulfilment of the tabernacle/temple's mission.

Chapter 11: The Suffering Messiah. Given the centrality of the temple in the Hebrew Bible, it is no surprise the promised Messiah will be both priest and sacrifice. Key passages in Isaiah and Zechariah are considered along with discussion of how these were interpreted within Jewish tradition.

Chapter 12: Resurrection in the Hebrew Bible. Death, evil, and suffering are a consequence of sin in the Hebrew Bible. Therefore, the promised Messiah must conquer these. Resurrection and new creation is central to the reign of the Messiah.

PART THREE: HEBREW BIBLE AND THE MESSIAH

> **BOX 7. SUMMARY OF PART THREE**
>
> *Chapter 13: Son of Man, the Ascended King.* The Messiah of the Hebrew Bible and Jewish tradition is both Son of Man and the promised son of David. Jesus' ascension is interpreted within the light of passages in Daniel and the Psalms on the ascension of King Messiah.
>
> *Chapter 14: Jesus the Promised Messiah.* This final chapter sums up the extent to which Jesus' death, resurrection, and ascension are consistent with the Hebrew Bible's promised Messiah.

Part Three considers a key determinant of the prior probability of the resurrection—Jesus himself. If he is the Messiah, we expect the Hebrew Bible to promise a divine savior whose sacrificial death will be followed by exaltation—demonstrated by his resurrection and ascension. In this context, the prior probability of Jesus' resurrection is increased.[5]

If Jesus is not the Messiah, we expect important divergences between the life of Jesus and the promises of the Hebrew Bible. In this case, the prior probability of Jesus' resurrection is close to impossible, as we can be certain God would not vindicate this heretic.

---

5. Of course, this has much in common with Swinburne's model—however his prior is determined by the probability of a generic theistic God existing, the probability that he would become incarnate, and the probability of a super miracle (such as a resurrection) to authenticate his message.

Chapter 9

The Word (*Memra*) Made Flesh

9.1 INTRODUCTION

THERE ARE MANY OVERLAPS between the New Testament and Rabbinic Jewish depictions of the Messiah. This chapter focuses on a key difference—Christian belief in a divine Messiah. The first chapter of John's Gospel is probably the clearest statement of this doctrine. Jesus is the divine mediator between God and humanity:

> In the beginning was the Word [*Logos*], and the Word was with God, and the Word was God. He was with God in the beginning. Through him all things were made; without him nothing was made that has been made. (v1–3).

Rabbinic Jews, Muslims, and sceptics, often argue this view of God departs from the monotheism of the Hebrew Bible. It is commonly asserted that John's Gospel borrowed from Gnostic ideas about the *Logos* ("Word")—this view can be traced back to nineteenth century sceptics. They identified themes such as light and darkness, life and death, flesh and spirit shared in John's Gospel and Gnostic writings. However, as Don Carson notes, these are near-universal themes in numerous religions.[1] So the overlap is hardly surprising. Other scholars, such as Daniel Boyarin,[2] propose a Jewish origin for John's *Logos*:

---

1. Carson, *John*, 116.
2. A conservative rabbi, and scholar of early Judaism.

> Rather than seeing in the Logos of John a parthenogenetic birth from a Greek mother-father, foisted illegitimately on a "Jewish" Christianity... I think [it] highly conceivable to see this Prologue, together with its Logos doctrine, as a Jewish text through and through rather than, as it has often been read, a "Hellenized corruption" of Judaism.[3]

This chapter discusses the following topics:

- the Word in the Hebrew Bible;
- the Word in early Judaism;
- the Word outside of John's Gospel.

9.2 THE WORD IN THE HEBREW BIBLE

The Hebrew Bible speaks of a divine mediator, referred to as Lord (YHWH), yet distinct from the Lord (also YHWH). For example, the Word of the Lord often reflects the Lord's activities on earth (see Psalm 147:15, Psalm 107:20). The Word also meets with specific people like Abraham:

> Then the word of the Lord came to him: 'This man will not be your heir, but a son who is your own flesh and blood will be your heir.' He took him outside and said, 'Look up at the sky and count the stars—if indeed you can count them.' Then he said to him, 'so shall your offspring be.' (Genesis 15:3–4)

John 1:18 reflects this personification of the Word, "No one has ever seen God, but the one and only Son, who is himself God and is in closest relationship with the Father, has made him known." New Testament scholar Don Carson argues this verse likely alluded to Exodus chapters 33 to 34:[4] "The Lord would speak to Moses face to face, as one speaks to a friend" (33:11). Yet a few verses, later it reads, "you cannot see my face, for no one may see me and live" (v20).

On the surface, Exodus 33 is confusing. A passage in the Talmud (b. Yevamot 49b) asserts Manasseh killed Isaiah for claiming to see the Lord (Isaiah 6:1).[5] The sage argued Isaiah was contradicting Exodus 33:20.[6]

---

3. Boyarin, *Borderlines*, 31.
4. Carson, *John*, 129.
5. It should be noted there is no historical evidence to back up the sage's suggestion.
6. b. Yevamot 49b includes several other interpretations including: 1) Isaiah was

But, if that's the case, we could also argue Exodus 33:11 does the same. John's Gospel therefore argues the Son (the Word), addressed with the divine name, spoke with Moses (Exodus 33:11) face-to-face. In addition, that he is distinct from the Father, yet they share the divine name (Exodus 33:20).

Exodus 24:1 is another key text, "Then the Lord said to Moses, 'Come up to the Lord, you and Aaron, Nadab and Abihu, and seventy of the elders of Israel.'" The Lord said to Moses "Come up to the Lord [YHWH]", why did he not say, "Come up to me?" A passage in the Talmud addresses this controversy in a surprising way (b. Sanhedrin 38b). According to Rav Idit, the person addressed as Lord (YHWH) was an angel (in Hebrew "a sent one" or "messenger").

> Rav Nahman said: A person who knows how to answer the minim [heretic] as Rav Idit, let him answer, and if not, let him not answer. A certain min said to Rav Idit: "It is written, "And to Moses he said, come up unto the H' [the Lord]⁷ [Exod. 24:1]." It should have said, "Come up to me"! He [Rav Idit] said to him: "This was Metatron, whose name is like the name of his master, as it is written, "for My name is in him" [Exod. 23:21]: But if so, we should worship him!" It is written, "Do not rebel against him" [Exod.23:21]—Do not confuse him with me!" If so, then why does it say, "He will not forgive your sins'?" We have sworn that we would not even receive him as a guide, for it is written "If Your face goes not [do not bring us up from here]" [Exod.33:15]⁸

Boyarin explains the implications of this dialogue between the *min* ("heretic") and Rav Idit:

> God has been addressing the Jewish people as a whole (in [Exodus] chapter 23), informing them that he will send his angel before them and instructing them how to behave with respect to this angel. He then turns to Moses and tells him to come up to H' (the Tetragrammaton), implying quite strongly that H' is not the same person as the speaker of the verse. Rav Idit turns back to the

---

killed by Manasseh for referring to the Jewish people in a derogatory manner ("people of unclean lips'). However, once again there is no indication in the text this happened. 2) Isaiah's vision was a metaphorical vision. Only Moses saw the Lord. Although this resolves the potential contradiction between Ex. 33:20 and Isaiah 6:1, this creates a contradiction between Ex 33:11 and 33:20. References to the Babylonian Talmud are to the William Davidson Edition unless stated otherwise.

7. H' is short for HaShem, commonly used in Judaism to refer to the covenantal name of God.

8. b. Sanhedrin 38b, quoted in Boyarin, *Borderlines*, 120–21.

previous chapter and remarks that verse 21 there explicitly says that "My name is in him [that is, in the angel]." Metatron, that angel, therefore could be called by the name H', and it is to him that Moses is being instructed to ascend.[9]

Jewish tradition often identified Metatron as Enoch or the archangel Michael. But this is problematic because the Hebrew Bible never called Enoch or Michael YHWH. Exodus 23–24 is consistent with later New Testament teaching on the unity and plurality of God (e.g., Matthew 10:40; John 3:16–17).

9.3 THE WORD IN EARLY JUDAISM

This understanding of a divine mediator in the Hebrew Bible was common among Jews in the first-to-fourth centuries:

> Although official rabbinic theology sought to suppress all talk of the Memra or Logos by naming it the heresy of "Two Powers in Heaven" (b. Hag.15a), before the rabbis, contemporaneously with them, and even among them, there were many Jews in both Palestine and the Diaspora who held on to a version of monotheistic theology that could accommodate this divine figure linking heaven and earth.[10]

In chapter 4, I argued the Hebrew Bible teaches that the Word, along with the Spirit, created the world. The early targums—Aramaic paraphrases of the Hebrew Bible written in the first-to-fourth centuries—referred to this person as the *Memra* (or *Logos*). When the Lord interacted with his creation, he was usually identified as the *Memra*.[11] They also distinguished the *Memra* from the Lord (see for example, Targum Neofiti Exodus 3[12] and Genesis 17[13]).

Philo, a Hellenistic Jew, also wrote about the *Logos* (the Greek equivalent of *Memra*). The *Logos* in his writings was often equal to the intelligible

---

9. Boyarin, *Borderlines*, 121.

10. Boyarin, *Logos*, 547. He cites Targum Neofiti on Exodus 3.

11. McNamara, *Genesis*, 37.

12. Boyarin, *Logos*, 547.

13. McNamara, *Genesis*, 100: "And you shall circumcise the flesh of your foreskin and it will be a covenant-sign between my Memra [Hebrew text: "me"] and you." Paraphrase of Genesis 17:10–11.

world. But he also wrote of the *Logos* as a divine figure based on ancient Jewish tradition:

> Since Philo states that he relies on ancient Jewish tradition, his writings, including those pertaining to the exegesis of the names of God, may indicate the antiquity of the tradition. That Philo knows the issue suggests a possible origin well before the birth of Jesus.[14]

9.4 *LOGOS* DOCTRINE ONLY IN JOHN?

This understanding of the pre-existence of Jesus, and his active participation in the Hebrew Bible, was not limited to John's gospel. The apostle Paul also assumed Jesus was present with Israel in the past:

> For I do not want you to be ignorant of the fact, brothers and sisters, that our ancestors were all under the cloud and that they all passed through the sea. They were all baptized into Moses in the cloud and in the sea. They all ate the same spiritual food and drank the same spiritual drink; for they drank from the spiritual rock that accompanied them, and that rock was Christ. Nevertheless, God was not pleased with most of them; their bodies were scattered in the wilderness. (1 Corinthians 10:1–5)

The Messiah, in his pre-incarnate state, provided nourishment and protection to the Israelites during the desert wanderings:

> as the Rock who was with Israel, supplying them with "spiritual water" (v. 4), and as the one whom Israel thus put to the test (v. 9) . . . the same Christ who now supplies the Corinthians with the Spirit, and whom they are testing by going to pagan feasts, had already experienced such "testing" by Israel; and the Israelites had been overthrown in the desert so that they did not reach their goal. It is precisely the presence of Christ in Israel's story that will make all of this work as a warning to the Corinthians.[15]

---

14. Segal, *Powers*, 43.
15. Fee, *Pauline*, 94.

9.5 CONCLUSION

Boyarin, reflecting on the Jewish background to John 1, comes to a startling conclusion:

> Christian theology, far from "gradually draw[ing] away from Judaic tendencies," actually maintained a more *conservative* Judaic approach to the doctrine of God than did the Rabbis, and that it is they—if anyone—who drew away from earlier Jewish theology.[16]

This coherence between the Hebrew Bible's teaching on a divine mediator, and the New Testament's teaching about Jesus as that divine mediator, is key to weighing up the prior probability of his resurrection. If Christianity is just a Hellenized corruption of Judaism, it is close to impossible that Jesus is the Messiah. Since it is close to impossible that God would authenticate this heresy by raising him from the dead.

However, if Jesus is the Word of the Lord, active in creation of the universe, and ministering to God's people throughout history, the prior probability looks very different. It is likely that God would provide a super-miracle, like Jesus' resurrection, to authenticate his mission.[17]

The next chapter will look at one of the central messages of the Hebrew Bible, a model of reality and redemption revealed by the tabernacle/temple system. It pointed forward to a divine mediator, God's priest-king, who will rescue his people through suffering and death.

---

16. Boyarin, *Borderlines*, 92.
17. Swinburne, *Resurrection*, 141.

Chapter 10

The Tabernacle and Temple

10.1 INTRODUCTION

MOST RABBINIC JEWS AND Christians consider the first five books of the Bible to be a single narrative. Some critical scholars have challenged this view, while other scholars continue to argue for the unity of the Pentateuch's message.[1] Yet most agree the first five books are foundational to the rest of the Hebrew Bible. Therefore, if we want to know what the Messiah will be like, here is the place to look. According to Biblical theologian Michael Morales, and many other scholars, Leviticus is where the central teaching of the Hebrew Bible can be found.[2]

The book of Exodus finishes with the tabernacle—filled with God's glory. However, there is an unresolved problem, how can sinful people enter God's place? "Moses could not enter the tent of meeting because the cloud had settled on it, and the glory of the Lord filled the tabernacle" (Exodus 40:35). This recalls Genesis 3, where cherubim blocked the way to the garden (and therefore God's presence) after the fall. Leviticus presents the tabernacle sacrifices and rituals as the solution: "For the life of a creature is in the blood, and I have given it to you to make atonement for yourselves on the altar; it is the blood that makes atonement for one's life" (17:11).

Many Rabbinic Jews now question the centrality of atonement in the Hebrew Bible. For example, Rabbi Singer argues "the Church would

---

1. For example, Sailhamer, *Pentateuch*, 1–78.
2. Morales, *Ascend*, 24.

be hard-pressed to point to a single incident in the Hebrew Scriptures in which a sacrifice atoned for an egregious sinner."[3] For example, Leviticus 17:11 "does *not* imply that the only method of atonement is blood. This verse explains that when a sin sacrifice is offered, every ritual associated with the blood must be conducted properly, in order for the offering to be valid."[4] However, many earlier Rabbinic commentators took a different position. For example, Rashi, perhaps the preeminent commentator of Jewish tradition, taught atonement was at the heart of this verse: *"For the soul of the flesh*: of every creature is dependent upon the blood, and therefore, I have given it to atone for the soul of man. [In this way,] one "soul" [namely, the blood of a sacrifice] shall come and atone for another soul."[5]

Rabbi Singer correctly points out that the sin offering [or purification offering] only atoned for unintentional sins.[6] We will consider this offering in more detail later. However, this was not the only atoning sacrifice.[7] Below we will focus on the day of atonement (*Yom Kippur*)—the central festival of ancient Israel, where the high priest made atonement for intentional and unintentional sins. The guilt offering (*asham*) also atoned for specific intentional sins (Leviticus 6:1–7).

This chapter will focus on the tabernacle and temple as a model of atonement—with an emphasis on the Book of Leviticus. The follow topics will be covered:

- the purpose of temples in the Hebrew Bible: Eden, Mount Sinai, the Tabernacle/Temple;
- atonement in the Hebrew Bible;
- the day of atonement and the central message of the Torah.

10.2 TEMPLE/TABERNACLE IN THE HEBREW BIBLE

Table 3 shows the progression of the Pentateuch, from creation and fall in Genesis to the tabernacle. Morales argues that the Genesis creation account,

---

3. Singer, *Biblical*, 68.
4. Singer, *Biblical*, 69.
5. Rashi, *Leviticus*, 17:11.
6. Singer, *Biblical*, 69.
7. Wenham, *Leviticus*, 89.

Mount Sinai, and the Tabernacle all show a "mediated return to Eden."[8] Throughout the Scriptures the cosmos is described either as a tabernacle or a house where God dwells (e.g., Psalm 19:4; 78:23; Job 9:8). As seen in chapter 4, the tabernacle is a model of Eden, a promise that God will dwell again with his people, "Then the cloud covered the tent of meeting, and the glory of the Lord filled the tabernacle." (Ex. 40:34)

	Creation	Mount Sinai	Tabernacle
Tripartite division	Heavens (Genesis 1:1)	Summit: only Moses may enter (Exodus 24:1–2, 12–18)	Holy of holies: only the high priest may enter
	Earth (Genesis 1:1)	Second zone: partway up mountain accessed by the priesthood and elders (Exodus 24:9–11)	Holy place: accessed by the priesthood
	Seas (Genesis 1:9–10)	Base of the mountain: accessed by the people (Exodus 19:10–12)	Outer court: accessed by the people
Presence of YHWH	Lord God walking in the garden (Genesis 3:8)	Glory of YHWH (Exodus 24:15–16)	Glory of YHWH (Exodus 40:34)
Sabbath	God rested on the seventh day (Genesis 2:1–3)	On the seventh day, the Lord calls to Moses from within the cloud (Ex. 24:15–18)	The day of atonement is to be a day of sabbath rest (Leviticus 16:31)
Veiled presence of YHWH	After the fall, cherubim guard the way to the garden (Genesis 3:24)	When Moses ascended cloud covered mountain (Exodus 24:15–18)	Curtain with embroidered cherubim guards the way to the holy of holies. High priest may only enter through a cloud of incense. (Exodus 40)

Table 3. Comparisons between the Genesis creation account, Mount Sinai, and the Tabernacle

10.3 YOM KIPPUR (DAY OF ATONEMENT)

The first two verses of Leviticus 16 present the problem of sinful humanity entering God's presence:

> The Lord spoke to Moses after the death of the two sons of Aaron who died when they approached the Lord. The Lord said to Moses: "Tell your brother Aaron that he is not to come whenever he

---

8. Morales, *Ascend*, 101.

chooses into the Most Holy Place behind the curtain in front of the atonement cover on the ark, or else he will die. For I will appear in the cloud over the atonement cover."

The reader is reminded of Nadab and Abihu's[9] death in Leviticus 10. To avoid their fate, Aaron and future high priests must not enter the Most Holy Place (where the Lord appears). The high priest may only enter behind the curtain annually (Leviticus 16:3):

> The reason why Aaron may not enter the innermost sanctuary whenever he likes is that it houses the ark on which the mercy seat [atonement cover] is found. It is there that God comes to his people . . . Now he dwells among them in the innermost part of the sanctuary.[10]

10.3.1 Atonement and Purification of the High Priest

The high priest needed to offer a burnt offering and a sin offering to make atonement and purification for his sins. Given the importance of the tabernacle/temple as a teaching aid for the people, this points forward to the Messiah who must make atonement for his people's sins. Leviticus describes these sacrifices in earlier chapters:

- burnt offering (Leviticus 1): the Hebrew word (*olah*), often translated as burnt offering, means to ascend; "Its main function was to atone for man's sin by propitiating God's wrath";[11] The high priest needed to acknowledge his sin and guilt, to be thankful for God's blessing, and "resolve to live according to God's holy will all the days of his life."[12]
- sin (purification) offering: these sacrifices were for unintentional sins (4:1–35) and sins of omission (5:1–13); the focus was purification, "sin not only angers God and deprives him of his due, it also makes his sanctuary unclean . . . The purification offering purifies the place of worship, so that God may be present among his people."[13]

---

9. Aaron the high priest's sons.
10. Wenham, *Leviticus*, 229.
11. Wenham, *Leviticus*, 63.
12. Wenham, *Leviticus*, 63.
13. Wenham, *Leviticus*, 89.

The high priest went behind the curtain, sprinkling the blood from the sin offering on the atonement cover (16:11, 14). But he had to enter the Most Holy Place in a thick cloud of incense (16:12–13):

> Entry into the holy of holies is fraught with danger. To protect him from the wrath of God, the high priest has to prepare a censer full of hot charcoal taken from the altar of burnt offering in the outer court and put in it fine incense . . . The purpose of the incense-smoke was to create a screen which would prevent the High Priest from gazing upon the Holy Presence.[14]

The next stage of the ritual was to make atonement for the people. The high priest casted lots for two goats—one for the Lord and one for the scapegoat (16:8).[15] The goat for the Lord would become a sin offering for the people (16:15–18). The high priest went behind the curtain again. He sprinkled the blood on the atonement cover, tent of meeting, and the altar. This was "because of the uncleanness and rebellion of the Israelites" (16:16).

The scapegoat was then sent out into the wilderness, taking Israel's sins with him. Aaron must place his hands on the goat transferring all the sins of the Israelites onto the scapegoat (16:21–22). The symbolism is straightforward. "This ceremony removes the sins from the people and leaves them in an unclean place, the desert."[16] The day of atonement, central to the tabernacle/temple sacrificial system, had a clear aim:

> By cleansing the sanctuary they permit the holy God to dwell among an unholy people (vv16–17; cf. Isa. 6:3ff.; Ps. 15; 24:3ff.). Verse 17 underlines the fact that only one man, the high priest, may enter into the holy of holies. Under both testaments there is but one mediator between God and man (cf. 1 Tim 2:5).[17]

---

14. Wenham, *Leviticus*, 231.

15. The Hebrew word is "Azazel" a debated term. It could either be the name of a demon, total destruction, or a rocky place. See Wenham, *Leviticus*, 233–34; and Wright, *Azazel*, 536–37.

16. Wenham, *Leviticus*, 233.

17. Wenham, *Leviticus*, 233.

10.4 CONCLUSION

The tabernacle is a model of the cosmos, so these rituals have a broader application.[18] The day of atonement reflects the promise of "a reversal of Eden's expulsion."[19] Atonement is central to the Pentateuch and the Hebrew Bible; it allows sinful humans to live with God again. Someone must die in our place, to atone for our sins and turn away the wrath of God. If Jesus is the Messiah, we expect him to provide sacrifice for our sins, cleanse us, make a way back to the Father.

---

18. Morales, *Ascend*, 171.
19. Morales, *Ascend*, 177.

Chapter 11

The Suffering Messiah

11.1 INTRODUCTION

THE NEW TESTAMENT DEPICTS suffering as key to the Messiah's mission. He must be "delivered into the hands of men" (Mark 9:31). Rabbinic Jews, Muslims, and sceptics alike consider this a departure from the Hebrew Bible's promise of a victorious king.

> And who was Jesus? He was a crucified criminal. He appeared in public as an insignificant and relatively unknown apocalyptic preacher from a rural part of the northern hinterlands. At the end of his life he made a pilgrimage to Jerusalem with a handful of followers. While there, he ended up on the wrong side of the law and was unceremoniously tried, convicted, and tortured to death on criminal charges. That was the messiah? That was just the opposite of the messiah.[1]

Early followers of Christianity reinterpreted passages from the Hebrew Bible to justify Jesus' shameful death. If so, there is no chance God would raise Jesus from the dead—a failed candidate for the Messiah. Jewish scholar Daniel Boyarin challenges this summary of early Judaism.

> many who hold this view hold also that Isaiah 53 was distorted by the Christians from its allegedly original meaning, in which it referred to the suffering of the People of Israel, to explain and account for the shocking fact that the Messiah had been crucified.

---

1. Ehrman, *Triumph*, 48–49.

The Suffering Messiah

This commonplace view has to be rejected completely. The notion of the humiliated and suffering Messiah was not at all alien within Judaism before Jesus' advent, and it remained current among Jews ... well into the early modern period.[2]

In this chapter I will consider the following themes:

- evidence for a suffering Messiah before the time of Jesus;
- whether the Messiah was meant to be victorious king, suffering servant, or both;
- passages from the Hebrew Bible on a suffering Messiah: Zechariah 12–13, Psalm 22, and Isaiah 53.

11.2 BELIEF IN A SUFFERING MESSIAH BEFORE JESUS?

Several documents from the Dead Sea Scrolls (DSS)—written before Jesus' time (approximately 100 BCE)—provide important evidence of ancient belief in a suffering Messiah. For example, Israel Knohl, Professor Emeritus at Hebrew University Jerusalem, argued certain hymns from the DSS point to belief in a suffering Messiah.[3]

Martha Himmelfarb, former Director of Judaic Studies at Princeton, also points to the Apocryphon of Levi—where a suffering servant will bring atonement for Israel.[4] The Great Isaiah scroll (1QIsa^a), the oldest and most complete manuscript of the book of Isaiah (dated approximately 100 years before Jesus) also supports a Messianic interpretation of the final servant song. The text is similar to the later standard Hebrew (Masoretic) text. Yet there is an important difference. The servant is anointed above all others, almost certainly a reference to the Messiah (in Hebrew "the anointed one").

> At Isaiah 52:14, in place of MT [Masoretic Text]'s "His appearance was so marred, beyond human semblance"—1QIsa^a reads *mashahti*, "I have *anointed*": "so have I anointed his appearance beyond that of any (other) man."[5]

---

2. Boyarin, *Gospels*, 132.
3. Knohl, *Servant*, 5–26.
4. Himmelfarb, *Messiahs*, 64.
5. Himmelfarb, *Messiahs*, 63.

Part Three: Hebrew Bible and the Messiah

11.3 A SUFFERING MESSIAH IN THE HEBREW BIBLE?

11.3.1 Zechariah 12: the One They Have Pierced

One of the most famous passages on the suffering Messiah is from Zechariah:

> And I will pour out on the house of David and the inhabitants of Jerusalem a spirit of grace and supplication. They will look on me, the one they have pierced, and they will mourn for him as one mourns for an only child, and grieve bitterly for him as one grieves for a firstborn son. (Zechariah 12:10)

John's Gospel (19:34–37) cites this passage when writing about Jesus' death. This passage points forward to Jesus as the one who would bring healing to Israel through his death:

> The flow of water and blood are often referred to as being medical evidence that Jesus was really dead. However it seems unlikely that this was what John had in mind. Rather, he regarded the water and the blood as scriptural evidence that Jesus was really the promised Messiah. Water and blood are the twin symbols of cleansing in the Old Testament; thus when Jesus was pierced on the cross, John saw the fountain for cleansing promised in Zechariah 13:1 flowing out from his side.[6]

There is evidence from the Talmud (b. Sukkah 52a) that at least some Rabbinic Jews considered Zechariah 12 to be about the Messiah. The "pierced one" was *Mashiach ben Yosef* (Messiah son of Joseph). As seen above, the Davidic Messiah was not the only Messiah figure in Jewish tradition. Himmelfarb pointed out these texts spoke of a priestly Messiah:

> ... in ancient Israel both kings and priests were anointed, making them messiahs in the literal sense, and it goes back as far as Zechariah's prophecies at the very beginning of the Second Temple period ... For Zechariah, Zerubbabel, the Persian governor descended from David, and Joshua the high priest (Zech 3–4, 6:9–15) are two "sons of oil" (Zech 4:14).[7]

---

6. Duguid, *Zechariah*, 279.
7. Himmelfarb, *Messiahs*, 101.

11.3.1.1 Meaning of Zechariah 12

Zechariah 1–8 focuses on the building of the second temple, led by Zerubbabel and Joshua. Chapters 9–14 look to an apocalyptic future widely cited in the book of Revelation.[8] The second temple was small and currently unimpressive. But there will come a time when God sends his representative to bless Israel. The Messiah will be a victorious king—he will defeat God's enemies (Zechariah 9:1–8). Yet he will be gentle and humble (Zechariah 9:9) and will be killed (Zechariah 12:10):

> The final word of Zechariah 9–14 and New Testament alike is grace not judgement. Though the shepherd be rejected (Zc. 11:8–9) and pierced by his own people (Zc. 12:10; 13:7–9), though the covenant be broken (Zc. 11:10) and a worthless anti-shepherd be allowed to rule over God's people for a while, yet that is not God's final word. For God brought again from the dead our Lord Jesus the great shepherd of the sheep, by the blood of the eternal covenant, so that he might be the God of peace.[9]

In Zechariah 12, Israel mourns their divine king—who was pierced: "They will look on me, the one they have pierced, and they will mourn for him as one mourns for an only child, and grieve bitterly for him as one grieves for a firstborn son" (Zechariah 12:10). Michael Brown, scholar of Near Eastern languages, argues the mourners are turning to God. He is the only one referred to in the first person throughout this chapter (e.g., "I will keep a watchful eye on Judah," v4):

> "They will look on me the one they have pierced." It is perfectly clear, therefore, that the me in this verse is the Lord himself—as rendered in the Jewish translations cited above [Sukkah 52a and the Septuagint]—suggesting the real possibility that the Hebrew text is speaking about the Lord Himself who was pierced.[10]

The death of the suffering Messiah will bring cleansing from sin: "On that day a fountain will be opened to the house of David and the inhabitants of Jerusalem, to cleanse them from sin and impurity" (Zechariah 13:1). Verses 7–9 continue the account of this suffering Messiah.[11] He is the shepherd (King) struck by the sword. Yet he will bring God's people back to him:

---

8. Beale, *Revelation*, 1081–1158.
9. Duguid, *Zechariah*, 280.
10. Brown, *Messiah*, 149–50.
11. identified by Ibn Ezra as *Mashiach ben Yosef* (Messiah Son of Joseph).

"They will call on my name and I will answer them; I will say, 'They are my people,' and they will say, 'The Lord is our God.'" (Zechariah 13:9)

11.3.2 Psalm 22 in Jewish Tradition

Psalm 22 is another passage about the suffering Messiah. For example, Rashi, an influential Jewish commentator, considered this psalm to be about "the time of our redemption in the days of our Messiah". *Pesikta Rabbati* (approximately seventh century CE), also considered Psalm 22 to be about the Messiah (*Mashiach ben David*). Psalm 22 primarily shaped the midrash's description of the Messiah's suffering. The message of *Pesikta Rabbati* has a lot in common with Isaiah 53. The Messiah does not come at the end of history. He comes to suffer for each generation: ". . . this homily understands the messiah to be suffering for the sins of each generation. Because of the suffering he has endured."[12]

11.3.2.1 *Meaning of Psalm 22*

The Gospels also considered Psalm 22 to be about the Messiah. For example, Jesus recites words from this Psalm on the cross:

> At noon, darkness came over the whole land until three in the afternoon. And at three in the afternoon Jesus cried out in a loud voice, "Eloi, Eloi, lema sabachthani?" (which means "My God, my God, why have you forsaken me?" [Psalm 22:1]) (Mark 15:33–34).

He experienced great physical suffering, "My mouth is dried up like a potsherd, and my tongue sticks to the roof of my mouth; you lay me in the dust of death. Dogs surround me, a pack of villains encircles me; they pierce my hands and my feet." (Psalm 22:14–16) The psalm appears hopeless. But there is promise of vindication: "For he has not despised or scorned the suffering of the afflicted one; he has not hidden his face from him but has listened to his cry for help." (Psalm 22:24)

---

12. Himmelfarb, *Messiahs*, 84.

11.3.3 Isaiah 53: the Suffering and Rejected Servant

Most modern Rabbinic Jews believe Isaiah 53 (technically, Isaiah 52:13—53:12) is about Israel (the "collectivist view"). However, appendix 1 shows this interpretation emerged quite late in Jewish writings (after 1000 CE) likely in response to persecution of Jews in medieval Europe. Many passages in the Rabbinic literature (such as the Talmud, Targum of Jonathan, midrashim, and the writings of major rabbis) affirmed the servant was the Messiah. Many passages in the New Testament also connected the servant of Isaiah 53 with the Son of Man (for example, Mark 10:45) and the Messiah (for example, Romans 15:21, 1 Peter 2:21–25).

Isaiah 53 is the final servant song in a series of four poems (42:1–9; 49:1–6; 50:4–11). The first servant song (42:1–9), is interpreted by numerous Christian (for example Matthew 3:17; Matthew 12:17–21; Mark 1:11; Luke 3:22) and Jewish sources[13] as Messianic. The next servant song makes clear there are two servants: Israel (49:3) and the servant who brings Israel back to God (49:6). The third song calls disobedient servant Israel (50:1–2) to listen to the obedient servant's voice (50:5–6, 10).

Isaiah 53 explains how the suffering servant will redeem Israel and then the world. He was "despised and rejected by mankind." (52:14, 53:3). The servant performed the role of a priest whose ministry extended beyond Israel, he will "sprinkle many nations" (52:13). Yet, it is *his* life that is given as a guilt offering (53:10). The servant was "pierced for our transgressions . . . crushed for our iniquities." (53:5–6) In this famous chapter of the Hebrew Bible, the priest is also the sacrifice that cleanses his people, not only for Israel, but for the world.

Hebrew Bible texts such as Isaiah 53 (written hundreds of years before the New Testament), Zechariah 12–13, and Psalm 22 are the foundation for belief in a suffering Messiah:

> These diverse images are drawn together in the New Testament and applied to Jesus . . . The many different images were freely combined and transformed by the New Testament writers, to show how all the eschatological promises of the Old Testament had been fulfilled in Jesus, who is both final prophet and great high priest, suffering servant and coming king, good shepherd and sacrificial lamb.[14]

---

13. For example, Targum of Jonathan, *On Isaiah*, chapter 42; Rambam, *Mishnah Sanhedrin*, 10:1; Metzudad David, *On Isaiah*, 42. However, Rashi and Ibn Ezra disagree.

14. Duguid, *Zechariah*, 280.

11.4 CONCLUSION

We reflected on the consensus of the Messiah as a victorious king (see chapter 13 for further discussion). Later in the chapter, we saw that the Hebrew Bible also promises he will suffer. Of course, modern Rabbinic Jews rarely consider these passages to be about the Messiah. Yet Jewish tradition grappled for many centuries with how to reconcile passages about a suffering Messiah, and other passages that highlight his exaltation. Many concluded the Messiah would be victorious, but that he would also suffer—without seeing the need to resolve the paradox. Other Rabbinic Jews proposed two Messiahs:

- *Mashiach ben Yosef* (Messiah son of Joseph): the suffering servant
- *Mashiach ben David* (Messiah son of David): the victorious king

Christianity resolved this dilemma by positing that Jesus will first come as the suffering Messiah and return as the victorious king. Jesus' death is consistent with the Hebrew Bible's plan for redemption. His followers claimed he was the promised priest and sacrifice. Passages like Psalm 22 and Isaiah 53 not only spoke of a suffering Messiah—they point to his vindication. Suffering and death are not the end of the story. The Hebrew Bible's teaching on resurrection will be considered in the next chapter.

Chapter 12

Resurrection in the Hebrew Bible

12.1 INTRODUCTION

ACCORDING TO JON LEVENSON, a Jewish scholar, many modern Jews are uncomfortable about resurrection beliefs. For example, Abba Hillel Silver, a key figure in American Judaism in the mid-twentieth century, considered the resurrection of the dead, "a late and degraded development in Jewish thought, a borrowing from foreign sources."[1]

Understandably, the prominent place of resurrection in Christian doctrine, has led many modern Jews to distance themselves from these beliefs, "the Christians, vulnerable to a crude superstition about a god-man who came back from the dead, have perverted the Hebrew Bible by introducing something altogether foreign into it."[2] However, as Levenson points out, this modernist view, is condemned as heresy by the Mishnah (200 CE), "the great law code of rabbinic Judaism."[3]

> And these are the ones who do not have a share in the World-to-Come: He who says that the resurrection of the dead is not in the Torah, [he who says] that the Torah is not from Heaven, and the skeptic.[4]

---

1. Levenson, *Resurrection*, 2.
2. Levenson, *Resurrection*, 3.
3. Levenson, *Resurrection*, 24.
4. Levenson, *Resurrection*, 24.

This inhouse debate within Judaism, of course, is relevant to Christians. If the modernists are correct, the prior probability of Jesus' resurrection is close to zero. If the Hebrew Bible does not promise resurrection, then Easter looks like an *ad hoc* response to Jesus' embarrassing death. This chapter considers the following topics:

- the meaning of resurrection in the Hebrew Bible and first century Palestine;
- key Hebrew Bible passages on resurrection (Daniel 12, Isaiah 24–27, Isaiah 53);
- what does it mean that Jesus was raised on the third day, according to the Scriptures?

12.2 RESURRECTION AND LIFE AFTER DEATH

There is little doubt that belief in resurrection was common in first century Palestine:

> from burial customs to the fomenting of revolution, belief in resurrection influenced and energized many concrete aspects of first-century Jewish life. Resurrection was not a strange belief added on to the outside of first-century Judaism. Except for the Sadducees and those who insisted on a final disembodied state, resurrection had been woven into the very fabric of first-century Jewish praying, living, hoping and acting.[5]

As twenty-first century people, we often think of resurrection as another word for life after death, a belief common in most religions. Yet this does not reflect its first-century usage:

> Many people think that "resurrection" is just an old-fashioned religious word for the survival of our souls after the inevitable deaths of our bodies. In fact, however, resurrection envisions the return of the whole person, body and soul together, not simply the continuing survival of his or her "spiritual" dimension.[6]

At that time, many Greco-Romans saw death as an opportunity to escape from the physical world. Others approached death with fatalistic

---

5. Wright, *Resurrection*, 3.
6. Madigan and Levenson, *Resurrection*, xii.

resignation. N.T. Wright argues resurrection belief was grounded in the theology of the Hebrew Bible. Jews believed in the redemption of the physical creation:

> the reversal or undoing or defeat of death, restoring to some kind of bodily life those who had already passed through that first stage. It belonged with a strong doctrine of Israel's god as the good creator of the physical world. It was the affirmation of that which the pagan world denied.[7]

Scholars debate when resurrection was first explicitly taught in the Hebrew Bible. Yet Jon Levenson, Professor of Jewish Studies at Harvard, points out the seeds for this doctrine are there from the beginning:

> it is thus both an innovation and a restatement of a tension that had pervaded the religion of Israel from the beginning, the tension between the Lord's promise of life, on the one hand, and the reality of death, on the other. In the case of resurrection, the last word once again lies not with death—undeniably grievous though it is—but with life. Given the reality and potency ascribed to death throughout the Hebrew Bible, what overcomes it is nothing short of the most astonishing miracle, the Divine Warrior's eschatological victory.[8]

12.3 RESURRECTION IN THE HEBREW BIBLE

12.3.1 Daniel 12

Probably the clearest Hebrew Bible passage on resurrection is found in the twelfth chapter of Daniel:

> At that time Michael, the great prince who protects your people, will arise. There will be a time of distress such as has not happened from the beginning of nations until then. But at that time your people—everyone whose name is found written in the book—will be delivered. Multitudes who sleep in the dust of the earth will awake: some to everlasting life, others to shame and everlasting contempt. Those who are wise will shine like the brightness of the heavens, and those who lead many to righteousness, like the stars for ever and ever. (Daniel 12:1–3)

---

7. Wright, *Resurrection*, 1.
8. Levenson, *Resurrection*, 216.

Levenson points out Daniel 12 builds on several earlier texts (such as Isaiah 24–27, Isaiah 53, Ezekiel 37).[9] For example, "Multitudes who sleep in the dust of the earth" likely refers to Genesis 3:9.[10] The promise of resurrection from the dead and reversal of the fall is based on Isaiah 24–27. Daniel 12 emphasizes, "the thought that the salvation which is to occur at this time will not be limited to those who were alive but will extend also to those who had lost their lives."[11] God will judge those who have persecuted his people. "The condemnation of the wicked no longer involves their simply ceasing to exist or their being dispatched to Sheol, never to rise from there. Now both groups awake from death, but to different verdicts."[12]

12.3.2 Isaiah 24–27

Chapters 24-27 of Isaiah's prophecy are dated by critical scholars to the fifth or sixth century BCE and even earlier by traditional scholars.[13] Alec Motyer, the late Old Testament scholar, outlines the context of this passage:

> The world-wide song, entitled "Glory to the Righteous One" ([Isaiah]24:16a), is now heard in detail as the world pilgrimage arrives in Zion ... In the imagery Isaiah is using, the pilgrims to Zion move through a ruined world, and their song dwells on the marvel of their rescue and the power of the Lord over all the power of the enemy.[14]

These chapters show how intertwined resurrection is with the defeat of death, justice, and the promise of a new creation:

> That the omnipotent God of deliverance "will destroy death forever" and revive the dead (Isa 25:8; 26:19) is readily understandable in [this] context ... For resurrection is part of a larger scenario of national deliverance in which God at long last makes good on his promises to his people Israel.[15]

---

9. Levenson, *Resurrection*, 215.
10. Young, *Daniel*, 256.
11. Young, *Daniel*, 256.
12. Levenson, *Resurrection*, 213.
13. Levenson, *Resurrection*, 201.
14. Motyer, *Isaiah*, 207.
15. Levenson, *Resurrection*, 213–14.

Isaiah 25:6–8, full of evocative images of the new Jerusalem,[16] may be recalling the image of Exodus 24 when Moses and the elders ate with the Lord on the mountain:[17]

> On this mountain the Lord Almighty will prepare a feast of rich food for all peoples, a banquet of aged wine—the best of meats and the finest of wines. On this mountain he will destroy the shroud that enfolds all peoples, the sheet that covers all nations; he will swallow up death forever. The Sovereign Lord will wipe away the tears from all faces; he will remove his people's disgrace from all the earth. The Lord has spoken. (Isaiah 25:6 –8)

As seen in Part One, "mountain" is often a symbol of the temple or sanctuary in the Hebrew Bible. This passage in Isaiah looks forward to the fulfilment of Exodus 24. Isaiah 25 and Exodus 24 look back to Eden and the reversal of the curse, a new earth where death and suffering are no more. God and humanity will dwell together for eternity.

The next chapter of Isaiah continues this theme: "But your dead will live, Lord. Their bodies will rise. Let those who dwell in the dust wake up and shout for joy." (Isaiah 26:19) Although Isaiah used figurative language, many scholars (both Christian and Jewish[18]) view this as a promise of bodily resurrection:

> the verse is a promise of life for the world, the fulfilment of 25:6–10a. But if this is so, then while the main thrust of the terminology is used figuratively of the resurrection of the wicked into salvation and the strong city, we need to recall that 25:7-8 looked forward to the abolition of death itself. In this regard, the terms of the present verse go beyond the figurative to the literal and declare a full resurrection, including the resurrection of the body.[19]

12.3.3 Isaiah 53

As I argued in the previous chapter, Isaiah 53 (52:13—53:12) speaks of the servant's atoning death. Yet the passage also promises his vindication:

---

16. Motyer, *Isaiah*, 208.
17. These images are built on in Revelation 21.
18. For example, Ibn Ezra, *On Isaiah*, 26:19; Radak, *On Isaiah*, 26:19.
19. Motyer, *Isaiah*, 219.

and though the Lord makes his life an offering for sin, he will see his offspring and prolong his days, and the will of the Lord will prosper in his hand. After he has suffered, he will see the light of life and be satisfied; by his knowledge my righteous servant will justify many, and he will bear their iniquities. (Isaiah 53:10–11)

These verses constitute an early promise of the resurrection:

> Among the immediate antecedents of Dan 12:1–3 is Isa 52:13—53:12, which seems to speak (admittedly with considerable obscurity) not only of the post-mortem vindication and exaltation of a faithful but mistreated servant of the Lord but also of his being awarded new life in the process.[20]

12.4 RESURRECTION ON THE THIRD DAY

The New Testament states several times that Jesus was raised on the third day according to the Scriptures (the Hebrew Bible).[21] Many have challenged whether such a passage exists. But Michael Brown, a Messianic Jew and scholar in Near Eastern Languages, points out these arguments are misleading. "As a Jew schooled in the Scriptures from his childhood Paul was not thinking of just one passage but of several passages that pointed to the Messiah's resurrection on the third day."[22] There are many examples of rescue, salvation, and restoration on the third day in the Hebrew Bible.[23] For example, in the restoration of Israel in Hosea 6:2 "After two days he will revive us; on the third day he will restore us, that we may live in his presence." This pattern is also recognized in the Rabbinic literature (e.g., Bereishit Rabbah 56:1). Genesis 22 narrates the famous account where God commands Abraham to sacrifice Isaac on Mount Moriah. On the third day of their journey (v4), the angel of the Lord said to Abraham: "Do not lay a hand on the boy." (v12) *Pirkei DeRabbi Eliezer*[24] suggested the Messiah

---

20. Levenson, *Resurrection*, 213.
21. For example, First Corinthians 15:4; Luke 24:46.
22. Brown, *Jewish*, 181–82.
23. For example, Jonah 2:1–9; Esther 5:1–2; 2 Kings 20:1–8.
24. A midrash traditionally ascribed to Rabbi Eliezer ben Hyrcanus (1st or 2nd century CE).

would take a similar journey as Isaac. The midrash asserts that Isaac's release was a figurative resurrection.[25]

12.5 CONCLUSION

Belief in resurrection was a central aspect of first century life for many Palestinian Jews. This chapter has focused on passages specifically on resurrection hope. Scholars implore us to view resurrection within the deeper narrative of the Hebrew Bible. If Jesus is the Messiah and was "pierced for our transgressions" then it is not unsurprising that God would vindicate his faithful servant by raising him from the dead.

---

25. *Pirkei DeRabbi Eliezer*, 31:10.

Chapter 13

Son of Man, the Ascended King

13.1 INTRODUCTION

THIS CHAPTER CONTINUES THE theme of the vindication of the Messiah. Herman Bavinck, a theologian from the nineteenth century, pointed out we cannot separate Jesus' resurrection from his death or ascension.

> Cross and crown, death and resurrection, humiliation and exaltation lie on the same line. As Jesus himself put it after his resurrection: It was necessary that the Christ should suffer these things and so enter his glory.[1]

Jesus' resurrection was the first step in being: "exalted to the highest power, dignity, and honor conceivable . . . A Priest-King is seated on the throne of the universe and is still looking forward to his greatest exaltation when he comes again for judgment."[2] Yet for many of us, the ascension seems an anti-climax.

> Wouldn't evangelism be a whole lot easier if Jesus was still on earth. Imagine He was still living somewhere in Palestine so that people could go to see Him. Imagine that scientists had studied Him over the years and could verify that He was over 2,000 years old . . . The ascension seems a bad strategy. It removes the key

---

1. Bavinck, *Dogmatics*, 3:423.
2. Bavinck, *Dogmatics*, 3:446–47.

piece of evidence that substantiates the claims of Christianity. It's as if our best player by far was substituted as the game was beginning.[3]

This chapter traces key ascension themes in the Hebrew Bible, and why Jesus' ascension was necessary:

- the ascension of the Priest-King: ascension themes related to the temple, and the Davidic Messiah;
- the Son of Man: the apocalyptic King seated on a throne next to the Ancient of Days;
- Son of Man in the Gospels: Jesus' most common self-description and the Hebrew Bible background to these references.

13.2 ASCENSION: TEMPLE AND THRONE

The Hebrew word *olah* (to "go up" or to "ascend") has deep connections with the temple.[4] For example in chapter 10, I noted the burnt offering is literally an "ascension offering". The sacrifice ascends to the throne of heaven. Ascension was also used to describe Moses meeting the Lord at Mount Sinai:

> with the sense of going up to or ascending to the Lord. It came to be a regular term for the ascent to Mount Zion, or Jerusalem, and for going up to the Temple, while within the Temple it was used for ascension into the Holy of Holies.[5]

The enthronement Psalms (such as 2, 24, 68) also spoke of ascension. These psalms had a dual meaning: "with regard to ascent to royal sovereignty, but beyond that there lies the thought of the enthronement of Yahweh himself."[6] For example, Psalm 24 asks the question, "Who may ascend the mountain of the Lord? Who may stand in his holy place?"

> The Psalmist calls on the gates of Mount Zion to swing open because someone is coming who can ascend the hill of the LORD— the King of glory. This is the king of God's people, the human son

3. Chester and Woodrow, *Ascension*, 9.
4. Torrance, *Resurrection*, 107.
5. Torrance, *Resurrection*, 107.
6. Torrance, *Resurrection*, 107.

of David. But it is also God Himself, the LORD Almighty. He may stand before God in the holy place. For He has clean hands and a pure heart.[7]

Psalm 110 also includes ascension themes of royalty and priesthood. The king enthroned at the right hand of YHWH (110:1), is "a priest forever, in the order of Melchizedek" (110:4). I will come back to this Psalm later, as it was cited extensively in the New Testament (for example, Acts 2:32–36; Hebrews 1:3; 8:1). Several Rabbinic texts (such as b. Avot D'Rabbi Natan 34:4 in the Talmud, second half of the third century CE) also interpreted Psalm 110 as Messianic, as did First Enoch.[8]

13.3 SON OF MAN IN THE HEBREW BIBLE

Daniel 7 depicts an apocalyptic figure, a king who rules over many nations, "one like a son of man."

> In my vision at night I looked, and there before me was one like a son of man, coming with the clouds of heaven. He approached the Ancient of Days and was led into his presence. He was given authority, glory and sovereign power; all nations and peoples of every language worshiped him. His dominion is an everlasting dominion that will not pass away, and his kingdom is one that will never be destroyed. (Daniel 7:13–14)

The Son of Man was the most common title used by Jesus about himself. The phrase was "meaningless for a Greek"[9] but often used in the Hebrew Bible and in first century Palestine. Many places in the Hebrew Bible, this word has the straightforward meaning of "person" (e.g. Ezekiel 2:1, Daniel 8:17). But Daniel 7 is different—the focus is on an apocalyptic figure. An angel later interpreted Daniel's vision (Daniel 7:15–28). God's kingdom will triumph; God's king (the one like a son of man) will rule over the whole earth in an everlasting kingdom. Jewish tradition considers the "one like a son of man" to be the King Messiah.[10]

---

7. Chester and Woodrow, *Ascension*, 90.
8. Pao and Schnabel, *Luke*, 371–72.
9. Hengel and Schwemer, *Judaism*, 557.
10. Rashi, *On Daniel*, 7:14; Metzudat David, *On Daniel*, 7:14; b. Sanhedrin 98a.

13.3.1 Why Thrones?

One of the key debates about this King in Daniel 7, is whether he is divine. As we saw in chapter 9, belief in a divine mediator was common in the first century.[11] Many Jews considered this view consistent with the monotheism of the Hebrew Bible. Yet this belief was later condemned as heresy, possibly because of its similarities with Christian doctrine. A key element of this debate was on the meaning of the plural word "thrones."

> As I looked, "thrones were set in place, and the Ancient of Days took his seat. His clothing was as white as snow; the hair of his head was white like wool. His throne was flaming with fire, and its wheels were all ablaze." (Daniel 7:9)

Alan Segal pointed out, "In the apocalyptic vision ascribed to Daniel, two thrones appear in heaven, which imply two different figures to fill them."[12] Who sits on these thrones? Early midrash (such as The Mekhilta of R. Ishmael Bahodesh 5), suggest Daniel 7 "must be taken to demonstrate that God may be manifested either as a young man or as an old man."[13] However, as Segal noted:

> [Daniel 7] may easily be describing two separate, divine figures. More than one throne is revealed and scripture describes two divine figures to fill them. One sits and the other seems to be invested with power, possibly enthroned. The Ancient of Days may be responsible for judgment, but delegates the operation to a "son of man" who accomplishes judgment by means of a fiery stream. That this "son of man" is young or that his dominion is to be merciful, ostensibly the point of the reference, is hardly evident in the text.[14]

13.3.2 Riding in the Clouds

When Daniel spoke of "one riding in the clouds" he used a common phrase in the Hebrew Bible (see for example, Deuteronomy 33:26-27; Psalm 104:3; Psalm 18:10-18; Isaiah 19:1; Nahum 1:3). In every instance, it refers to

---

11. Boyarin, *Borderlines*, 112-27; Segal, *Powers*.
12. Segal, *Powers*, 40.
13. Segal, *Powers*, 35.
14. Segal, *Powers*, 35-36.

God.[15] So when Jesus asserted this verse was about him, it is no surprise the high priest cried "blasphemy!" Jesus defined himself as Daniel 7's Son of Man (Mark 14:60–65).

Morales also noted a link between Daniel 7 and the day of atonement. Annually the high priest entered the holy of holies (an image of heaven) through a cloud of incense. Therefore "Daniel envisions an Adam-like figure approach God's throne with the clouds of heaven we are probably to understand this as a priestly image."[16]

13.4 SON OF MAN IN THE GOSPELS

Jesus referred to himself as son of man 81 times in the gospels, and 69 in the synoptics alone.[17] As with the Hebrew Bible, son of man had different meanings in the gospels, depending on context. NT scholar Don Carson classified these into three main categories:

- the earthly son of man (the everyday meaning of "I");
- the suffering Son of Man (focusing on the death and resurrection of Jesus);
- the apocalyptic Son of Man (alluding to Daniel 7).

I will focus below on references to the suffering and apocalyptic Son of Man.

13.4.1 Suffering Son of Man

The first key reference in Mark, is after Peter's confession that Jesus is the Christ. From this point on, Jesus' teaching pivots to his suffering, "He then began to teach them that the Son of Man must suffer many things and be rejected by the elders, the chief priests and the teachers of the law, and that he must be killed and after three days rise again." (Mark 8:31)

We will struggle to find a suffering Messiah in Daniel 7. As we saw above, the focus is on a victorious king. According to RT France, an NT scholar, Jesus was likely referring to a range of passages in the Hebrew Bible such as Zechariah 9–14, Psalm 22, Isaiah 53 which spoke of a suffering

15. Young, *Daniel*, 154.
16. Morales, *Ascend*, 172.
17. Carson, *Matthew*, 248.

Messiah.[18] Yet, the suffering of the Son of Man will not end in defeat, he will be raised from the dead and ascended to heaven in victory.

13.4.2 The Apocalyptic Son of Man

Although Jesus often spoke of the suffering Son of Man, he also used the term in direct reference to Daniel 7, for example his trial:

> Again the high priest asked him, "Are you the Messiah, the Son of the Blessed One?" "I am," said Jesus. "And you will see the Son of Man sitting at the right hand of the Mighty One and coming on the clouds of heaven." The high priest tore his clothes. "Why do we need any more witnesses?" he asked. "You have heard the blasphemy. What do you think?" (Mark 14:60–64)

Jesus' statement in Mark 14:62 likely reflects this understanding of a divine mediator (for further discussion see chapter 9).[19] He claimed to be the Son of Man who will be seated at the right hand of the Father. The Book of Enoch,[20] written by Jewish mystics somewhere between 100 BCE and the early first century, took a similar interpretation of Daniel 7.[21] Most scholars think Jesus' response to the high priest also referenced Psalm 110.[22]

13.5 CONCLUSION

In summary, the Hebrew Bible promised the Messiah would experience both suffering and exaltation. Therefore, if Jesus was the Messiah, his death, resurrection, and ascension are consistent with these teachings. Jesus' ascension "demonstrates his exaltation from humiliation to royal majesty,

---

18. France, *Mark*, 335.

19. It is important to distinguish between the "binitarianism" of the "two powers' doctrine and Jesus' teaching in the gospels. I am only observing some overlap between his teaching and the "two powers' doctrine, clearly such views downplay the divinity of the Holy Spirit and therefore are not identical with the teachings of the New Testament.

20. The main difference was that the 1 Enoch considered the son of man to be Enoch. The "head of days' [Ancient of Days] sits on the throne to judge. His head is "white like wool" (1 Enoch 46:1) and with him is one like a son of man who also sits on a throne (1 Enoch 61:8; 62:2–9; 69:27–29). 3 Enoch, written around the 5th century CE, is even clearer. The son of man is a divine angel (Metatron) who sits on a throne next to the Ancient of Days.

21. Bock, *Enoch*, 233.

22. Bock, *Enoch*, 235.

but through crucifixion and sacrifice, for the power and glory of the Royal Priest are bound up with his self-offering in death and resurrection."[23]

---

23. Torrance, *Resurrection*, 111.

Chapter 14

Jesus the Promised Messiah

14.1 INTRODUCTION

SCRIPTURE PRESENTS, "JESUS IN the context of a rich, complex historical drama. Jesus is the expectation of God's people over a period of several thousand years before his birth . . . God's people began to look for a deliverer, one who would save them from the effects of the fall."[1] Chapters 9 to 13 have sketched out key motifs in the Hebrew Bible and how they relate to Jesus' mission:

- the Word (*Logos* or *Memra*);
- the Tabernacle/Temple;
- the suffering servant;
- resurrection and the defeat of death;
- ascension of the Priest-King.

This chapter recaps on these themes and implications for the prior probability of Jesus' resurrection.

14.2 JESUS THE WORD

In chapter 4, I argued the Hebrew Bible speaks of a divine mediator (YHWH) who, with the Spirit, was responsible for creation (Genesis 1:1–3;

---

1. Frame, *Apologetics*, 139.

Psalm 33:6). He spoke face to face with Moses, Abraham, and many others. Yet he was distinct from YHWH who no one may see and live (Exodus 33:20). In the first century, Jewish tradition referred to this person as the Word (in Aramaic *Memra* and in Greek *Logos*). In a first century context, identifying Jesus as the Word was an outrageous claim. The man they had seen with their eyes, and heard with their ears, was the divine mediator of the Hebrew Bible.

It was not only John's Gospel that portrayed him as divine mediator. Jesus makes a similar affirmation in Matthew's Gospel, "All things have been committed to me by my Father. No one knows the Son except the Father, and no one knows the Father except the Son and those to whom the Son chooses to reveal him" (11:27; see also Luke 10:22 and John 1:18). It is no surprise that this divine mediator would come to earth once more as the promised Messiah.

14.3 JESUS AND THE TABERNACLE/TEMPLE

In chapter 10, I argued the tabernacle was a model of the cosmos, illustrating God's mission to dwell once more with sinful humanity. Jews and Christians alike consider the first five books of the Hebrew Bible to be the foundation for all theology. Therefore, if Jesus is the Messiah, the tabernacle must be at the centre of his mission, as it is in the Torah/Pentateuch. John 1:14 makes this explicit connection, he "tabernacled" (*eskeneson*) among us: "The Word became flesh and made his dwelling [tabernacled] among us. We have seen his glory, the glory of the one and only Son, who came from the Father, full of grace and truth." (John 1:14) Jesus' incarnation fulfilled the main aim of the temple—that God would dwell with humanity on earth.[2]

14.4 JESUS THE SUFFERING SERVANT

After the fall, cherubim guarded the entrance into the garden of Eden, keeping people from the presence of God (Genesis 3:24). Leviticus showed sinful people could not come into the presence of YHWH without atonement. Only the high priest could enter the holy of holies annually on the day of atonement (*Yom Kippur*). *Az milifnei vereishit*, seventh century

---

2. Morales, *Ascend*, 261.

Jewish liturgy, connected the high priest's role at *Yom Kippur* with the suffering Messiah of Isaiah 53.[3] Of course, for Christians, both figures point to Jesus:

> So Israel learns from the Old Testament the nature of man's plight, the sort of sacrifice needed to deal with sin, the sort of suffering that must be involved, the remarkable combination of divinity and humanity required for the work of salvation, the divine self-giving ... Suddenly all the pieces of the puzzle come together in Jesus. Hundreds of prophecies and narratives were involved, all pointing in various ways, from various perspectives, in only one direction—to Jesus.[4]

The suffering servant fulfils the promise of the temple to bring atonement and purification of God's people. Furthermore, this blessing that starts with Israel (John 4:22), overflows to people from all nations who turn to the Messiah (John 7:38).

> The Crucifixion and Death of Jesus involved a double motion, in terms of the Tabernacle. The sacrifice was made outside the Tabernacle in the courtyard on the altar. Then, on the day of atonement the High Priest took the blood into the Most Holy and presented it before the Throne of God (Leviticus 16:15). Just so, we see the Lamb of God sacrificed outside the gate, and then He presents His Death before the Father's throne (Hebrews 9:7, 23–26).[5]

The New Testament constantly returns to the tabernacle/temple to explain Jesus' death, resurrection, and ascension. For example, all three synoptic Gospels report the tearing of the temple curtain at the point of his death: "And when Jesus had cried out again in a loud voice, he gave up his spirit. At that moment the curtain of the temple was torn in two from top to bottom." (Matthew 27: 50–51)[6] The symbolism is clear. Jesus' death had torn the barrier between heaven and earth.

---

3. Himmelfarb, *Messiahs*, 89.
4. Frame, Apologetics, 141.
5. Jordan, *Eyes*, 268.
6. See also Mark 15:38 and Luke 23:45.

14.5 JESUS' RESURRECTION AND THE DEFEAT OF DEATH

Throughout the Hebrew Bible there is the promise that death will not triumph. After the fall, and the entry of death, Adam names his wife Eve—"the mother of all the living" (Genesis 3:20). The Lord promises to "swallow up death forever" (Isaiah 25:8). One day, there will be a new heaven and new earth, where evil and suffering are no more (Isaiah 65–66). Although the Hebrew Bible rarely, if at all, spoke of the Messiah's resurrection, there is good reason to think resurrection is consistent with his mission:

- if the Messiah is a victorious King, his victory must include victory over death, otherwise it is no victory at all;
- if the Messiah must suffer and die, resurrection is powerful vindication.

John's Gospel proclaims Jesus' resurrection as the fulfilment of the temple's mission, "'Destroy this temple, and I will raise it again in three days.' . . . the temple he had spoken of was his body" (John 2:19–21). These verses connect Jesus' resurrection with the promise of a new creation.[7]

14.6 JESUS' ASCENSION

The Hebrew Bible promises the exaltation of the Messiah, the Priest-King, to the throne of heaven (e.g., Psalm 110). On the day of atonement, the high priest went behind the curtain into the holy of holies (a symbol of heaven). The Book of Hebrews proclaims that Jesus' ascension is the reality to which this ceremony pointed:

> But when Christ came as high priest of the good things that are now already here, he went through the greater and more perfect tabernacle that is not made with human hands, that is to say, is not a part of this creation. He did not enter by means of the blood of goats and calves; but he entered the Most Holy Place once for all by his own blood, thus obtaining eternal redemption. (9:11–12)

Jesus' ascension represents the victory of the King Messiah. The enthroned King is both human son of David and the Lord Almighty (Psalm 24).

---

7. Jordan, *Eyes*, 266–67.

14.7 JESUS THE MESSIAH

14.7.1 No One Else Has Come Close

As argued in the introduction to Part Three, the mission of the Messiah is central to the Hebrew Bible. We have traced how Jesus's life, death, resurrection, and ascension meet these expectations. There is no figure in history that compares to Jesus in fulfilment of these criteria.

Although the focus of Part Three has been thematic, it is also important to point out specific Messianic prophecies met by Jesus. Once more, there is no person in recorded history who has come close to meeting these explicit criteria. Of course, they may meet one or two of these elements, but fail on multiple other criteria. For example, Michael Brown points out:[8]

- Jesus was born in Bethlehem (Micah 5:2);
- he was born before the destruction of the second Temple, as the prophets predicted (e.g., Daniel 9:24–27);[9]
- his followers claimed he was a healer (e.g., Isaiah 35:5–7; 49:6–7);
- he was rejected by his own people (e.g., Isaiah 49:4);
- he suffered before exaltation (Psalm 22; Zechariah 9:9).

14.7.2 Promise of a Worldwide Church

Many have argued Jesus' followers later invented stories to make it appear he was the Messiah. Yet there is a promise we can observe in the present.[10] Passages in the Hebrew Bible predict that people from many nations will follow the Messiah (e.g., Genesis 49:10; Isaiah 42:4; Isaiah 49:6; Zechariah 8:23). In addition, most Jewish people will reject him (Isaiah 49:4).

But are these examples of modern Christian anachronism—claiming these verses are Messianic? This is unlikely. Rabbinic Jews also agree that the Messiah's mission will extend to all nations. For example:

---

8. Brown, *Jewish*, 153.

9. There is no space to get into the detail her, but for further details see Brown, *Jewish*, 86–111.

10. Brown, *Jewish*, 159–61.

- *Genesis 49:10*, Rashi interpreted this verse as reference to the coming of the King Messiah,[11] as does Ramban,[12] Sforno,[13] and many other Rabbinic commentators;
- *Isaiah 42:4*, in chapter 11 we saw several influential Rabbinic texts (Targum of Jonathan, Rambam on Mishnah Sanhedrin, Metzudad David) stated that this servant song was about the Messiah.

14.7.3 Fulfilment of a Worldwide Church

In New Testament times, this was a very high bar to meet. Michael Brown puts this into perspective:

> Just consider how utterly absurd it would have seemed if as you stood at the foot of the cross as Yeshua suffered a torturous, ignominious, shameful death, someone told you, "Two thousand years from now . . . Hundreds of millions of people from all world religions will forsake their idols and their dead traditions and will instead become followers of the God of Israel through him."[14]

Lamin Sanneh, a scholar of World Christianity, argued "Few developments in our day have been more striking and less anticipated than the emergence of Christianity as a world religion."[15] Some sceptics may consider this an exaggeration—the worldwide spread of Christianity was simply due to European colonialism. However, Sanneh argues this growth, occurred despite colonialism. The declining influence of Christianity in the West has been accompanied by unprecedented growth in the global South and East.

> First, the colonial empires that were Christianity's accompanying frame were waning when the religion commenced its surprising forward thrust. New faith communities came into being without a colonial order there to maintain them. Instead of Christianity fading away along with the empire, it unexpectedly grew and spread . . . In the wake of the worldwide Christian resurgence,

---

11. Rashi, *On Genesis*, 49:10.
12. Ramban, *On Genesis*, 49:10.
13. Sforno, *On Genesis*, 49:10.
14. Brown, *Jewish*, 160.
15. Sanneh, *Christianity*, 3.

societies and cultures on every continent and in most countries continue to be attracted to the church.[16]

14.7.4 An Argument From Popularity?

A potential rebuttal to Brown and Sanneh's celebration of a worldwide church, is to argue they are making an argument from popularity. Hundreds of millions of Christians from all nations does not guarantee the truth of Christianity. However, this fails to understand their point.

Several hundred years before the Gospels, the Hebrew Bible promised the Messiah would be rejected by fellow Jews. Yet it also promised people from many nations would put their faith in him. The Gospels and Acts asserted Jesus was that promised Messiah. There is no way authors of these first century[17] texts could know about the twentieth and twenty first century events described by Brown and Sanneh. A prophecy made hundreds of years before the birth of Jesus, the extremely unlikely event of a worldwide community of believers in the Messiah, has seen fulfilment in our times.

14.8 CONCLUSION

Part Two focused on how judgments about the nature of reality inform the prior probability for Jesus' resurrection. Part Three has focused on whether Jesus is the Messiah promised in the Hebrew Bible, another important component of the prior. If Jesus is not the Messiah, and therefore a heretic, it is close to impossible God will raise him from the dead. Part Three has considered several passages, widely agreed by Jewish tradition and Christians, on the Messiah:

> Here we have a wide variety of human authors, writing across many centuries, with very different interests, concerns, styles, and levels of intellectual sophistication, saying many different things, and yet, at the same time, saying one thing: Jesus is coming, and this is what he will be and do.[18]

---

16. Sanneh, *Christianity*, 3.
17. Of course, some would argue second century texts.
18. Frame, *Apologetics*, 141.

PART FOUR

The Evidence for Jesus' Resurrection

RECAP

PARTS ONE TO THREE *have been building up to this section—evidence for the resurrection. In Part One, I argued Hume's views on miracles remain foundational for many atheists. Although probably unfamiliar with Bayes's rule, Hume's rejection of miracles depended on what we now call "prior probabilities" or "priors." In other words, before assessing evidence that a miracle happened, we must consider the initial probability of that miracle. I have argued the prior for Jesus' resurrection depends on two main factors—the nature of reality, and if Jesus is the Messiah, assessed in Parts Two and Three (see Figure 4).*

Part Two focused on the nature of reality. If ultimate reality is founded on impersonal energy, then Hume is correct, miracles are close to impossible. If mind-first approaches are true, miracles are possible. But super miracles,[1] like the resurrection, are extremely unlikely given the finite nature of gods. Part Two compared how well these worldviews account for the existence of the universe, success of science, suffering, and evil. I argued that, overall, Christianity and unipersonal theism best account for these data.

Part Three focused on whether Jesus is the Messiah, another important determinant of the prior. Though unipersonal theists are open to the possibility of miracles, the probability of Jesus' resurrection is also close to impossible for them. If Jesus is not the Messiah (as, for example, argued by Rabbinic Jews), then it is close to impossible God would raise him from the dead.

---

1. I am using this in a similar way to Swinburne, in the sense of a miracle which indicates the supreme authority of God.

PART FOUR: THE EVIDENCE FOR JESUS' RESURRECTION

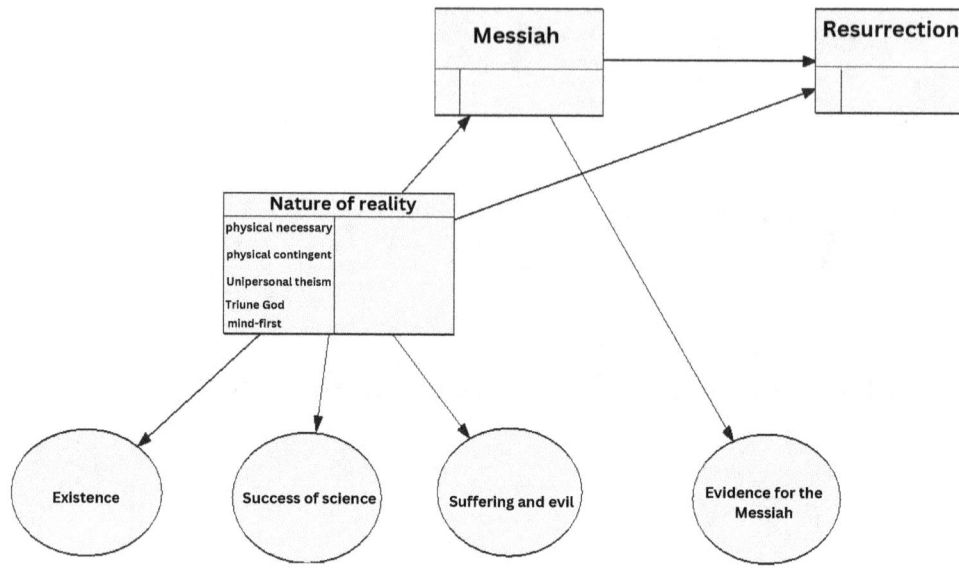

Figure 4. Main factors impacting on the prior for Jesus' resurrection

However, if Jesus is the Messiah, and his resurrection is consistent with the Messiah's mission, then this increases the prior. I argued in Part Three, Jesus' death, resurrection, and ascension are consistent with the Messiah's mission as set out in the Hebrew Bible. Parts Two and Three challenge Hume's assertion that the prior for Jesus' resurrection is close to impossible. The consistency of Christianity with data on the nature of reality, and evidence that Jesus is the Messiah, suggests the prior is higher than asserted by Hume. Now that the key factors for the prior have been considered, it is now time to assess evidence for Jesus' resurrection.

INTRODUCTION TO PART FOUR

Many scholars, both atheist and Christian, try to pit the early creed of First Corinthians 15 and the canonical Gospels against each other. Yet these battles are unnecessary. Both sets of sources have complementary strengths.

The creed in First Corinthians 15 is the earliest source of evidence for Jesus' resurrection—perhaps within a few years of Jesus' death. These verses show belief in Jesus' death and resurrection were at the heart of the early church—from the beginning. But the details are sparse—as we would

Part Four: The Evidence for Jesus' Resurrection

expect in a creed. Paul's letter to the Corinthian church does not set out to tell a detailed story of these events, nor does the creed. That was the aim of the four canonical Gospels.

While sceptics try to pick holes in the creed, because of its brevity, they have opposite concerns regarding the length of the Gospels. The extra content is explained away as legendary embellishment. Yet these differences can equally be accounted for by the different purposes of the creed (and the wider purposes of a letter to the Corinthian church) compared with documents setting out to give an account of the life, death, and resurrection of Jesus.

The four canonical Gospels provide a later but more detailed account of the evidence for Jesus' resurrection (dated from approximately 65 to 110 CE).[2] I will argue that the creed and the Gospels are consistent on all the main points (see Box 8 for a plan of Part Four).

BOX 8. SUMMARY OF PART FOUR

Chapter 15: First Corinthians 15. The focus is on the early creed, verses 3–5, but also considers verses 6–8 on the appearances to Paul, James, and the 500.

Chapter 16: Matthew and Mark's Gospel. Compares the similarities and differences between Matthew and Mark's Gospels.

Chapter 17: Luke and John's Gospel. Focuses on Luke and John's Gospels;

Chapter 18: Summary and Conclusions. Compares the similarities and differences across the four Gospels and First Corinthians 15:3–8.

---

2. Jesus' death was in approximately 33 CE.

Chapter 15

First Corinthians 15, An Early Creed

15.1 INTRODUCTION

FIRST CORINTHIANS IS USUALLY dated to the mid-fifties CE.[1] Yet most scholars believe Paul cited an *early creed* in chapter 15—about Jesus' death and resurrection. Most consider it to be constructed *within two to three years after Jesus' death*.[2] Ehrman is rightly tentative, but acknowledges, "this is very ancient tradition about Jesus. Does it go back even to before the time when Paul himself joined the movement around 33 CE, some three years after Jesus died? If so, it would be very ancient indeed!"[3] NT scholars Martin Hengel and Anna Maria Schwemer summarised the significance of this early confession.

> The fact that such reported confessional statements are formulated at all is grounded in the fact that the resurrection of Jesus could not be proclaimed as a pure testimony of faith without reference to a real event . . . Rather, there was a need to emphasize at the same time the eyewitness testimony of those to whom the risen one had appeared, who saw him and thus, according to the opinion of the earliest communities, really perceived him. For the persons involved the confession was based on real, indeed, from

---

1. Ehrman, *Jesus*, 138.
2. Wright, *Resurrection*, 319.
3. Ehrman, *Jesus*, 138.

their perspective, one must say objective events, which were kept in memory and testified.[4]

Of course, for Christians, the testimony from the word of God about Jesus' resurrection is clear and sufficient. But the early church did not try to separate faith and history in a way that is natural to us. Paul spoke with the authority of an apostle called by Jesus Christ (First Corinthians 1:1). Yet he saw no conflict in repeating the early creed, with its careful preservation of eyewitness testimony. In what follows, I will pursue four main themes:

- which verses contain the early creed;
- First Corinthains 15: 3–5—Jesus' death, burial, resurrection, and appearances to the twelve;
- First Corinthians 15:6–8—appearances to Paul, James, and the 500;
- objections: such as whether these verses referred to real world perceptions or visions; if the creed denied Jesus' empty tomb.

15.2 THE EARLY CREED: AT LEAST VERSES 3–5

> For what I received I passed on to you as of first importance: that Christ died for our sins according to the Scriptures, that he was buried, that he was raised on the third day according to the Scriptures, and that he appeared to Cephas, and then to the Twelve. (First Corinthians 15:3–5)

Most scholars agree the creed includes verses 3–5. Ehrman argues the creed ends at "Cephas"—the beginning of verse 5.[5] However, there is good reason to think it continues till "the Twelve"—end of verse 5. Antony Thiselton points out Paul rarely referred to "the Twelve".[6] He preferred to use the term apostles, so this phrase likely reflects earlier tradition.[7]

---

4. Hengel and Schwemer, *Judaism*, 660.
5. Ehrman, *Jesus*, 139.
6. Thiselton, *Corinthians*, 1203–1204.
7. Thiselton, *Corinthians*, 1205.

PART FOUR: THE EVIDENCE FOR JESUS' RESURRECTION

15.3 FIRST CORINTHIANS 15: 3–5

15.3.1 He Was Buried

According to NT Wright, the purpose of mentioning Jesus' burial was to show:

> Jesus was really and truly dead . . . second, to indicate that when Paul speaks of resurrection in the next phrase it is to be assumed, as anyone telling or hearing a story of someone being raised from the dead would assume in either the pagan or the Jewish world, that this referred to the body being raised to new life, leaving an empty tomb behind it.[8]

However, First Corinthians 15 does not mention Jesus' empty tomb. According to Bart Ehrman, this may be significant:

> There we are told simply "that he was buried"—not that he was buried by anyone in particular . . . this should give us pause . . . My hunch is that it is because he knew nothing about a burial of Jesus by Joseph of Arimathea, or the way in which Jesus was buried.[9]

Yet many scholars think the creed implies the empty tomb. Hengel and Schwemer argue it would be unthinkable for Paul, a former Pharisee, to speak of Jesus' burial and resurrection whilst denying the empty tomb.

> For Palestinian Jews of a Pharisaic character—and Paul was a former Pharisee—the resurrection was only imaginable as a bodily resurrection from the grave. It is wrongheaded when it is stressed time and again that the stories of the empty tomb are late legends without exception, with the rationale that it is not spoken of in the oldest confession of 1 Cor15.3ff. In the conciseness of the confession statements we must assume that the statement "that he was buried" with the following statement "he was raised on the third day" together imply the tradition of the empty tomb, with the reference to burial admittedly still being ambiguous when taken on its own.[10]

---

8. Wright, *Resurrection*, 321.
9. Ehrman, *Jesus*, 141–43.
10. Hengel and Schwemer, *Judaism*, 664.

15.3.2 Objection: Bodily Resurrection or Vision?

Some sceptical scholars suggest the creed in First Corinthians 15 meant Jesus "appeared" spiritually after his ascension. Some have translated the Greek word *ophthe*, used in these verses, as either "seen by" or "appeared to." Word use alone cannot determine Paul's intention.[11] Bart Ehrman acknowledges Paul spoke about people who believed they had seen the risen Jesus, "he is assuming, with his readers, that Jesus really was raised . . . since Jesus was raised bodily from the dead . . . The resurrection for Paul is not a spiritual matter unrelated to the body."[12] Allison argues this depiction of the resurrection is consistent with the later Gospels:

> all know stories in which people ostensibly see the risen Jesus. Even were one to judge all these stories to be late, it is easier to imagine that they represent not some unprecedented interpretation of the confessional [*opthe*] but rather stand in continuity with it.[13]

Influential Bible scholar Rudolph Bultmann insisted "an historical fact which involves a resurrection from the dead is utterly inconceivable!"[14] He dismissed numerous New Testament passages that spoke of the historical reality of Jesus's resurrection as later embellishments. Yet even he acknowledged, "There is however one passage where St Paul tries to prove the miracle of the resurrection by adducing a list of eyewitnesses (1 Cor. 15: 3—8)."[15] Theologian Bruce Ware argues there are no examples in Ancient Greek literature where the word (*eigero*) used in verse 4 relates to ascension:

> As we have seen, [*egeiro*] does not mean to rise in the sense that a balloon rises into the air, but in the sense of arising to stand. In resurrection contexts the verb does not therefore denote that the dead ascend or are assumed somewhere; rather, the verb signifies that the corpse, lying supine in the grave, gets up or arises to stand from the tomb.[16]

---

11. Wright, *Resurrection*, 323.
12. Ehrman, *Jesus*, 137.
13. Allison, *Resurrection*, 43.
14. Bultmann, *Kerygma*, 1:39.
15. Bultmann, *Kerygma*, 1:39.
16. Ware, *Resurrection*, 494.

15.3.3 On the Third Day According to the Scriptures

I have already discussed in chapter 12, the concept of the third day in the Hebrew Bible—where God acted in redemption and salvation for his people. The early church were quick to note this connection with Jesus' resurrection on the third day. A famous example is Hosea 6:1–3 but there are several similar verses (such as Exodus 19:11, 16; Genesis 22:4; 2 Kings 20:5).

15.3.4 The Twelve

This section of the creed names specific eyewitnesses of Jesus' resurrection—Cephas (Peter) and his closest disciples (the Twelve)—likely within a few years of Jesus' death. Of course, by then, Judas had betrayed him. So "the Twelve" probably referred to the eleven remaining disciples or included Matthias, who later replaced Judas. This is not uncommon in antiquity. For example, Dale Allison points out Octavian and Mark Antony continued to refer to themselves as the triumvirate even after Marcus Aemilius Lepidus had been overthrown.[17]

15.4 FIRST CORINTHIANS 15:6–8

15.4.1 The Five Hundred

> After that, he appeared to more than five hundred of the brothers and sisters at the same time, most of whom are still living, though some have fallen asleep. Then he appeared to James, then to all the apostles, and last of all he appeared to me also, as to one abnormally born. (1 Corinthians 15:6–8)

There is disagreement among scholars whether verses 6–8 are part of the earlier creed—or added by Paul. At the latest, these verses reflect Christian belief fifteen to twenty-five years after Jesus' death. Most likely, some aspects were earlier. Some scholars argue the 500 was a reference to Luke's Pentecost account in Acts 2. But that passage was about the Holy Spirit, not Jesus.[18] Thiselton points to Matthew 28:16–20 as one possible occasion. Although Matthew only mentions the eleven in this story.

---

17. Allison, *Resurrection*, 62.
18. Wright, *Resurrection*, 324–25.

it is part of Matthew's distinctive ecclesiology that the Great Commission . . . is addressed *to the eleven* as authoritative leaders and teachers. It is beyond question, on the other hand, "that traditional elements underlie at least some of the material". . . Although it cannot be identified with certainty, this example is sufficiently plausible to allay fears that 15:6 could find no possible place in the traditions which find their way into the gospel narratives.[19]

15.4.2 Paul

NT scholar Craig Keener draws several contrasts between the Acts narratives on Paul's conversion and later visions (e.g. Second Corinthians 12:1). He argues Paul spoke in First Corinthians 15 about a specific incident—his conversion:

> the revelation in 2 Cor 12:2–4 was a secret one, in contrast to his conversion, and belonged to a larger series of visions as a believer in Jesus (12:1; Acts 26:16). Paul himself speaks of meeting Christ (1 Cor 15:8) in a manner distinct from his later visions (2 Cor 12:1).[20]

According to Keener, theophanies in the Hebrew Bible, are the closest background to Paul's conversion (Acts 9, 22, 26).[21] Much like the Hebrew prophets and leaders of the past, God met Paul face-to-face and commissioned him to be an apostle.[22] As argued in chapter 9, John's Gospel states when Moses, and other saints of the Hebrew Bible, saw the face of God they saw Jesus (John 1:18; John 8:58; 12:41). There are many examples of appearances of God in the Hebrew Bible that involve seeing (for example Genesis 18–19, Exodus 33:11).

15.4.3 Objection: Paul's Experience Similar to the Twelve?

In the Gospels and Acts, there is a clear distinction between Jesus' appearances before and after his ascension. Jesus appeared to many of his disciples, including the twelve, to equip them to be witnesses to his resurrection.

---

19. Thiselton, *Corinthians*, 1206.
20. Keener, *Acts*, 271.
21. Keener, Acts, 274–79.
22. Bruce, *Acts*, 467.

After Jesus' ascension, his appearances were fewer and of a different nature. Paul, as we saw above, was commissioned to be an apostle to the Gentiles; Stephen, an early martyr, received comfort in his trials; John at Patmos received apocalyptic revelation.

Some sceptics argue First Corinthians 15 implies Jesus' appearances to the twelve were much the same as Paul's experience of the ascended Jesus. If so, assuming the primacy of Paul, the resurrection accounts in the Gospels were pious inventions. However, as Dale Allison points out, this assumes too much:

> why should we presume that Paul's encounter, in Leslie Houden's words, "was generally admitted to be of the same sort as its predecessors'? . . . Paul does not subjoin his experience to those before it with a simple "and then". . . He rather prefaces "appeared also to me" with "last of all as to one aborted," cryptic words which in some way distinguish him from others.[23]

15.4.4 James

Most scholars[24] agree James, mentioned here, is the brother of Jesus. Paul and James became followers of Jesus after his resurrection.[25] Paul makes clear in Galatians he considered James an apostle (Galatians 1:19). The book of Acts also portrays him as a central figure, along with Peter, in the early church (e.g., Acts 15:13). There is no explicit reference to James in any of the resurrection accounts in the canonical Gospels, but he may have been present in the group alluded to in Acts 1:6–9.[26] It is hard to account for his influence in the early church except that James had seen the risen Jesus.

15.5 CONCLUSION

Most scholars agree First Corinthians 15:3–5 is an early creed composed up to five years after Jesus' death. These verses affirm he was raised bodily from the dead—for that is what resurrection meant to most first century Jews. There is more debate about whether the early creed included all, or

---

23. Allison, *Resurrection*, 224–25.
24. See Thiselton, *Corinthians*, 1207 for further details.
25. Thiselton, *Corinthians*, 1207.
26. Thiselton, *Corinthians*, 1207.

First Corinthians 15, An Early Creed

some parts, of verses 6–8. At the latest, they reflect Christian belief fifteen to twenty-five years after Jesus' death. These verses show that Paul and James claimed to see Jesus after his resurrection—along with 500 others. First Corinthians 15: 3–8 shows belief in Jesus' physical resurrection was a central feature of the early church from the beginning.

The Gospels offer a more detailed account of the final events of Jesus' death, resurrection, and ascension. *Chapters 16 and 17* will argue that when read side-by-side the four canonical Gospels provide a coherent account of these events. I will also explore some of the major differences between them. Finally, *chapter 18* will argue for consistency between the Gospels and the early creed of First Corinthians 15.

Chapter 16

Mark and Matthew

16.1 INTRODUCTION

MANY SCEPTICS HAVE POINTED out differences between the Gospel resurrection accounts. For example, Charles Templeton, a former evangelist, and critic of Christianity argued, "The four descriptions of events . . . differ so markedly at so many points that, with all the good will in the world, they cannot be reconciled."[1] The next two chapters will explore whether this is in fact the case.

I will argue there is a *common thread* that runs through these accounts. For example, all four Gospels mentioned Jesus' crucifixion and burial in Joseph of Arimathea's tomb. Jesus' female disciples were also first to witness his empty tomb in all four Gospels. Three of the four Gospels narrated various occasions when his disciples saw Jesus. They made clear he had a physical body, yet it was somehow different. N.T. Wright called this "*transphysicality*:"

> Jesus is almost routinely depicted in these stories as having a human body with properties that are, to say the least, unusual. The same Lukan text that tells us that Jesus ate broiled fish, and invited his followers to touch him and see he was real, also tells us that Jesus appeared and disappeared at will, that at one of these appearances two close friends and colleagues did not recognize him.[2]

---

1. Cited in Strobel, *Easter*, 44.
2. Wright, *Resurrection*, 605.

Mark and Matthew

This chapter discusses the following topics:

- overlap between Mark and Matthew's Gospels;
- apparent differences;
- summary of Mark's resurrection account: the short and long ending; Jesus' death, burial, and empty tomb;
- summary of Matthew's resurrection account: Jesus' death, burial, and empty tomb; Jesus' appearance in Galilee.

16.2 OVERLAP BETWEEN MATTHEW AND MARK

It is generally accepted that Matthew and Mark are based on similar sources:

> There are moments when it sounds as though we are listening to a version of the same text, though from this passage alone it would be impossible to say which of them has used the other. Even so, out of 136 words in the equivalent Matthew passage (28:1–8) there are only thirty-five which are matched in Mark.[3]

Yet there is an important difference. Mark ends the account early (16:8) while Matthew continues the narrative with Jesus' appearances to the disciples.

16.3 APPARENT DIFFERENCES

Despite the many similarities, reading the Gospels side-by-side you may notice some apparent differences. Most of these are trivial. For example, who were the women present at Jesus' death, burial, and empty tomb?

> Mark and Matthew mention three women named Mary throughout their Gospels: the mother of Jesus, the mother of James the Younger and Joses/Joseph, and Mary Magdalene. Luke mentions four women named Mary: the mother of Jesus, Mary Magdalene, the sister of Martha, and the mother of James. John mentions four women named Mary: the mother of Jesus, Mary Magdalene, the sister of Martha and Lazarus, and the wife of Clopas.[4]

---

3. Wright, *Resurrection*, 590.
4. Licona, *Gospels*, 210.

Part Four: The Evidence for Jesus' Resurrection

In addition to several Marys, the Gospels also mention the following women present at Jesus' death, burial, and empty tomb:

- Joanna
- Salome
- the mother of the sons of Zebedee (John and James)
- the sister of Mary mother of Jesus.

This raises a few questions. First, why all the Marys? One reason is the popularity of the name in the first century. Approximately 30% of women in Palestine at the time were named Mary or Salome.[5] Second, are these eight different women (four Marys plus four other women)? Or do the Gospel authors use slight variations in naming them? There are various views but in the end:

> one can only speculate pertaining to whether some of the women mentioned in one Gospel are variants of women mentioned in the parallel accounts. The differences notwithstanding, one is hard pressed to conclude that the accounts stand in contradiction, since Luke mentions "women" at the crucifixion and burial without providing the number and names three women and "others with them" at the empty tomb. Each evangelist may have included the names of the women from whom came the testimony upon which their narrative relied.[6]

N.T. Wright points out these surface ambiguities would be expected if the resurrection accounts were early and unvarnished. Later accounts would likely have had more time to iron out apparent inconsistencies. These differences seem to reflect "the hurried, puzzled accounts of those who have seen with their own eyes something which took them horribly by surprise and with which they have not yet fully come to terms."[7]

---

5. Licona, *Gospels*, 210.
6. Licona, *Gospels*, 212.
7. Wright, *Resurrection*, 612.

16.4 MARK

16.4.1 Mark's Lost Ending?

Mark's resurrection account is shorter than those found in the other Gospels. Most scholars agree the longer endings of Mark are not in the original. He finishes in an enigmatic manner, "Trembling and bewildered, the women went out and fled from the tomb. They said nothing to anyone, because they were afraid." (Mark 16:8)

Most conclude Mark intended to stop at 16:8.[8] "It is, they argue, appropriate to a gospel which has traded heavily in paradox to end on a paradoxical note."[9] However, influential scholars, like France and Wright propose an alternative solution. The ending may have been lost:

> Did Mark mean to break off at 16:8? Did he really intend his whole gospel, admittedly in rough Greek, to end with *ephobounto gar*, "for they were afraid"? Where did the two extra endings come from, and what would Mark have thought of them?[10]

In addition, many ancient scrolls are damaged at both ends, consistent with the possibility of Mark's ending being lost. It is not possible to decide definitively which explanation is correct.

16.4.2 Jesus' Death

Mark's account of Jesus' death is full of allusions to the Hebrew Bible. For example, he cried out in a loud voice from Psalm 22:1, "My God, my God, why have you forsaken me?" (15:34). This is a psalm on the suffering son of David (the Messiah) who dies for his people (see Part Three). When Jesus breathed his last, "The curtain of the temple was torn in two from top to bottom" (15:36). In Part Three we saw that the temple is a key theme throughout the Hebrew Bible. This reference to the curtain likely concerns the holy of holies, a symbol of the barrier between God and his people—caused by sin. Which in turn points back to Eden after the fall. Jesus' death was bringing about a new creation, when the dwelling of God would be with his people (for example, Isaiah 65–66; Ezekiel 48).

---

8. France, *Mark*, 670.
9. France, *Mark*, 670–671.
10. Wright, *Resurrection*, 616–17.

16.4.3 Jesus' Burial and Empty tomb

Mark 16 is a combination of the down-to-earth and the incomprehensible:

> This is not the stuff of a heroic epic, still less of a story of magic and wonder, and yet what underlies it is an event beyond human comprehension . . . It is in this incongruous combination of the everyday with the incomprehensible that many have found one of the most powerful and compelling aspects of the NT accounts not of Jesus' resurrection (for there are none) but of how the first disciples discovered that he had risen.[11]

Consistent with the other three Gospels, Mark reported that Jesus was buried in Joseph of Arimathea's tomb (15:27–42). Mary Magdalene and Mary, the mother of Joseph, saw where he was laid (15:47). After the Sabbath, Mary Magdalene, Mary the mother of James, and Salome went to anoint Jesus' body. As they approached the tomb, a young man dressed in a white robe (likely an angel) told them Jesus was raised from the dead (16:5–7).

This Gospel ends in verse 8 with the silence of the women. This may lead some to argue, because Mark did not mention any resurrection appearances, these must have been invented later. But, of course, First Corinthians 15 shows that cannot be the case (see chapter 15).[12]

16.5 MATTHEW

16.5.1 Death, Burial, and Empty Tomb

Most of the main points mentioned in Mark are also found in Matthew:

- Jesus quoted Psalm 22:1 on the cross (27:46);
- the temple curtain is torn in two from top to bottom (27:51);
- Jesus was buried in the tomb of Joseph Arimathea (27:57–60);
- Jesus' female disciples (Mary Magdelene and "the other Mary") saw the empty tomb (28:1–10).

Because of these similarities, most scholars think Matthew's account of Jesus' resurrection is dependent on Mark—with the women as the first

---

11. France, *Mark*, 675.
12. Allison, *Resurrection*, 126.

witnesses of his empty tomb and appearance. Yet Matthew chose to tell the story in his own way:

> They do not go into the tomb as they do in Mark; Matthew has the women confronted not simply by a "young man" as in Mark, or "two men in dazzling clothes" as in Luke, but by a palpable angel looking like lightning.[13]

16.5.2 Appearance in Galilee

Both Matthew and Mark reported that Jesus would appear in Galilee (Mark 16:7; Mathew 26:32, 28:7). The Galilee appearance in Matthew is focused on Jesus' exaltation he has "all authority in heaven and on earth." Virtually identical to "your kingdom, your will be done, on earth as it is in heaven" in the Lord's prayer (Matthew 6:10).[14] Indicating that Matthew considered Jesus' resurrection a sign that the kingdom of God had begun.

An important sign of authenticity, Matthew reported that "some doubted." The author would be unlikely to include this detail if he was inventing a story to convince or inspire people. "This forces us to look for another explanation. An obvious one is that here, as in the other canonical resurrection narratives, the risen Jesus both was and was not "the same" as he had been before."[15] Matthew 28 is focused on showing God's kingdom had begun with Jesus' resurrection. He now "holds the role that had been marked out for the Messiah in Psalms 2, 72 and 89, which became concentrated in such imagery-laden figures as the "son of man" in Daniel 7."[16]

I will argue in the next chapter that Luke builds on this theme where he includes an account of Jesus' ascension as fulfilment of these promises. The main account of Jesus' death and resurrection remains the same in Luke and John's Gospels. Yet as before, there are some variations in how they told the story.

---

13. Wright, *Resurrection*, 640.
14. Wright, *Resurrection*, 643.
15. Wright, *Resurrection*, 644.
16. Wright, *Resurrection*, 643.

Chapter 17

Resurrection Accounts in Luke and John

17.1 INTRODUCTION

LUKE, LIKELY WRITTEN LATER, is thought to have used Mark. But the relationship between the texts is not straightforward:

> If Luke has "used" Mark, we must conclude either that he has done so very freely or that he has had another source alongside, which he has almost exclusively preferred. Or maybe "using" in this case means that he had the scroll of Mark on the table but was so accustomed to telling the story his own way that he glanced at it, decided he could do without it, pushed it to one side and got on without further reference to it.[1]

John's is the most enigmatic of all the canonical Gospels. It shares the main points of the synoptics (Matthew, Mark, and Luke) but takes its own path from the beginning. Sceptical scholars have several doubts about the resurrection accounts in Luke's and John's Gospels. For example, atheist scholar Gerd Ludemann, considered Luke 24:36–43, "a figment of the imagination of the second Christian generation, arising from discussions within the community on the bodily nature of the 'Risen One.'"[2]

Dale Allison seeks a half-way option. He partly rejects the common narrative of modern sceptical scholars—that Luke and John's accounts reflect, "a trajectory from less literal to more literal . . . the seemingly solid

---

1. Wright, *Resurrection*, 590.
2. Ludemann, *Resurrection*, 111.

figures in Luke and John being later developments."[3] Yet, he is only mildly less dismissive of their historical validity:

> Now I personally remain hesitant to find history in the demonstrations of Luke 24 and John 20–21. I rather detect Christian apologetics here, an answer to the criticism that Jesus was merely a specter or hallucination.[4]

Whether doubts about increasingly physical appearances, or apologetical denial of hallucinations, these hypotheses pit Luke and John against Mark and Matthew. We will explore the extent to which these proposals are supported by the data.

17.2 LUKE'S GOSPEL

17.2.1 Jesus' Burial and Empty Tomb (24:1–12)

Luke, like the other canonical Gospel writers, chose to tell the story in his own way.[5] But his freedom of expression, is constrained:

> He does not feel free to modify substantially what must be considered very early tradition. His stories share with the other canonical ones the strange features . . . which simultaneously fit with the early Christian reflection on what resurrection actually involved while showing no signs of having borrowed from that reflection the developed theological or exegetical detail.[6]

The account of Cleopas and his friend on the road to Emmaus, and the focus on Jerusalem, is unique to Luke.[7] Yet, Acts 1 shows he was aware of many other appearances of Jesus over a forty-day period.[8] His account of Jesus' ascension is also more prominent than the other Gospels.

The opening section of Luke's resurrection account is like the corresponding section in Matthew and Mark where Jesus' female disciples witness the empty tomb.[9] A minor difference is that an angel spoke to

---

3. Allison, *Resurrection*, 226–27.
4. Allison, *Resurrection*, 229.
5. Morris, *Luke*, 363.
6. Wright, *Resurrection*, 647–48.
7. Morris, *Luke*, 363.
8. Marshall, *Luke*, 878.
9. Wright, *Resurrection*, 647–48.

the women in Matthew and Mark, whereas Luke (like John) mentioned two angels (24:4). There may be various explanations, for example that one angel was the main spokesman, and therefore "more prominent than his associates and maybe referred to without mention of others."[10] But more importantly, "these minor differences tell us that the accounts are independent."[11]

In addition to the women, Luke reported that Peter witnessed the empty tomb (24:12). On the surface, John 20:2–10 appears to contradict this account, which places Peter and the beloved disciple at the empty tomb. However, Cleopas and his companion make clear Peter was not alone: "Then some of our companions went to the tomb and found it just as the women had said, but they did not see Jesus." (Luke 24:24) Carson argues, "the plural should be given its natural force and taken as confirmation of the witness of the Fourth Gospel."[12]

17.2.2 Road to Emmaus (24:13–35)

None of the other Gospels contain this account of Jesus' appearance on the road to Emmaus.[13] It is understandable that other Gospel writers omitted this testimony of lesser-known disciples. There appears to have been testimony about a range of appearances, no one Gospel account claims to contain them all. In addition, according to Wright, this fits well with Luke's theme of journeying. "Much of Luke's gospel, like Acts, has journeying as its underlying motif: the walk to Emmaus becomes the vehicle for the central message Luke wants to convey about Easter and its meaning."[14]

The two disciples at first did not recognise him; they shared their perplexity at his death and claims of an empty tomb. Jesus then made himself known to them, "And beginning with Moses and all the Prophets, he explained to them what was said in all the Scriptures concerning himself." (24:27). According to Wright, chapter 24 returns to the opening themes of Luke's Gospel. The resurrection narrative is designed to mirror the prologue:

10. Morris, *Luke*, 364.
11. Morris, *Luke*, 364.
12. Carson, *John*, 636.
13. Morris, *Luke*, 366. He makes the intriguing suggestion that the unnamed companion could have been Luke.
14. Wright, *Resurrection*, 647.

> In the centre of the opening chapters is the story of the conception and birth of Jesus ... we cannot fail to notice the angel, announcing and explaining what is going on, and particularly the emphasis on Jesus as Israel's Messiah (1:32; 2:11, 26; 24:26, 46) ... Luke is telling the Easter story in such a way as to say: all that was promised in the prologue has now come true, though not in the way anyone imagined."[15]

17.2.3 Appearance to the Eleven and Others (24:36–49)

After he left them, Cleopas and his companion continued their journey to meet the eleven.[16] They shared with the disciples how they had seen Jesus. Once more he appeared amongst them (24:36). The focus of this narrative is the state of Jesus' resurrected body—that he is not a ghost.[17] He impelled them to touch and see his flesh and bones (24:39–40). He ate broiled fish to further reiterate his physicality, or transphysicality. Some sceptical scholars have suggested contradiction between Luke's understanding of Jesus' resurrection body, from Paul's statement "flesh and blood cannot inherit the kingdom of God" (First Corinthians 15:50). But as NT scholar I. Howard Marshall points out:

> the conflict is apparent rather than real. Paul is concerned with the nature of the body in the new life after the resurrection of the dead in the kingdom of God, while Luke is concerned with the appropriate form of manifestation of the risen Jesus in earthly conditions, and his narrative makes it plain that although Jesus has flesh and bones he is able to appear and vanish in a way that is not possible for ordinary men. Both writers agree that resurrection is concerned with the body and not with a bodiless soul or spirit.[18]

---

15. Wright, *Resurrection*, 649–50.
16. Jesus' leading disciples minus Judas Iscariot.
17. Marshall, *Luke*, 900–901.
18. Marshall, *Luke*, 900.

PART FOUR: THE EVIDENCE FOR JESUS' RESURRECTION

17.2.4 Ascension (24:50–53)

Luke is the only Gospel author to write a direct account of Jesus' ascension.[19] For Luke, the ascension represents a "dramatic closure to the story of Jesus and then a hermeneutical key to the new history of the people of God."[20] We need not wait till the end of history for Jesus' vindication:

> the ascension and heavenly session provide that guarantee already. The ascension (not the resurrection or the parousia) thus becomes the climax of Jesus-history and *the* eschatological event, fulfilling all the prophetic hopes of Israel. And this eschatologizes what is left of history by setting it within the tension of his departure and still-impending return.[21]

Critical scholars have much to say about Luke's ascension narratives. Some have argued the parallel account in Acts contradicts Luke 24. Acts 1 states there were 40 days between Jesus' resurrection and ascension, whilst Luke's Gospel suggests a much shorter period. However, as theologian Douglas Farrow points out, "can we not allow him [Luke] the licence to condense before unfolding?"[22]

17.2.5 Ascension in Other Gospels

Does the lack of an ascension account in the other Gospels indicate a Lukan invention? We should not be too hasty, "the omission of an account of the event and its absence from the work itself are not the same thing."[23] It is not Luke, but Paul, who first spoke of Jesus' ascension (e.g., Romans 8:34; Ephesians 1:20; 2:6; Colossians 3:1).

The Gospels are also far from silent. In Part Three, I pointed out Mark's allusions to Daniel 7:13 (Mark 8:38; 13:26–31; 14:62). According to NT scholar France, these verses refer to Jesus' ascension and enthronement:

> Daniel 7:13–14 is, in other words, no less than Ps. 110:1 an enthronement oracle, and it is that universal and unending dominion which Jesus here declares that he himself will now receive . . . we

---

19. Discounting Mark's longer ending.
20. Farrow, *Ascension*, 16.
21. Farrow, *Ascension*, 17.
22. Farrow, *Ascension*, 16.
23. Farrow, *Ascension*, 20.

are clearly in the realm of vindication which was to begin with Jesus' resurrection and according to Luke to be more visibly confirmed by his ascension ... it would certainly be possible for Jesus' judges within their lifetime to see that the "Messiah" they thought they had destroyed had in fact been vindicated and exalted to the place of supreme authority.[24]

Matthew 28:16–20 also speaks about the implications of Jesus' ascension:

> Having atoned for the sins of his people, this coming Messiah—the last Adam, the seed of Abraham, the true Israel, greater to reign from the heavenly Mount Zion, from the right hand of God the Father. The commission of Matthew 28:18–20, then, is but the embrace of the inheritance promised in Psalm 2 (and Dan. 7).[25]

John's Gospel makes several references to Jesus' ascension. For example, in response to his disciples' grumbling, "Does this offend you? Then what if you see the Son of Man ascend to where he was before!" (6:61–62) In common with the synoptics, Jesus relates his ascension to the right hand of God as fulfilment of Daniel 7. Jesus' ascension is necessary for the descent of the Spirit (e.g., 7:39, 14:2, 16:2). Similarly, after his resurrection, Jesus told Mary, "Do not hold on to me, for I have not yet ascended to the Father" (20:17).

> That Jesus is in the process of ascending to his Father, on the way as it were, is in conformity with the significance of the ascension described in Luke 24:51; Acts 1:9—11 ... In that sense, in both John and Luke/Acts, Jesus is in process of ascending to the Father until the culminating ascension.[26]

17.3 JOHN'S GOSPEL

John's resurrection narrative shares the same basic framework of the other Gospels: Jesus' death, burial, empty tomb, and appearances to disciples. However, the precise accounts he used to tell this story are very different. "He agrees on the fact of the resurrection and he speaks of the empty tomb

---

24. France, *Mark*, 612–13.
25. Morales, *Ascend*, 235.
26. Carson, *John*, 645.

as do the others, but he lacks the stories the others tell, and he tells stories they do not."[27]

17.3.1 Death, Burial, Empty Tomb (John 19–20:1–10)

- Jesus' death on the cross is also viewed in terms of the Hebrew Bible (e.g., Psalm 22, Zechariah 12); but details included in all three synoptic Gospels are not reported by John (e.g., Jesus' calling out Psalm 22:1 from the cross, and the tearing of the temple curtain);
- in common with the synoptic Gospels, Jesus was buried in the tomb of Joseph Arimathea (19:38–42); however, John added that Nicodemus bought burial spices (19:39);
- like the synoptics, a female disciple (Mary Magdalene) was at the tomb first; she reported to Peter and the beloved disciple that the stone had been moved (20:1–2); this appears different from the other Gospel accounts where a group of women go to Jesus' tomb; Carson[28] and Ridderbos[29] think it more likely that Mary Magdalene went first alone, before joining a group of women later; whereas Morris[30] suggests the plural in 20:2, "They have taken the Lord out of the tomb, and *we* don't know where they have put him!" implied Mary was not on her own;
- John's narrative included an account of Peter and the beloved disciple witnessing the empty tomb (20:3–10).

17.3.2 Jesus' Appearance to Mary (20:11–18)

John suggests Mary Magdalene was the first to see Jesus after his resurrection. This story was "surely, with Luke's walk to Emmaus, one of the two most memorable resurrection appearance narratives."[31] At first, she did not recognize Jesus (20:14), in a similar way to the travellers on the Emmaus road (Luke 24:16), and the disciples in the boat in lake Tiberias

---

27. Morris, *John*, 731.
28. Carson, *John*, 635–36.
29. Ridderbos, *John*, 631–32.
30. Morris, *John*, 734.
31. Bauckham, *Gospel Women*, 283–84.

(John 21:4). Mary originally thought he was the gardener, until he uttered her name (John 20:16). Carson points out this tension between the continuity and discontinuity of Jesus' resurrection body with his earlier body is consistent with First Corinthians 15:35–58:[32]

- continuity: he eats food (Luke 24:41–43), can be touched (John 20:27), still bears the scars from his pre-resurrection body (20:20, 25, 27);
- discontinuity: he appears in an apparently locked room (John 20:19, 26), and is sometimes not recognised (initially).

17.3.3 Jesus' Two Appearances to the Disciples (20:19-23, 24-29)

The next appearance narrative was to a group of disciples, likely paralleled in Luke 24:36–42.[33] John adds the detail that the doors were "locked." Although in Greek the doors were literally "closed,"[34] the context (fear of the Jewish leaders) suggests "locked" is the correct translation.[35] After standing among them, he showed his hands and side (20:20). Luke 24:36–42 explained that the disciples were afraid he was a ghost.

Mary also did not initially recognise him (John 20:14). So Jesus "took steps to convince them of his identity and to take away their fear . . . The resurrection body has properties different from the body of flesh; yet it is not ethereal."[36] A week later, Jesus returns to the same house where the doors were again "locked" (20:24–29). This time the group of disciples included Thomas (20:27).

17.3.4 Jesus' Appearance at the Sea of Galilee (chapter 21)

Chapter 21 narrates Jesus' third post-resurrection appearance in John.[37] Verses 1–14 are located at the sea of Galilee (or Tiberias). The transphysicality of Jesus is once more at the centre of the story. The disciples failed to

32. Carson, *John*, 641.
33. Carson, *John*, 646; Morris, *John*, 744.
34. Morris, *John*, 745.
35. Carson, *John*, 646; Morris, *John*, 745.
36. Morris, *John*, 746.
37. The debate on whether this chapter was originally included in the John's Gospel is beyond the scope of this book. For a summary see Carson, *John*, 665–68.

recognise Jesus (21:4), but the miraculous catch of fish opened their eyes to his identity (21:5–14). At the same time, Jesus is disarmingly humble, cooking breakfast with the freshly caught fish (21:10–14). The rest of the chapter focuses on Jesus' restoration of Peter as a leader in the early church (21:15–25).

17.4 CONCLUSION

Atheist scholars, like Gerd Ludemann, argue for a gradual development in the accounts over time. The vision-like experiences of First Corinthians evolve into an increasingly "physical Jesus" as we move from Matthew through to Luke and John. Chapters 16 and 17 have challenged this interpretation—as Mark and Matthew also speak of bodily resurrection. In the next chapter, I will sum up these findings.

Chapter 18

Summary of Evidence for Jesus' Resurrection

18.1 INTRODUCTION

WHEN READING THE RESURRECTION accounts, there is a temptation to force "every last detail into an over-simple harmony, or . . . into an over-simple hermeneutic of suspicion."[1] I have argued when we read the accounts side by side, they tell a coherent story. As Carson points out, many of the alleged discrepancies are trivial in nature. "Only the assumptions scholars make about the nature of the descent of tradition, coupled with peculiarly modern and Western notions of precise reportage, could discern any difficulty."[2] This chapter has three main sections:

- comparison between resurrection accounts in the Gospels;
- comparison between First Corinthians 15 and the Gospels;
- Jesus' ascension and the worldwide church.

18.2 SUMMARY OF GOSPEL RESURRECTION ACCOUNTS

All four accounts agree on the most important details (see Table 4):

---

1. Wright, *Resurrection*, 614.
2. Carson, *John*, 632.

Part Four: The Evidence for Jesus' Resurrection

- Jesus' death by crucifixion;
- his burial in Joseph's tomb;
- Jesus' female disciples were first to witness his empty tomb;
- angel(s) announced Jesus' resurrection to his female disciples.

Events narrated in the Gospels	Mark	Matthew	Luke	John
Buried in Joseph's tomb				
Female disciples first to witness the empty tomb				
Angel(s) announce Jesus' resurrection to his female disciples at the tomb				
Jesus' post-resurrection appearances to male and female disciples				
Jesus' Ascension				

Table 4. Summary of key aspects of the resurrection narrative in the four Gospels

Of course, there are differences (see Table 5). For example, Mark included no post-resurrection appearances. Luke only mentioned Jesus' post-resurrection appearances in Jerusalem. He reported that Peter was a witness to the empty tomb, while John included the beloved disciple along with Peter at the empty tomb. Mark and Matthew only mentioned the female disciples at Jesus' tomb. Although only Luke specifically reported Jesus' ascension; Matthew, Mark, and John all assume Jesus' exaltation and enthronement in heaven.

Events narrated in the Gospels	Mark	Matthew	Luke	John
Male disciples witness to empty tomb				
Jesus appears to disciples in Jerusalem				
Jesus appears to disciples in Galilee				

Table 5. Summary of minor differences between resurrection accounts in the four Gospels

Summary of Evidence for Jesus' Resurrection

18.3 COMPARING FIRST CORINTHIANS 15 AND THE FOUR GOSPELS

Sceptics often argue for an evolution in the Gospel accounts starting from Mark (no resurrection appearances) through to Luke and John (where there is a greater emphasis on the physical nature of Jesus' resurrection). The creed in First Corinthians, probably written within a few years of Jesus' death, challenges this conclusion. This section will show remarkable consistency between the earliest accounts of Jesus' resurrection and the later Gospels (see Table 6).

18.3.1 Jesus' Death

The four Gospels (Mark 15:21–41; Matthew 27:45–56; Luke 23: 26–49; John 19: 16–37) and First Corinthians (15:3) all report testimony that Jesus died. Yet evidence, and its significance, are never separated in the New Testament. His death is "according to the Scriptures" (First Corinthians 15:3). As argued in chapter 11, various passages in the Hebrew Bible (such as Psalm 22; Isaiah 52:13—53:12; Zechariah 12–13) taught the Messiah would suffer. The Gospels all present Jesus' death as fulfilment of these promises.

	Mark	Matthew	Luke	John	First Cor 15
Jesus' Death					
Burial in Joseph's tomb					
Empty tomb					
Appearances to the twelve					
Appearances to female disciples					

Table 6. A summary of evidence for Jesus' resurrection

18.3.2 Burial in Joseph's Tomb

First Corinthians 15:4 reports that Jesus was buried. All four Gospels provide further detail that he was buried in the tomb of Joseph of Arimathea, a member of the Sanhedrin (Mark 15:42–47; Matthew 27:57–61; Luke 23:50–56; John 19:38–42).

There are minor differences. John added the observation that Nicodemus went with Joseph and bought the spices (John 19:39). Mark and Luke focus on Jesus' female disciples watching where Jesus was buried and their preparation of the spices and perfumes for burial (Mark 16:1; Luke 23:55–56). This is not necessarily contradictory. It is far from surprising that some miscommunication may have resulted between Nicodemus and Joseph on the one hand, and Jesus' female disciples on the other, regarding who would prepare the spices for his burial.

18.3.3 Empty Tomb

All four Gospels report that Jesus' tomb was empty (Mark 16: 1–8; Matthew 28:1–12; Luke 24:1–8; John 20: 1–10). First Corinthians 15 does not mention the empty tomb, but as we saw above it reports that Jesus was buried. Ehrman argues, on this basis, that Paul was unaware of testimony about the empty tomb.[3] Yet, we should be cautious about arguments from silence. An obvious explanation is the concise nature of the pre-Pauline creed.[4]

18.3.4 Appearances to the Twelve and Other Disciples

First Corinthians 15:5 includes appearances to the twelve and other disciples. This is consistent with appearances to members of the twelve in the Gospels (e.g., Matthew 28: 16–20; Luke 24:36–49; John 20–21). Although Mark's Gospel (16: 6 –7) did not include an appearance of Jesus, an angel announced that he was risen so is consistent with this expectation.

It is no surprise, given the focus of the Gospels (to testify about Jesus' life, death, and resurrection), that they report more detail than First Corinthians 15. A key addition is their unanimous testimony that the female disciples were first to see him (e.g. Matthew 28: 9–10; John 20: 11–18). The brevity of the early creed, and scepticism about female eyewitnesses in the first century,[5] likely explains the omission (see chapter 15 for further discussion).

---

3. Ehrman, *Jesus*, 141–43.
4. Allison, *Resurrection*, 129.
5. Allision, *Resurrection*, 154–62.

Summary of Evidence for Jesus' Resurrection

18.3.5 Appearances to Paul and James

Jesus' appearances to Paul and James (First Corinthians 15:7–11) were not recorded in the Gospels. In the case of Paul, this is expected as his testimony about Jesus is a few years after the period covered in the Gospels. The appearance to James is more enigmatic, although he may have been present (but unnamed) in one of Jesus' appearances to groups of disciples.

18.3.6 Jesus' Ascension and the Worldwide Church

In the Gospels, Jesus often referred to himself as the apocalyptic Son of Man promised in Daniel 7 (e.g., Mark 14:62). His death, resurrection, and ascension begins the fulfilment of the Hebrew Bible's promise that God would dwell with his people from many nations (e.g., Genesis 49:10; Isaiah 42:4; Psalm 22; Psalm 87). The book of Acts records the start of this fulfilment, the inclusion of the Gentiles (non-Jews) into the blessings of Israel. The mission of the Holy Spirit to all nations follows the ascension of Jesus (Acts 2: 1–13). The apostle Peter (a Jew) was later led to share the Gospel to Cornelius (a Gentile) and his friends. At first, Peter was reluctant, yet the Holy Spirit came upon Cornelius and his friends as confirmation (Acts 11:17). The apostle Paul, when preaching in Athens, pointed to Jesus' resurrection as a sign of his worldwide authority (Acts 17:30–31).

18.4 CONCLUSION

Part Four has assessed the evidence for Jesus' resurrection from the earliest available accounts—First Corinthians 15:3–8 and the four canonical Gospels. They testify that God has sent Jesus, the promised Messiah. His death, resurrection, and ascension redeems a worldwide community who turn back to him in faith. If God raised Jesus from the dead, we would expect this kind of evidence.

There is very early evidence. For example, the creed of First Corinthians 15:3–5 was likely written at most five years after Jesus' death—naming the twelve as eyewitnesses to Jesus' postmortem appearances. The rest of the account (v6–8) included further eyewitnesses (Paul, James, and the 500). The four Gospels, with their focus on the life, death, and resurrection of Jesus, provide more detailed accounts of these events.

Part Four: The Evidence for Jesus' Resurrection

Sceptics counter that these sources are unreliable—as there are differences between them. However, this "does not mean nothing happened."[6] Proposed "contradictions" between the Gospels, often "turn on too little information."[7] Both the harmonizer and the sceptic want to pin down every mechanical step:

> This lack of information, coupled with modern assumptions about the way ancient editors and communities constantly cut up their sources and patched them together into new pieces, has led to several ingenius but unbelievable constructions.[8]

Part Five will consider this same evidence, but through the lens of those who deny Jesus' resurrection. If there was no resurrection, how best to account for this evidence?

---

6. Wright, *Resurrection*, 614.
7. Carson, *John*, 633.
8. Carson, *John*, 633.

PART FIVE

Naturalistic Explanations

PART FOUR ASSESSED EVIDENCE *for Jesus' resurrection. I looked at two main sets of sources:*

- *First Corinthians 15:3–8—an early creed (up to five years after Jesus' death) included in at least verses 3—5, verses 6-8 are at most 15-20 years after Jesus' death.*
- *The four canonical Gospels (Matthew, Mark, Luke, and John)—these are usually dated between 20-80 years after Jesus' death.*

I have argued that these two sets of sources provide a consistent account of Jesus' death, burial, resurrection, and ascension.

INTRODUCTION TO PART FIVE

In Part Two we looked out at our world, to investigate the nature of reality—the first stage in estimating the prior (the probability before assessing the evidence) for Jesus' resurrection. Part Three focused on Jesus. Does his life reflect the Hebrew Bible's expectations of the Messiah? Another key determinant of the prior. Part Four assessed evidence from the earliest resurrection accounts. The aim of Part Five is to look at these same data from a different lens. If there was no resurrection, how best to explain these accounts? This is the final set of data needed for the model in Part Six.

Debates on the merits of naturalistic explanations can be exasperating. It seems inevitable that Christians and atheists will talk past each other.

Part Five: Naturalistic Explanations

Philip Goff, an agnostic philosopher, illustrates this with a debate between Mike Licona and Bart Ehrman:

> Rather than disputing the history, a lot of time was taken up arguing about whether it is possible for a historian, as a "historian", to argue for a miracle. This seems to me a very silly thing to argue about. We could define the word "historian" however we wish. Surely the interesting question is what we have reason to believe.[1]

For example, Bart Ehrman's position on miracles, arguably misappropriating Hume, appears untestable. For him, miracles cannot be established historically:

> It's always easy to scream "anti-supernatural bias" when someone does not think that the miracles of one's own tradition can be historically established; it's much harder to admit that miracles of other traditions are just as readily demonstrated. But the view I map out here is that none of these divine miracles, or any others, can be established historically.[2]

Christians are often no better. Many apologists appear to think refuting all naturalistic explanations will leave the resurrection hypothesis as victorious. Alex O'Connor, a popular sceptic, has argued these attempts are hampered by a selection effect.[3] For Christians, the resurrection hypothesis is the last option standing. But sceptics exclude this much earlier because "extraordinary claims require extraordinary evidence"—for them some form of naturalistic hypothesis (e.g., bereavement hallucinations) is the final remaining option. Both sides often ignore a key factor—the prior probability for Jesus' resurrection.

Parts Two and Three explored how our worldviews impact on these judgments. Part Five evaluates a wide range of naturalistic explanations for testimony about Jesus' empty tomb and postmortem appearances (see Box 9).[4] Many of these arguments seek to apply psychological explanations to the disciples' experiences. Below I will provide an extensive summary of relevant psychological data on bereavement hallucinations, conversion disorder,

---

1. Goff, *Miracle*, §2.
2. Ehrman, *Jesus*, 144.
3. Scrivener, *Argument*, 22:26 to 31:43.
4. Based on Andrew Loke's categories.

Part Five: Naturalistic Explanations

"mass hysteria", distorted memory and cognitive dissonance theory. Each chapter is relatively independent, so readers can focus on topics of interest.[5]

BOX 9. SUMMARY OF PART FIVE

Chapter 19: Naturalistic explanations for the empty tomb. This chapter looks at several naturalistic explanations including the "unburied hypothesis," "remained buried hypothesis," "removed by friends, enemies, or neutral party hypotheses."

Chapter 20: Visions or hallucinations. Probably the most popular naturalistic explanation, this chapter reviews data on bereavement hallucinations, experimental induction of hallucinations, and group visions.

Chapter 21: Conversion disorder and mass hysteria. Conversion disorder (or functional neurological symptom disorder) is a popular explanation for Paul's experience of Jesus. "Mass hysteria" (or mass psychogenic illness) is often used to account for group appearances of Jesus.

Chapter 22: Distorted memories. Of course, testimony for Jesus' resurrection is largely dependent on memories. This chapter considers a range of issues from the psychological literature including false memories, whether confidence is associated with accuracy, and recent trends on the reliability of memory.

Chapter 23: Cognitive dissonance theory (CDT). We are resistant to changing our cherished beliefs. I assess attempts to apply CDT to a naturalistic explanation for the disciples' experiences.

---

5. It is possible to skim, or skip, chapters of less interest and still follow the argument of the book. Reading chapter 24 will probably be sufficient to follow the next stage of the argument.

Part Five: Naturalistic Explanations

> **BOX 9. SUMMARY OF PART FIVE**
>
> *Chapter 24: Summary.* This final section of Part Five summarises the previous five chapters and considers naturalistic theories proposed by Ehrman, Allison, and Ludemann which include a combination of hypotheses assessed earlier.

Chapter 19

Naturalistic Explanations for the Empty Tomb

19.1 INTRODUCTION

NATURALISTIC EXPLANATIONS FOR THE empty tomb must face inconvenient evidence. First, the canonical Gospels are unanimous that female disciples were the first witnesses of Jesus' empty tomb. This presents challenges for those who claim the Gospels were a later invention:

> Now, given their low social status and inability to serve as legal witnesses, it's quite amazing that it is women who are the discoverers of and principal witnesses to the empty tomb. If the empty tomb story were a legend, then it is most likely that the male disciples would have been made to be the first to discover the empty tomb.[1]

Christianity's critics could dismiss these accounts because their source was "half-frantic women."[2] Josephus, writing in first century Palestine, summarised the legal norms of the time, "Let not the testimony of women be admitted, on account of the levity and boldness of their sex."[3] This is consistent with *Sifre Deuteronomy 190* and much of the Mishnah.[4]

---

1. Craig, *Reasonable Faith*, 562.
2. Allison, *Resurrection*, 154.
3. Craig, *Reasonable Faith*, 562.
4. Allison, *Resurrection*, 157.

PART FIVE: NATURALISTIC EXPLANATIONS

A second challenge is the church's origin in Jerusalem. The church's growth and proclamation began there too. Carson argues this would be unthinkable without the empty tomb:

> Historically, the preaching and the rapid growth of the early church are alike unexplainable apart from the empty tomb. Even on the doubtful supposition that all the first Christians were dupes or hallucinating enthusiasts, the Jewish authorities, though they had every incentive to do so, could not come up with the body of the man whose execution they had organized. Theologically, the empty tomb rules out any reinterpretation of "resurrection" that makes it indistinguishable from mere immortality.[5]

Despite the difficulty of the task, several naturalistic hypotheses have been proposed (see Box 10).[6]

BOX 10. NATURALIST EXPLANATIONS FOR THE EMPTY TOMB

Andrew Loke, Associate Professor of Philosophy, proposed that all naturalistic explanations for Jesus' empty tomb can be reduced to eight categories:

- apparent death (or "swoon") hypothesis;
- escape hypothesis;
- unburied hypothesis;
- removal by non-agents (such as earthquakes) hypothesis;
- removal by friends hypothesis;
- removal by enemies hypothesis;
- removal by neutral party hypothesis;
- remained buried hypothesis.

---

5. Carson, *John*, 638.
6. I will consider apparent death (or "swoon"), and escape theories in chapter 22.

Naturalistic Explanations for the Empty Tomb

19.2 UNBURIED HYPOTHESIS

Scholars including Bart Ehrman, Dominic Crossan, and David Aus, have proposed that Jesus was never buried.[7] Since there was no tomb, there was no empty tomb. This explanation usually involves two main assumptions:

- the invention of Joseph of Arimathea;
- the authorities would not allow Jesus, an executed criminal, to be buried.

19.2.1 Doubts About Joseph of Arimathea

Some sceptics point out Joseph of Arimathea is never mentioned outside the Gospels.[8] There is also debate on whether Arimathea was an actual place.[9] As discussed in chapter 15, Ehrman's suspicions about Joseph of Arimathea begin in First Corinthians 15. The terse creed says only, "he was buried" (v4), not "in Joseph's tomb." Moreover, Ehrman argues this, "created an imbalance with the second portion of the creed where he does name the person to whom Jesus appeared [Cephas]."[10]

Dale Allison is less impressed. He considered this argument "ill considered."[11] There are numerous linguistic challenges of reconstructing the parallelism proposed by Ehrman. Most importantly, the formula in v. 5 is not "appeared to Cephas" but "appeared to Cephas, then to the Twelve." One fails to see how to fashion a linguistic twin for that with nothing but the singular, "Joseph of Arimathea."[12]

Ehrman's next step is also problematic. He suggests Acts 13:29 is an example of pre-Markan tradition, indicating a hostile burial and no mention of Joseph of Arimathea.[13] There are a few issues. First, Acts is generally considered to be written after Mark. "It is far from self-evident that we have here a distinct tradition of the burial."[14] Second, as F.F. Bruce pointed out,

---

7. Allison, *Resurrection*, 95.
8. Allison, *Resurrection*, 95.
9. Allison, *Resurrection*, 97.
10. Ehrman, *Jesus*, 153.
11. Allison, *Resurrection*, 107.
12. Allison, *Resurrection*, 107.
13. Ehrman, *Jesus*, 154–56.
14. Allison, *Resurrection*, 102.

Acts 13:29 refers to Jesus' burial by Jewish leaders, which is consistent with burial by Joseph of Arimathea a member of the Sanhedrin.[15]

19.2.2 Burial of Executed Criminals

If Jesus was not buried in Joseph's tomb, what happened to his body? Both Crossan and Ehrman argue executed criminals were often eaten by scavenging animals.[16] However, there is insufficient data to estimate how usual this was.[17] The key question is whether Roman officials were willing to grant requests for the burial of crucified victims. *Digesta*, a codification of Roman law, suggests this was the case: "The bodies of those who are condemned to death should not be refused their relative; and the Divine Augustus, in the Tenth Book of his life, said that this rule had been observed."[18] Philo's account written in 38CE is consistent with this edict:

> families, at least during holidays and during the rule of some Roman prefects, could recover crucified bodies. There is a parallel between the families' obtaining permission to recover the corpses of the victims during holidays and Joseph of Arimathea's similar action on the eve of the Passover.[19]

As is Josephus's writings, in first century Palestine: "The Jews are so careful about funeral rites that even malefactors who have been sentenced to crucifixion are taken down and buried before sunset."[20]

19.2.3 Shared Grave?

For argument's sake, we may grant Jesus' "burial" in a shared grave. If so, would no one be able to identify his dead body? According to Allison, a passage from the Talmud (m. Sanhedrin 6:5–6) challenges this assumption:

> The rabbinic text presupposes that even in the case of a criminal buried dishonorably, relatives could claim the skeleton after some time had passed . . . If relatives could collect the bones of an

---

15. Bruce, *Acts*, 259.
16. Allison, *Resurrection*, 104.
17. Allison, *Resurrection*, 104.
18. Cited in Allison, *Resurrection*, 104.
19. Cook, *Burial*, 211.
20. Allison, *Resurrection*, 104.

executed criminal after the flesh had fallen off, then those bones were not in a jumbled pile but must have been deposited in such a way as to allow for later identification.[21]

19.3 REMOVAL BY NON-AGENTS

A further possible explanation for an empty tomb, is the non-agent removal of Jesus' body. For example, Allison suggested an earthquake may have accounted for the removal of the stone, and the disappearance of Jesus' body. However, evidence from the Gospels states that Jewish authorities assumed the tomb was empty. They argued the disciples stole Jesus' body. If this naturalistic explanation was valid, we would expect Jewish leaders to argue Jesus' body was under the rubble of a broken tomb.[22]

19.4 REMOVAL BY FRIENDS

This is probably the earliest naturalistic explanation of all. Matthew 28:11–15 records that Jewish authorities claimed the disciples had stolen Jesus' body. However, this is difficult to justify given testimony about guards at Jesus' tomb (Matthew 27:62–66). It is unclear how anyone could have removed Jesus' body without their knowledge.

Some argue reports of guards was an apologetic strategy.[23] However Carson points out an invented story would more likely state the guards were present from Friday not Saturday.[24] Since this leaves a period when friends or thieves could have stolen Jesus' body without detection.

19.5 REMOVAL BY ENEMIES

Allison suggests it was possible the Jewish authorities stole Jesus' body and disposed of it to avoid people venerating the tomb. The leaders then accused the disciples of stealing his body. However, it would have been a safer

---

21. Allison, *Resurrection*, 148.
22. Loke, *Resurrection*, 140–41.
23. Allison, *Resurrection*, 152.
24. Carson, *Matthew*, 654.

strategy for the Jewish leaders to announce they had dumped Jesus' body. Why complicate the matter by bringing guards into the story?[25]

19.6 REMOVAL BY A NEUTRAL PARTY

Another option is that tomb robbers had stolen Jesus' body. However, the guards' presence at the tomb also makes this unlikely (see above). Although there was a period between Friday and Saturday when the tomb was unguarded, the "soldiers would naturally check the tomb and report back to Pilate if it were already ransacked. Otherwise, they would be charged with dereliction of duty if it were found to be empty on their watch."[26] Therefore, it is more likely the Jewish authorities would have reported the theft immediately rather than a few days later.

19.7 REMAINED BURIED

Richard Carrier proposed that Jesus' body remained buried, but his disciples claimed he had received a second body.[27] Ludemann also suggested Jesus' body remained buried in an unknown location. He argues passages like First Corinthians 15 indicate, "Jesus was exalted from the cross directly to God."[28]

According to James Ware, professor of religion, there are two main problems with this argument. First, there are no examples of contemporary Jewish views of resurrection that posit no connection with the body in the tomb.[29] Second, there are no examples in Ancient Greek literature where *egeiro* (the word used for Jesus' resurrection) describes ascension or elevation (see chapter 15).

---

25. Loke, *Resurrection*, 139.
26. Loke, *Resurrection*, 140.
27. Carrier, *Empty Tomb*, 105–232.
28. Ludemann, *Resurrection*, 71.

29. This is not to deny heterogeneous beliefs within Second Temple Judaism, such as the Sadducees, who denied the resurrection. Only that resurrection was not used in the first century to describe apparitions.

NATURALISTIC EXPLANATIONS FOR THE EMPTY TOMB

19.8 CONCLUSION

As I argued at the start of this chapter, there are good reasons to posit the validity of the empty tomb narratives. For example, the centrality of Jesus' female followers is unlikely if these stories were invented. In addition, all naturalistic explanations considered above, face important difficulties. Considering these data together, the validity of the empty tomb accounts are likely:

> If Jesus had female followers, as everyone admits he did; and if some went up with him to Jerusalem, as we have no reason to doubt; and if a few of them witnessed the crucifixion, which is wholly probable given that crucifixions were designed to be public events, then a visit not long after entombment is nothing but expected.[30]

The next three chapters will consider naturalistic explanations for postmortem appearances of Jesus. *Chapter 20* examines the hallucination, or intramental, hypothesis. *Chapter 21* looks at functional neurological symptom disorder (conversion disorder) and mass psychogenic illness. *Chapter 22* considers the potential for distorted memories.

---

30. Allison, *Resurrection*, 162.

Chapter 20

Visions or Hallucinations?

20.1 INTRODUCTION

MOST SCHOLARS ACCEPT THAT at least one disciple had some kind of experience after Jesus' death.[1] The precise nature of these experiences is widely debated. Box 11 summarises these naturalistic explanations. This chapter evaluates the most popular—the intramental hypothesis. Atheist scholars like Ludemann and Ehrman propose that post-mortem "appearances" were hallucinations or visions. They look to the psychological literature for possible explanations.

Dale Allison offers a half-way option. He "eschew[s] accounting for the appearances of Jesus wholly in terms of typical appearances of the dead."[2] However, he also suggests visions may contribute to an explanation. This chapter discusses the following themes:

- defining hallucinations and illusions;
- how frequent people in non-clinical populations experience hallucinations (general populations, people who are bereaved, psychology experiments);
- how common non-clinical populations have insight they experienced a hallucination;

1. Habermas and Licona, *Resurrection*, 52–56.
2. Allison, *Resurrection*, 222.

- group hallucinations or visions;
- application of these data to the disciples' experiences.

BOX 11. NATURALISTIC EXPLANATIONS FOR TESTIMONY OF JESUS' POSTMORTEM APPEARANCES

Loke[3] argues that all naturalistic explanations of the post-mortem appearances reduce to six categories:

- Legend hypothesis
- No experience hypothesis
- Intramental hypothesis (e.g., hallucinations or visions)
- Mistaken identity hypothesis
- Escape hypothesis
- Apparent death ("swoon") hypothesis

20.2 DEFINING HALLUCINATIONS AND ILLUSIONS

Hallucinations are a perceptual experience "by an awake individual in the absence of appropriate stimuli from the environment or from the body."[4] Many psychologists consider hallucinations to be on a spectrum of severity. They can occur in clinical (e.g., people with a psychotic disorder like schizophrenia) and non-clinical populations (people not diagnosed with a psychiatric disorder). People with a psychiatric disorder often find it difficult to distinguish hallucinations from real life events. Their symptoms have a profound impact on everyday life. People from non-clinical populations often have more insight about experiencing hallucinations. Most current models posit primarily neuroscientific explanations for these phenomena.[5]

In the fields of psychology and psychiatry, seeing ghosts, angels, or gods are generally categorised as hallucinations (i.e., a false perception). Whereas

---

3. Loke, *Resurrection*, 24–25.
4. Peyroux, *Hallucinations*, 3.
5. E.g., Collerton, *Visual Hallucinations*, 105208.

the religious and parapsychological literature often refers to these experiences as visions. Psychologist Karina Kamp proposes the term sensory and quasi-sensory experiences as a bridge between these two literatures.[6]

Perceptual illusions are another important term to define. The famous neuropsychologist Richard L. Gregory[7] proposed several types of illusion:

- ambiguities (e.g., mist, shadows);
- distortions (e.g., Muller-Lyer illusion where one line looks large than the other despite being the same length);
- paradoxes (e.g., "magic mirrors" in fairgrounds that distort our body shape);
- fictions (e.g., Kanizsa triangle, where our brain sees a triangle that is not there).

20.3 HALLUCINATIONS IN NON-CLINICAL POPULATIONS

20.3.1 General Population

A recent systematic review and meta-analyses[8] estimated an annual incidence of 2% for hallucinations and delusions in non-clinical populations.[9] These estimates are based on fifteen studies and included 56,089 people.[10] These data were collected mainly from large population studies, using well validated measure of hallucinations or delusions.

20.3.2 Bereaved Population

Studies of bereaved populations are usually smaller in size and use less well-defined measures.[11] Rates of quasi-sensory experiences are often

6. Kamp, *Bereavement*, 1367–1381.
7. Gregory, *Illusions*, 1–4.
8. This means a statistical combination of data from a comprehensive set of studies.
9. i.e., outside of a psychotic condition like schizophrenia.
10. Staines, *Experience*, 1007. The 95% confidence interval was 1% to 3%, which can be interpreted (approximately) as 95% certainty that the true effect lies between 1% and 3%. The estimate of incidence for adults, and across all age subgroups, was the same despite some variation among age-groups.
11. Castelnovo, *Hallucinatory*, 266–74.

higher than in the general population. It is difficult to tell whether these are genuine differences or an over-estimate due to less robust methods. I could not find any recent systematic reviews in this population. But several reviews have informed my estimates.[12] These reviews identified eighteen relevant studies. For a more detailed summary, see appendix 2.

Feeling a sense of presence of the dead during bereavement is common (approximately 30–60%).[13] However, more specific "perceptual-like" experience is lower:

- tactile (median=5%, range=1 to 25%);
- visual (median=14%, range=2 to 48%);
- auditory (median=15%, range=2 to 35%);
- verbal (median=12%, range=4 to 70%).

Experiences in a single modality appear more common than in multiple modalities (for example visual and auditory, median=6%, range=4 to 9%). All estimates were associated with considerable uncertainty—in particular verbal quasi-sensory experiences ranged from 4% to 70%. As discussed above, this may reflect variation in how these experiences are measured or potentially different populations studied.

20.3.3 Experimental Induction of Hallucinations

Studies where psychologists induce "hallucinations" may also offer applicable data.[14] For example, experimenters ask participants to imagine hearing music, or they might deprive participants of sensory experience to induce a hallucination. An important limitation to these experiments is a potential lack of applicability to actual hallucinations:

> . . . the main critique of the voice-hearing paradigms reviewed here is that they lack a fundamental aspect of the voice-hearing experience with regards to the nature of internally generated stimuli (i.e., having human characteristics) . . . the challenge remains to develop a paradigm in which participants' internally generated

---

12. Castelnovo, *Hallucinatory*, 266–74; Kamp, *Bereavement*, 1367–1381; Streithorn, *Systematic Review*, 1–81.

13. Castelnovo, *Hallucinatory*, 268.

14. See for example Anderson, *Experimental*, 101635. This paper reports a systematic review of 49 studies.

stimuli can be attributed externally in a way that more closely represents inner speech [or other modalities].[15]

Second, there are important demand characteristics that may bias results. This means participants often try to guess the aim of the experiment and report information they think will be helpful. Third, most non-clinical participants are aware they are not perceiving real sights or sounds.[16]

20.3.4 Insight Into Whether Hallucinations are Real?

Ehrman argues "one of the most striking features of this research is that those who experience such visions [during a period of bereavement] almost always assume, and wholeheartedly believe, that they are veridical".[17] However, Anna Castelnovo (a psychiatrist), points out that people are often aware hallucinations (or visions) are not real:

> No matter how vivid such visions maybe, to the extent that some people behave in response to them, reality testing [they know that these experiences are not reflective of "reality"] seems preserved, at least in the absence of conditions such as pathologic grief reactions, sub-threshold or overt psychiatric/neurologic disorders, sensory/cognitive impairment, or drug/alcohol abuse.[18]

This also appears to be the case in other non-clinical populations. For example, Toh and colleagues found that:

- only 13% of non-clinical individuals were strongly convinced their quasi-sensory experience was real;
- 44% considered these experience as "not real";
- 28% had "some doubt" or thought the experience "possibly real."[19]

Studies suggest non-clinical populations are better able to distinguish imagined and real events—compared to people with schizophrenia.[20]

---

15. Anderson, *Experimental*, 101635.
16. Anderson, *Experimental*, 101635.
17. Ehrman, *Jesus*, 195.
18. Castelnovo, *Hallucinations*, 272.
19. Toh, *Hallucinations*, 5.
20. Garrison, *Hallucinations*, 197–207.

There is also evidence of potential differences in brain structure[21] between non-clinical populations and people with schizophrenia.[22]

20.4 Group Quasi-Sensory Experiences?

The group nature of the disciples' experiences present a significant challenge to the "intramental hypothesis." By standard psychiatric definitions of hallucinations, "it is unreasonable to think that causal mechanisms internal to each person in a group simultaneously generated similar experiences."[23]

For those willing to abandon a naturalistic explanation, Allison points to literature where participants report group visions.[24] Lifetime prevalence is low in surveys where this phenomenon has been investigated (between 0.8% and 4%, see Table 7).[25] In addition, of those reporting an experience in the presence of others, their companion(s) often did not share that experience, or there was insufficient evidence (e.g., 87%[26] and 45%[27]).

Study	No. of people surveyed	Visual	Auditory	Any
Palmer 1979[28]	622	-	-	4%
Kalish and Reynolds 1973[29]	434	-	-	2%
Sidgwick 1874[30]	17,000	0.6%	0.2%	0.8%

Table 7. Prevalence of group visions

---

21. Researchers compared the length of the paracingulate sulcus (PCS)—a structure in the brain thought to be important for discerning the difference between perceived and imagined information—in people with schizophrenia and non-clinical populations.

22. Garrison, *Parasingulate*, 733–41.

23. Loke, *Resurrection*, 100.

24. Allison, Resurrection, 236–61.

25. This is not necessarily a comprehensive list of surveys, but were the only ones I was able to identify.

26. Kalish, *Phenomenological Reality*, 217.

27. Sidgwick, *Hallucinations*, 304.

28. Palmer, *Psychic*, 228–29.

29. Kalish, *Phenomenological Reality*, 209–21.

30. Sidgwick, *Hallucinations*, 25–401.

PART FIVE: NATURALISTIC EXPLANATIONS

An additional difficulty for naturalistic explanations are the number of individuals who witnessed Jesus' postmortem appearances. First Corinthians 15:5, dated up to five years after Jesus' death, states he appeared to the Twelve. This may have included Matthias, who replaced Judas as a member of the Twelve, or possibly the eleven—minus Judas. Either way, this is a far larger number than reported for most group apparitions. I identified fifty-one cases of group apparitions from Allison's citations.[31] Of these, forty-seven (92%) were witnessed by five or less people, three group apparitions were witnessed by six to ten people (6%). Allison identified only one case, in Russia in 1832, where it was claimed more than eleven witnessed the apparition. However, this case was not authenticated by additional witnesses and was reported sixty years after the event.[32] Therefore, this spiritual apparition hypothesis, posits a rare subset (eleven or more witnesses) to an already rare event (claims that a group saw the same vision).

20.4.1 Doubts About the Samuel Bull Case

Of the apparition cases experienced by six or more people, the "appearance" of Samuel Bull is most controversial. The family had been living in dilapidated conditions, "they had to live in a dreadfully crowded and unhappy condition. This state of things had continued for several months, although continued effort has been made to find better housing."[33] During investigation of these ghostly appearances, the family were moved to a new residence. Therefore, there is a possibility that the family's testimony may have been motivated by the aim of securing better housing.[34] Further reasons to doubt the veracity of their testimony include that "appearances" of Samuel Bull stopped once the family moved house; and that no one else, outside the immediate family, witnessed them.

Allison is more sanguine.[35] He notes that Lord Balfour[36] and John George Piddington, members of the Society of Psychical Research (SPR), were persuaded by the family's testimony. Allison cites another SPR

---

31. Allison, *Resurrection*, 218.
32. Flammarion, *Mystery*, 349.
33. Balfour and Piddington, *Haunting*, 296.
34. O'Connell, *Resurrection*, 535.
35. Allison, *Resurrection*, 256–57.
36. A former Prime Minister. However, if Allison factors in Lord Balfour's social status to assess his credibility, to be balanced he should also take into account Balfour's White supremacist and anti-Semitic views, which are at least as pertinent.

168

member (Andrew MacKenzie) who claimed to have interviewed "two senior officials of the local council who were employed there at the time of the haunting that they had never heard of this experience of the Bull family."[37]

However, questions remain unanswered. MacKenzie offered sparse detail about the local council officers' testimony. We do not know who they were, their role in the Bull case, nor their connection to MacKenzie. It is unclear why Allison is certain about MacKenzie's clarification but dismisses Luke or John's clarifications as apologetics.

Assuming the material is genuine, and not apologetics, we also do not know when MacKenzie spoke to these council officials. *The Unexplained* was published in 1966. Balfour died in 1930—so this testimony may have been obtained more than three decades later. Memories of key life events, like a local earthquake or wartime, remain reliable over many decades.[38] However, longer term recall for more mundane events is often limited.[39]

20.5 APPLICATION TO JESUS' APPEARANCES

20.5.1 Appearances to Individual Disciples

Studies of bereavement hallucinations are likely to be the most relevant. First century Jews, as well as the wider Greco-Roman population, were aware of quasi-sensory experiences.[40] However there are several reasons to question the applicability of this data:

- there are important cultural differences; so it is unclear if these estimates are higher or lower than expected in first century Palestine;

- quasi-sensory experiences are not well defined or consistently measured in studies of bereaved populations;

- non-clinical populations have greater insight on the distinction between real and quasi-sensory experiences; therefore it is uncertain whether these experiences would lead the disciples to believe Jesus was raised from the dead (I will explore these uncertainties further in chapters 25 and 26).

---

37. MacKenzie, *Unexplained*, 14.

38. See chapter 22 for further details; see also Berntsen and Thomsen, *Memories*, 242–57.

39. See chapter 22; and Er, *Flashbulb*, 503–17.

40. Wright, *Resurrection*, 64.

Experiencing a sense of presence of the dead is common. But visions of the dead are less common, particularly the multimodal experiences reported in the Gospels. For example, Mary speaks with, hears, sees, and touches Jesus. Two studies reporting estimates for visual and auditory experiences ranged from 4% to 9% (see section 20.3.2).

20.5.2 Appearances to Small Groups

Studies estimating the incidence or prevalence of "shared visions" are sparse (see Table 7). So it is difficult to tell how likely it would have been for the disciples to have experienced a shared vision. An alternative explanation is mass psychogenic illness—considered in the next chapter.

20.5.3 Appearance to Paul

Bereavement hallucinations are less relevant to Paul, since it is unlikely he met Jesus. Some NT scholars have argued Paul experienced a psychiatric condition. However this is based on very limited data.[41] Incidence rates of hallucinations in the general population are more relevant. Paul's experience of Jesus was within a defined period, perhaps three-to-four years after Jesus' death.[42] These experiences are not impossible, but not that common (affecting, on average, 2% of the population). Of course, it is unclear whether these estimates generalise to first century Palestine.

20.5.4 Appearance to James

Information on the appearance to James (First Corinthians 15) is limited. The Gospels state that James (the brother of Jesus) was not a disciple during Jesus' lifetime. Therefore, there is some overlap with the experience of Paul, although he was not a persecutor of the early church. Whether James' postmortem experience of Jesus occurred before or after he joined the disciples is unclear. However, First Corinthians 15 appears to group Paul and James as separate from the appearance to the twelve.

---

41. Even if we want to "diagnose" Paul with some psychotic condition, the incidence and prevalence of such conditions is even lower than non-clinical populations (approximately 1%) so this only succeeds in reducing the probability of the explanation.

42. Ehrman, *Christianity*, 46.

20.6 CONCLUSION

The goal of this chapter has been to estimate the prevalence and incidence of quasi-sensory experiences in non-clinical populations. We have no way of knowing whether these rates were higher or lower in first century Palestine. This uncertainty equally applies to naturalistic arguments positing these phenomena.

The next chapter will summarise other relevant psychological literature. For example, some NT scholars have argued the apostle Paul developed conversion disorder; others apply the concept of "mass hysteria" to account for group appearances.[43]

---

43. Ludemann, *Resurrection*, 175–76.

Chapter 21

Conversion Disorder and "Mass Hysteria"

21.1 INTRODUCTION

PAUL'S CLAIM TO HAVE witnessed the risen Jesus presents sceptics with difficulties. There is little reason to think he was mourning the death of Jesus, so bereavement hallucinations are unlikely. It stretches credibility to think Paul wanted to have a vision of Jesus. Some sceptics have argued Paul's experience of Jesus can be accounted for by *conversion disorder*. This psychiatric condition is now known as *functional neurological symptom disorder (FNSD)*.

Sceptics (such as Gerd Ludemann[1]) are also fond of positing the influence of *"mass hysteria"* or *mass psychogenic illness (MPI)*—similar to FNSD but thought to occur among groups rather than individuals. MPI grew in prominence in the late eighteenth century—although reports go back to at least medieval times. Many of the modern New Testament proponents of group hallucinations continue to draw on some of these earlier ideas. The validity of the term has been contested by leading sociologists in the field:

> Given the variety of often conflicting hypothesized causative mechanisms and the ambiguity of symptom criteria, the existence of MPI as a mental disorder entity has yet to be convincingly established.[2]

1. For example, Ludemann, *Resurrection*, 175–76.
2. Bartholomew, *Psychogenic*, 298.

Below I will consider the validity of FNSD and MPI as potential naturalistic explanations for Jesus' resurrection.

21.2 FUNCTIONAL NEUROLOGICAL SYMPTOM DISORDER (FNSD)

To avoid misunderstanding, conversion disorder does not relate to "religious conversion." The term comes from psychoanalytic theory, the conversion of subconscious conflicts into neurological or physical symptoms.[3] FNSD is now the standard term (see box 12 for a summary), as conversion disorder had pejorative undertones.

This is a rare condition. Annual incidence (the number of new cases in a year) is between 4 and 12 per 100,000 (0.004% to 0.01%).

BOX 12. DIAGNOSTIC CRITERIA FOR FUNCTIONAL NEUROLOGICAL SYMPTOM DISORDER

The Diagnostic and Statistical Manual of Mental Disorder (DSM-5), official diagnostic guide for the American Psychiatric Association, list four main criteria:[4]

- one or more symptoms that impact bodily movement or the senses;
- incompatibility between the symptoms and recognized medical conditions;
- these symptoms are not explained better by another medical condition;
- significant levels of stress or impairment in everyday functioning.

---

3. Bergeron and Habermas, *Psychiatric*, 165–66.
4. Aybeck, *Neurological*, 064.

PART FIVE: NATURALISTIC EXPLANATIONS

21.3 MASS PSYCHOGENIC ILLNESS (MPI)

MPI is a little like a cluster of cases of functional neurological symptom disorder (FNSD) in a group or community. However, MPI is not recognised in either DSM-5 or ICD-11 (standard diagnostic guides for the American Psychiatric Association and the World Health Organization). This reflects, as discussed above, the disputed nature of the concept.

A second issue, for those proposing MPI as a potential explanation of individual or group hallucinations, is that these symptoms are rarely reported in case studies. I consulted two key reviews—which identified 98 reports.[5] Of these, only two reported hallucinations (none reported group hallucinations).

Between 1880 and 1886, several young people on Pitcairn islands (famous for the "mutiny on the bounty") experienced "temporary madness."[6] Rosalind Young, a resident of Pitcairn Islands, described various symptoms including "distorted vision", "losing all recollection of former events", "the mind became an utter blank", "the power of speech was taken away".[7] These symptoms lasted up to two years. Although some of these young people experienced hallucinations, none claimed to have shared visions or hallucinations. In addition, it is questionable whether the symptoms reported at Pitcairn Islands are comparable to the disciples' experiences in the Gospels.

The second case was reported in West Malaysia, 1978.[8] Seventeen students (sixteen girls and one boy) reported nightmares, fainting, screaming, laughing, and trances. One male student experienced, what appears to be, a hypnogogic hallucination.[9] An experience that happens when drifting between being awake and asleep. No other visions or hallucinations were reported by any other student.

21.4 VISIONS OF MARY

But what about the visions of Mary at Fatima in 1917 or Zeitoun in 1968? In Fatima, children (aged between six and nine years) reported seeing a

---

5. Wessely, *Hysteria*, 109–20; Bartholomew, *Psychogenic*, 281–306.
6. Kalgaard, *Pitcairn*, 4722.
7. Young, *Pitcairn*, 216–17.
8. Lee, *Hysteria*, 78–88.
9. Lee, *Hysteria*, 83.

vision of Mary; rumour spread she would perform a miracle on October 13. A gathering of approximately 70,000 people claimed to see a solar phenomenon—the Sun seemed to fall to the earth.

There are difficulties with classifying this incident as a group hallucination. First, we do not know the cause of this "vision." Claiming it was a hallucination is jumping to conclusions. Second, Allison proposes a helpful alternative, that the crowd may have seen a rare meteorological phenomenon.[10] In other words, if there is a naturalistic explanation, it is more likely to be a perceptual illusion than a group hallucination.

In 1968, there were several sightings of a "shining apparition with a large halo" of the Virgin Mary—at Zeitoun Coptic Orthodox Church in Egypt.[11] After the second "appearance," large crowds gathered of up to 100,000 people. Many claimed to see a similar apparition. Some have explained these sightings as an electromagnetic phenomenon. As before, the most likely naturalistic explanation is a perceptual illusion rather than a hallucination or vision.

21.4.1 Fraud in Ezkioga?

O'Connell reports an example of Marian "visions" that could, at least in part, be explained by fraud.[12] William Christian Jr. investigated events in Ezkioga, Spain in the 1930s. Blood had poured from the hands of those who had "seen" visions of Mary. However, counter-testimony soon emerged. After being stunned by blood dripping from the hand of Ramona (a visionary), a local citizen "lowered his eyes in awe and [saw] to his surprise a razor blade on the ground."[13] After examination by two doctors, it was concluded her wounds were self-inflicted, likely by a razor blade.[14] Further suspicions were raised by claims that a picture had bled during several prayer sessions. When questioned why it was not kept behind glass, the owner's response was less than convincing, "through a female seer the Virgin had forbidden it."[15]

---

10. Allison, *Resurrection*, 250.
11. For further details see Allison, *Resurrection*, 294–300.
12. O'Connell, *Resurrection*, 200.
13. Christian, *Visionaries*, 51.
14. Christian, *Visionaries*, 51.
15. Christian, *Visionaries*, 200.

PART FIVE: NATURALISTIC EXPLANATIONS

21.5 PAREIDOLIA

Pareidolia involves "seeing" faces (or patterns that are not actually there) in everyday objects. This may be explained by the creativity of our brains, discerning patterns in complex data. Some false positives (seeing things when they are not there) may be a downside to this generally beneficial neuropsychological function.

Most of us, at one time, have probably experienced this phenomenon. For example, when my children were younger, we would often gaze at the clouds and share what shapes we saw. Of course, we did not literally think these clouds were dragons or rabbits! Many occurrences of pareidolia are religious in nature. For example, Allison notes some online photos of clouds, where people claim to see the face of Jesus.[16] He suggests, why not think the disciples did something similar?

The analogy seems to me an over-reach. As Andrew Loke points out, when people see Jesus' face in burnt toast or in clouds, this does not mean they are claiming to see Jesus' resurrection body:

> It is one thing to say that pareidolia is common . . . It is another thing to say it is common for people to believe that they have literally seen Jesus' body (face) after pareidolia.[17]

A sceptic might respond that Loke's critique may apply to twenty-first century people. But were not people in the first century far less sceptical? He challenges this assumption. Ancient people were also questioning of these kinds of perceptions. For example, Loke quotes Titus Livius (died in 17 CE), on reports of a phantom navy in the sky. Titus responded with scepticism, "when once men's minds have been excited by superstitious fears they easily believe these things."[18] Similarly, the early church historian, Eusebius considered Constantine's claims to have seen a cross of light in the sky, "hard to believe."[19] N.T. Wright also provided a detailed review of ancient Greco-Roman scepticism about bodily resurrection.[20]

---

16. Allison, *Resurrection*, 250.
17. Loke, *Divine and Resurrection*, 213.
18. Livius 21.62, cited in Loke, *Divine and Resurrection*, 212.
19. Cited in Loke, *Divine and Resurrection*, 212.
20. Wright, *Resurrection*, 32–84.

21.6 APPLICATION OF THIS LITERATURE TO JESUS' APPEARANCES

21.6.1 Appearance to Paul

Diagnosing a psychiatric condition in someone from a different time and culture is challenging. The low annual incidence rate for FNSD introduces further uncertainty. We know far too little about Paul's mental state and circumstances to make this judgment. Paul reported altered vision (temporary blindness), which is consistent with a sensory subtype of FNSD. However, hallucinations are not included in diagnostic criteria and are probably reflective of a different condition.[21] Therefore, this is unlikely to be a valid explanation of Paul's experience of Jesus.

21.6.2 Appearances to Small Groups

In the previous chapter, I assessed the possibility that Jesus' disciples had shared quasi-sensory experiences. An alternative explanation is to posit similarities with reports of Marian visions—such as those reported in Fatima or Zeitoun. However, comparisons are problematic. First, naturalistic explanations for these sightings are more likely to reflect meteorological or electromagnetic phenomena. Perceptual illusions are an unlikely explanation for most of the claims that Jesus appeared to groups of disciples. O'Connell proposes several reasons why:[22]

- Jesus was seen close-up: I might confuse my wife and her sister (they are of a similar height and shape) from a distance—but not when they are sitting a few feet away; Jesus' female disciples were close enough to clasp his feet (Matthew 28:9), so mistaken identity is unlikely;
- substantial duration of appearances: I may mistake you for someone else if we exchanged brief greetings at a large conference, but this is less likely if we sat together over lunch; several appearances include Jesus spending time with his disciples and eating together (e.g., Luke 24:36–43);
- unobstructed view of Jesus: if my view of the game is obscured by people standing in front of me, there's a good chance I may misidentify

---

21. McWhirter, *Pseudohallucinations*, P230.
22. O'Connell, *Resurrection*, 206.

who scored; it requires considerable imagination to think Mary or Peter's view of Jesus was somehow obscured when conversing with him (John 21:15–23)!

A further challenge is that group apparitions tend to be primarily visual not multimodal.[23] Testimony about group appearances in the Gospels report that Jesus spoke, as well as being seen and touched by his disciples. Allison dismisses Luke's account (e.g. 24:40—43) as an apologetic legend to promote bodily resurrection.[24] Yet Mark's narrative makes little sense if the angel was announcing Jesus' spirit had gone to heaven—the empty tomb is superfluous. Matthew's account also describes Jesus in physical terms:

> So the women hurried away from the tomb, afraid yet filled with joy, and ran to tell his disciples. Suddenly Jesus met them. "Greetings," he said. They came to him, *clasped his feet* and worshiped him. Then Jesus said to them, "Do not be afraid. Go and tell my brothers to go to Galilee; there they will see me." (Matthew 28:8–10)

21.6.3 Appearance to the 500

"Mass hysteria", or mass psychogenic illness (MPI), is a common naturalistic explanation for the appearance to the 500. But there are several issues. First, applying Western worldviews to different cultural contexts can lead to anachronism.[25] In addition, these explanations are often barely distinguishable from subtraction stories motivated by:

> unsubstantiated or antiquated assumptions of crowd behaviour... which do not vary considerably from their original formulations. While European social scholars used various psychiatric studies on hypnosis in the early 1880s to construct a model of collective hallucination, mass hypnosis or extreme forms of *folie a deux* psychosis.[26]

Second, there are doubts regarding the validity of the category "mass hysteria" or mass psychogenic illness. Third, hallucinations are a relatively

---

23. There are some exceptions, e.g. Mrs Bull reported feeling a sense of touch from Samuel Bull.
24. Allison, *Resurrection*, 217.
25. Bartholomew, *Mass Psychogenic Illness*, 281–306.
26. Bartholomew, *Psychogenic*, 297.

Conversion Disorder and "Mass Hysteria"

uncommon feature of MPI.[27] Fourth, examples in the literature do not appear analogous to the appearance to the 500, since none involve a group vision/hallucination.

Visions of Mary have also been proposed as analogous. However, the only clear overlap is that large groups of people claimed to witness a supernatural event. Which does not take us very far. In addition, it is far from clear what best explains events at Fatima and Zeitoun.

Finally, Allison also suggests that pareidolia may have explained the appearance to the 500. However, as argued above, it is hard to see how people seeing faces in a cloud led them to believe Jesus was raised from the dead.

21.7 CONCLUSION

In summary, naturalistic explanations have attempted to apply a range of psychological and sociological concepts to explain the disciples' experiences after Jesus' death. However, these suggestions lack plausibility:

- hallucinations are not a characteristic symptom of conversion disorder, which is an already rare condition;
- hallucinations or visions are also rarely reported in MPI—a disputed concept in the psychological and sociological literature;
- events in Fatima or Zeitoun lack applicability to the disciples' experience.

Chapter 22 will assess another set of psychological literature, memory research, used in naturalistic explanations of the resurrection data. We will also consider the escape hypothesis, apparent death hypothesis, and the lying hypothesis.

---

27. Granting that, as stated above, MPI as a distinct condition itself is contested.

Chapter 22

Distorted Memories and Other Explanations

22.1 INTRODUCTION

UNTIL THE MID-1990S, MOST psychologists considered memory to be "broadly reliable."[1] However, DNA evidence began to overturn an increasing number of criminal convictions. This led to rapid growth in research on the unreliability of eyewitness memory. This research has been filtering down into New Testament studies and popularised by Ehrman's *Jesus Before the Gospels*.[2] The Gospels are based on testimony. The validity of this testimony depends on the memories of witnesses. Could this be based on false memories? Overconfidence about vivid recollections?

The psychological literature has moved on since Ehrman's book.[3] For example, an influential study, published a few years later, kick-started a "replication crisis" in psychology.[4] Researchers were only able to replicate the findings of a third to a half of all studies they investigated. This started a period of reflection across the discipline. Influential figures in memory research, began to question whether the focus on the "sins" of memory had led us to forget the "virtues" of memory.[5] The impact of memory loss

---

1. Brewin, *Memory*, 121.
2. E.g., Ehrman, *Gospels*, 130.
3. First published in 2016.
4. Open Science Collaboration, *Reproducibility*, 943.
5. Baddeley, *Memory*, 55–59.

(e.g., through Alzheimer's disease or various forms of amnesia) shows our everyday functioning depends on the reliability of memory.

There is growing evidence of an unrealistically negative view on the accuracy of memory. For example, Nicholas Diamond and colleagues asked memory scientists, and academics from other disciplines, to predict how well participants would recall verifiable real-world events. Memory scientists (40% accuracy) and other academics (30% accuracy) vastly underestimated the results—participants on average got 93–95% of events correct.[6] Although the debate rages on, recent studies are shifting the consensus:

> Prominently underpinning this view [scepticism about the reliability of eyewitness memory] are claims that the confidence we have in our memory has little relation to its accuracy, that it is easy to implant false memories of events that never happened, and that the public erroneously perceives memory as being like a video camera. We argue that these claims are exaggerated and do not challenge the traditional consensus concerning memory accuracy.[7]

This chapter considers Ehrman's arguments in the light of this new research.[8] We will also consider other potential naturalistic explanations. The following topics are discussed below:

- distorted memories (false memories, flashbulb memories, confidence and accuracy).
- lying hypothesis and evidence for martyrdom of Jesus' disciples;
- brief responses to less influential explanations (apparent death hypothesis, escape);

22.2 DISTORTED MEMORIES

22.2.1 False Memories

Ehrman gives the impression that it is straightforward to develop, or implant, false memories about events that did not happen:

6. Diamond et al., *Accuracy*, 1544–1556.
7. Brewin, *Memory*, 121.
8. To be fair to Ehrman, although focusing on memory distortions, he acknowledged that our memories are often reliable. So his position is less extreme than some NT scholars.

One of the fairly recent discoveries in the field is that distorted memories can be implanted in people's minds, for example, by hearing distorted information about a past event and then remembering it as part of the event. That can happen even with respect to events of one's own personal history. Psychologists have long known this is true of children: adults can be made to think that as a child they were once lost in a shopping mall, or that they accidentally but disastrously overturned a punch bowl at a wedding.[9]

For example, he cites a study by Seamon and colleagues that took forty undergraduate students on a campus tour.[10] These students were unaware they were taking part in a memory experiment. Half of the time, researchers asked them to perform familiar (e.g., check the Pepsi machine for change) or bizarre (e.g., propose marriage to a Pepsi machine) actions. In the other half of the experiment, researchers asked them to imagine performing these actions. Students were asked to recall from seventy-two actions/imaginations over two different sessions. Ehrman is partially correct. Memory is malleable and false memory is possible. Yet, on average, false memories/false beliefs were found for only 7–12% of actions on average.

Reassessment of other studies also suggest an over-estimate on the likelihood of false memories. For example, "one study found that it was apparently possible to implant a false memory of having committed a crime in 70% of participants."[11] Yet re-analyses of this study found that "over half of the 70% in fact reported false beliefs, not false memories."[12] Similarly a systematic review (a comprehensive summary of research on a topic), found:

> on average, 47% of participants were rated as having some recollective experience associated with the suggested false event, no matter how vague, uncertain, or speculative, only 15% of participants were classified as having fully accepted the false memory.[13]

These studies show it is possible to manipulate memory "in the lab." Yet it is rare for participants to fully accept the false memory. Some studies, viewed in isolation, may have over-estimated the problem:

---

9. Ehrman, *Gospels*, 139.
10. Seamon et al., *Pepsi Machine*, 752–56.
11. Brewin, *Memory*, 123.
12. Brewin, *Memory*, 123.
13. Brewin, *Memory*, 123.

Distorted Memories and Other Explanations

The fact that memory can be manipulated in the laboratory is important but does not by itself allow of any conclusion about how reliable memory is under normal, real life circumstances. Despite this, some organizations have endorsed statements such as "science shows that the memory of an honest witness who gives evidence in international arbitration proceedings can easily become distorted"[14]

22.2.2 Are Confidence and Accuracy Associated?

Vivid memories tend to inspire confidence in their accuracy. Ehrman proposes a common view that questions this intuition:

> But just because a memory is especially vivid does not mean that it is especially accurate. Many of us have a hard time believing that, at least when it comes to our own vivid memories. But it's true, and has been shown repeatedly.[15]

His summary of the evidence at the time was fair. However, it is now recognized this view was partly shaped by sub-optimal statistical methods:

> Regarding the confidence–accuracy relationship, eyewitness experts have largely considered confidence to be a poor predictor of accuracy for many... However, research conducted within the last 20 years has pointed to a new way of thinking about confidence and accuracy.[16]

For example, John Wixted and colleagues have pioneered the use of more appropriate statistical methods adapted from signal detection theory and medicine. Re-analyses of earlier studies has shown that "the confidence-accuracy relation is impressively strong."[17] This is not to deny that memory can become contaminated. Nor is it a denial that eyewitnesses can be confidently wrong. However, these findings indicate the dismissal of confidence, as a predictor of memory accuracy, was too hasty.

---

14. Brewin, *Psychology*, e7.
15. Ehrman, *Gospels*, 140–41.
16. Seale-Carlisle et al., *Eyewitness Memory*, 9.
17. Wixted et al., *Memory*, 328.

22.2.3 Should we Trust Vivid Memories?

We will see below, the disciples' willingness to suffer for their beliefs is a common argument for the veracity of their testimony. In response, Ehrman has suggested we do not even need to posit the disciples lied. The Gospel accounts may have been based on false memory.

> But it is also possible that people who invented stories really believed they happened ... if you imagine that something happened, even something implausible, it is very easy indeed for that imagination to become a memory and for that memory to be every bit as vivid as something that really did happen.[18]

Several studies have investigated emotive events known as "flashbulb memories." For example, Ehrman cited one by Neisser and Harsch on the memories of students about the Challenger disaster. These memories were frequently confused, and many could not even remember filling in a questionnaire at the time of the disaster.[19]

One of the lessons of the "replication crisis" is that taking the results of an individual study in isolation can be misleading. A later study by Neisser and colleagues[20] identified a key predictor of more reliable recall. Californian students had near-perfect accuracy (96–99%) remembering an earthquake in Loma Prieta (California) 18 months later. But Atlanta students had much less accurate recall (55% accuracy) for the same earthquake. These events were likely to be of greater relevance to Californians—which may explain their higher rates of accurate recall.

Researchers have replicated these findings elsewhere. For example, a study on memory of an earthquake in Marmara, Turkey—six months after the event.[21] People who lived in Marmara had near-perfect accuracy. Yet people who lived in another city (Mersin) performed far poorer on a memory test about that earthquake.

---

18. Ehrman, *Gospels*, 176.
19. Neisser, *Flashbulbs*, 9–31.
20. Neisser, *Earthquake*, 337–57.
21. Er, *Flashbulb*, 503–17.

22.3 LYING

The next naturalistic explanation works on two intuitive premises:

- We know that people lie.
- Just because the disciples reported seeing Jesus after his death does not mean they actually saw him.

Of course, it is possible the disciples lied. However, there are good reasons to think this explanation lacks plausibility:

> The apostles are supposed to have known best that there was not one single word of truth in the news of their master's resurrection... yet regardless of this, they are supposed to have spread the same story with a fire of conviction that sufficed to give the world a different form.[22]

Second, if these testimonies were a hoax, the disciples chose to suffer for a known lie:

> While many people throughout history would be willing to sacrifice everything (including their own lives) for what they believe to be true (even though it may not actually be true), no large group of people would be willing to sacrifice everything for what they do not believe to be true and be condemned by God after death for being false witnesses.[23]

22.3.1 Suffering and Persecution of the Early Disciples

Some sceptics question whether the disciples suffered for their testimony. However, the early church experienced persecution and hardship from the beginning.[24] This is unsurprising. If Jesus their leader was crucified—why would his followers expect an easy life? He also warned them they would suffer (e.g. Matthew 5:10–12; Mark 8:35; Matthew 10:39, 16:25; Luke 17:33, 9:24; John 12:25). Many were killed, beaten, or experienced hardship:

- Herod ordered the beheading of John the Baptist
- Stephen was stoned to death (Acts 6–8)

22. David Strauss, cited in Loke, *Resurrection*, 74.
23. Loke, *Resurrection*, 73.
24. McDowell, *Apostles*, 56.

Part Five: Naturalistic Explanations

- Herod Agrippa ordered the death of James the brother of John (Acts 12:12)
- The apostle Paul spoke of "troubles, hardships and distresses; in beatings, imprisonments and riots; in hard work, sleepless nights and hunger." (Second Corinthians 6:4–5)

There is also plenty of evidence from outside of the Bible. For example, Tacitus (115 CE) on the early persecution of Christians under Emperor Nero (54–58 CE).[25] Sean McDowell provides an extensive investigation of the evidence available on the suffering and martyrdom of each apostle. He argued there is strong evidence that four of the apostles were martyred.

Peter: For example, according to Bart Ehrman, First Clement mentions the martyrdom of Peter and Paul, somewhere between 64 and 170CE.[26] There is an "early and persistent tradition . . . that Peter was martyred for his faith."[27]

Paul: In addition to First Clement, McDowell once more identifies "early and persistent tradition that Paul was martyred for his faith."[28]

James, the brother of Jesus: McDowell argues there is strong evidence that James was executed by stoning.[29] Also, that it is very probably true, James was martyred for being Christian.[30] Most scholars agree. However some have pointed out Josephus' account does not mention the reason for James's death. Yet, Christians were often condemned as law breakers under

---

25. The Annals 15.44,2–5; cited in McDowell, *Apostles*, 76–77.

26. Ehrman, *Apostolic*, 1:24.

27. McDowell, *Apostles*, 154. In addition to the sources mentioned above he cites Ignatius, Letter to the Smyrneans 3.1–2, Letter to the Romans 4.3; Apocalypse of Peter 14.4; Ascension of Isaiah 4:2–3; the Acts of Peter; Dionysius of Corinth, Eusebius, *Ecclesiastical History* 2.25; Tertullian, Scorpiace 15 in support of this conclusion.

28. McDowell, *Apostles*, 192. In addition to First Clement, early sources include 2 Tim 4:6–8; Acts 19:21—28:31; Ignatius Letter to the Ephesians 12:2, Letter to the Romans 4.3; Letter to the Philippians 7:1; Dionysius of Corinth (Eusebius *Ecclesiastical History* 2.25); Irenaeus Against Heresies 3.1.1; Acts of Paul; Tertullian Scorpiace 15:5–6, The Prescription Against Heretics 24, 36.

29. McDowell, *Apostles*, 222. Early sources include Josephus *Antiquities* 20.197–203; Hegesippus *Hypomnemata* Book 5 as recorded in Eusebius *Ecclesiastical History* 2.23; Clement of Alexandria *Hypotyposes* Book 7 as recorded in Eusebius *Ecclesiastical History*, 2.1.4–5; *Second Apocalypse of James* 60.15–63.32.

30. McDowell, *Apostles*, 222. Early sources include Josephus *Antiquities* 20.197–203; Hegesippus *Hypomnemata* Book 5 as recorded in Eusebius *Ecclesiastical History* 2.23; Clement of Alexandria *Hypotyposes* Book 7 as recorded in Eusebius *Ecclesiastical History*, 2.1.4–5; *First Apocalypse of James*; *Second Apocalypse of James* 60.15–63.32.

Jewish law. So Josephus' account is not necessarily inconsistent with other early literature.

James, the son of Zebedee: McDowell argues there is strong evidence that James was martyred.[31] There is early and consistent evidence without any competing traditions.

Evidence on the martyrdom of the other apostles is less clear—so will not be considered here. For further details, see McDowell's dissertation quoted above. A further source of support, although an argument from silence, is that there is no evidence any of the apostles recanted.[32] There is good reason to think, given the harm it would have caused to Christianity, if such testimony existed it would have been used by their critics.

22.4 APPARENT DEATH (SWOON)

This explanation likely goes back to the nineteenth century—the assumption is that Jesus did not really die by crucifixion. This accounts for an "empty tomb"—since he either was never buried or escaped later. It also accounts for why the disciples saw Jesus after his "death," because he did not die. However, according to William Lane Craig, this explanation has been largely abandoned:

> how to explain the empty tomb, given Jesus' merely apparent death, since a man sealed inside a tomb could not move the stone so as to escape; how to explain the postmortem appearances, since as Strauss mused, the appearance of a half-dead man desperately in need of medical attention would hardly have elicited in the disciples the conclusion that he was the Risen Lord and conqueror of Death; and how to explain the anachronism of the origin of the disciples' belief in Jesus' resurrection, since seeing him again would lead them to conclude that he had not died, not that he was, contrary to Jewish thought (as well as their own eyes), gloriously risen from the dead.[33]

---

31. McDowell, *Apostles*, 314. Early sources include (Acts 12:1–2; Mark 10:39; Clement of Alexandria Book 7,
 Outlines (Eusebius *Eccl. Hist.* 2.9); Chrysostom *Homilies on the Acts of the Apostles* 26; Gregory of Nyssa; *Homily 2 On Stephen*; Philip of Side, Papias fragment).

32. McDowell, *Apostles*, 427.

33. Craig, *Reasonable Faith*, 373.

PART FIVE: NATURALISTIC EXPLANATIONS

22.5 ESCAPE

Many Muslims subscribe to the escape hypothesis. They find support in the Qur'an:

> That they said (in boast) "We killed Christ Jesus the son of Mary the Apostle of God"; but they killed him not nor crucified him but so it was made to appear to them and those who differ therein are full of doubts with no (certain) knowledge but only conjecture to follow for of a surety they killed him not.[34]

For Muslims, who believe the Qur'an is the Word of God, this is sufficient evidence to doubt Jesus' death by crucifixion and therefore also his resurrection. For non-Muslims, beliefs about Jesus' death written several hundred years later, that contradict much earlier accounts of both Christians and non-Christians, are of limited historical value. In addition:

> Against the escape hypothesis, it is unlikely that all the onlookers failed to recognize that it was not Jesus who was crucified in public. The enemies of Jesus who bothered to crucify him would have bothered to identify him correctly.[35]

22.6 CONCLUSION

This chapter has considered four naturalist explanations for postmortem appearances of Jesus: *apparent death, escape, lying, and distorted memories* (with greatest focus on the last two explanations). In response to the *lying hypothesis*, I considered evidence that the apostles Peter, Paul, James the brother of Jesus, and James the son of Zebedee were *martyred for their faith*. In addition, there is no evidence that any of the apostles recanted from their faith. This is *unlikely* if the apostles were lying. In response to the *distorted memories hypothesis*, I have assessed more recent psychological evidence which challenges the claims of NT scholars like Bart Ehrman.

The final naturalist explanation to be considered will be on cognitive dissonance. An explanation that has recently grown in popularity.

---

34. *Qur'an*, 4:157.
35. Loke, *Resurrection*, 119.

Chapter 23

Cognitive Dissonance Theory

23.1 INTRODUCTION

PETER KAY, A BRITISH comedian, often observes the absurdities of everyday life.[1] For example, when people run for a bus, but fail to catch it; why do they pretend they never needed it? They smoothly transition from running at full pace to a steady walk—in the hope no one noticed. Others might add in a few star-jumps and stretches, as if they are in the middle of a workout.

Of course, Kay is exaggerating, but his observation might be accounted for by cognitive dissonance. We do not want people to think we are stupid—or that we miscalculated—so we try to convince ourselves, and others, we did not really run for the bus. If we react in that way to minor disappointments, how much more so for other events?

If the Messiah was expected to be a victorious king—Jesus' death put an end to any hopes he was Israel's deliverer. Are New Testament citations of Isaiah 53 or Psalm 22 an attempt to resolve these feelings of cognitive dissonance? A strategy to keep the movement going, despite the obvious setback? We have already seen, in Chapter 11, this depiction of the Messiah's mission is overly simplistic. This chapter builds on that background to address these arguments.

Sceptics may also employ cognitive dissonance theory (CDT) as one component of a broader naturalistic explanation. For example, in chapter 20, we noted that people without a psychiatric disorder can often tell if they

---

1. Kay, *Bus*, 0.03 to 0.24.

have experienced a hallucination or vision. This makes it difficult to account for the disciples' belief purely through visions or hallucinations. CDT may then be deployed to fill this potential explanatory gap.[2] This chapter pursues the following four themes:

- the perils of using CDT to deconstruct the views of our opponents;
- summary of CDT;
- the best comparators for Christianity;
- attempts to apply CDT to the experiences of Jesus' disciples.

23.2 CHALLENGES IN DECONSTRUCTING BELIEFS

23.2.1 Risk of Correspondence Bias

Naturalistic explanations for Jesus' resurrection, including the application of CDT, are mainly proposed by atheists to explain beliefs they do not hold. It is therefore important to consider the potential for bias. The social psychological literature highlights several possible attributional biases. The correspondence bias is the most prominent example (see Box 13).[3]

BOX 13. CORRESPONDENCE BIAS

The correspondence bias is based on a common finding from psychological research, that we tend to judge ourselves (or people from our group) by different standards to how we judge others (or people from a different group). We tend to propose "dispositional" causes for others' behaviour, even when "situational" explanations are apparent:

Dispositional cause: when we judge a person's belief or behaviour is inherent to their personality—for example, Pete was late for the meeting because he is poor at time keeping.

---

2. Komarnitsky, *Dissonance*, §7.

3. Although there is often a limited awareness of this bias outside of the field of psychology.

> **BOX 13. CORRESPONDENCE BIAS**
>
> *Situational cause*: when we conclude someone's belief or behaviour reflects the situation, or the evidence—for example, Pete was late for the meeting because there was a lot of traffic.
>
> A classic example is the study by Jones and Harris, where American participants read out speeches written by their fellow students on Fidel Castro.[4] As you would expect, most participants concluded that pro-Castro students wrote positive speeches about Castro if they had a choice of what to write (*dispositional attribution*).
>
> However, when participants were informed there was a *situational cause*—that students were instructed what to write—they overwhelmingly continued to make *dispositional attributions* (positive speeches were written by pro-Castro students). Many studies have replicated these results, particularly in individualistic cultures.

New Testament scholar, Bermejo-Rubio's critique of NT Wright, is one potential example. For example, he asserts Wright's stance on CDT "*seems to be dictated by theological prejudices and fears.*"[5] Bermejo-Rubio posits a *dispositional attribution* (a type of "mind-reading") to Wright's beliefs about the application of CDT.

Bermejo-Rubio then applies a *dispositional attribution* to the wider outgroup, "Theologically-minded authors, however, *tend to rule out anything questioning the complete uniqueness of the movement they belong to.*"[6] This sounds like the ultimate attributional error, "negative outgroup [a group we do not belong to] behaviour is dispositionally attributed, whereas positive outgroup behaviour is externally attributed or explained away so that we preserve our unfavourable outgroup image."[7]

---

4. Jones and Harris, *Attributions*, 1–24.
5. Bermejo-Rubio, *Dissonance*, 126.
6. Bermejo-Rubio, *Dissonance*, 126.
7. Hogg and Vaughn, *Social Psychology*, 102–4.

PART FIVE: NATURALISTIC EXPLANATIONS

23.2.2 "We Are Unique, They Are All the Same"

Some further psychological background is needed before we move onto CDT. Social identity theory and social categorisation theory, some of the most influential social psychological theories, predict that social categorisation (e.g., stereotyping) accentuates group differences. Ingroup members tend to be categorised according to positive characteristics. For example, atheists may emphasise their love of scepticism, science, and logic. These positive characteristics are often contrasted with the negative characteristics of outgroups (e.g., unquestioning religious people who want to protect their beliefs from science). A key characteristic of this categorisation process—particularly in the individualist West—is an emphasis on the homogeneity (similarity) of the outgroup.

23.3 WHAT IS COGNITIVE DISSONANCE THEORY (CDT)?

Leon Festinger developed CDT in the 1950s. Social psychologists, Michael Hogg and Graham Vaughn, summarise the theory below:

> Festinger proposed that we seek harmony in our attitudes, beliefs and behaviour and try to reduce tension from inconsistency between these elements. People will try to reduce dissonance by changing one or more of the inconsistent cognitions (e.g., if in the case of the person having an extramarital affair, "What's wrong with a little fun if no one finds out?"), by looking for additional evidence to bolster one side or the other ("My partner doesn't understand me"), or by derogating the source of one of the cognitions ("Fidelity is a construct of religious indoctrination").[8]

Vaidis and Bran[9] point out the need to distinguish different stages of the cognitive dissonance process (see Figure 5):

- a triggering situation where there is an inconsistency between beliefs and reality (triggering situation)
- discomfort caused by this inconsistency (cognitive dissonance state)
- an attempt to reduce discomfort (regulation).

---

8. Hogg and Vaughn, *Social Psychology*, 221.
9. Vaidis and Bran, *Dissonance*, 1189.

A common issue is that people often focus on regulation strategies whilst neglecting earlier steps in the model.[10]

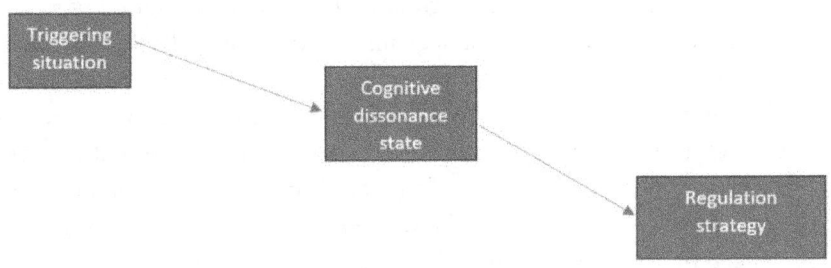

Figure 5. Three Stages of Cognitive Dissonance

23.4 GETTING THE COMPARATOR RIGHT

When trying to understand the origin of Christianity, it is interesting to compare the experiences of the disciples with other similar groups. But what do we mean by similar? Scholars, like N.T. Wright, have emphasised the importance of studying Jesus and the disciples in their original milieu of second temple Judaism. Some of the proponents of a CDT approach to Christian origins considerably broaden this scope for comparison.

23.4.1 The Millerites

Kris Komarnitsky,[11] writing for the WestStar Institute (formerly the Jesus Seminar), and Matthew Hartke (who has a popular YouTube channel and blog),[12] compare the experience of Jesus' disciples with religious movements in history. Komarnitsky explores a few examples including a North London Hassidic Jewish community in the twentieth century; and followers of Sabbattai Sevi in the seventeenth century.

---

10. Vaidis and Bran, *Dissonance*, 1189.
11. Komarnitsky, *Dissonance*, §4.
12. Hartke, *Dissonance*, §5.

I will focus on an example Komarnitsky and Hartke share—the nineteenth century Millerites. This group predicted the end of the world in 1844. Despite failed prophecy, the Millerite movement continues to this day, under a different name—the Seventh Day Adventists. Jesus' disciples had to adapt to Jesus' failure to fulfil Messianic prophecy. Like the Millerites, they had to adapt their core beliefs to avoid their movement imploding.[13]

The solution to failed prophecy for the Millerites follows this pattern. Hiram Edson—taking a walk in a cornfield—received the "insight from God" that 1844 was the time for the cleansing of the heavenly sanctuary, not the earthly one. This was a spiritualising of Miller's original prophecy. Ellen Harmon later had a series of similar visions. This explanation may fit the experience of the Millerites, "new revelation" comes through visions experienced by Hiram Edson and Ellen Harmon. However, I will argue below this argument fits Christianity less well.

The difficulty with Hartke and Komarnitsky's approach is that it is necessarily selective. It is not hard to find examples where the behaviour of members can be convincingly accounted for by CDT—as there have been many thousands of religious movements in the history of the world. Yet the sheer number of movements increases the temptation to pick at random those examples that seem to fit our argument, whilst neglecting evidence pointing in another direction.

Attempting to draw broad generalisations across disparate outgroups (people we disagree with) can also lead to further risk of bias in conclusions. Our tendency to think "we are unique, they are all the same" can lead us to highlight similarities and downplay differences. Intergroup biases can make it appear obvious that because CDT accounts well for the behaviour of some religious groups—it must also account for Christianity.

23.4.2 Revolutionary Movements

Being more specific about comparators helps guard against potential selection bias. Messianic movements, occurring at a similar time and place, are more suitable comparators with Jesus' disciples than a group of nineteenth century Americans. A more careful way of testing these assumptions is to examine:

---

13. Hartke, *Dissonance*, §6.

Cognitive Dissonance Theory

- if there were other Messiah candidates at a similar time in history where their leader died;
- if they adopted a similar strategy to Jesus' disciples.

Wright points out there were many messianic movements in second temple Judaism:

> many of the messianic movements between roughly 150 BC and AD 150 ended with the violent death of the founder. When this happened, there were two options open to any who escaped death: they could give up the movement, or they could find themselves another Messiah.[14]

Jesus famously claims in the Gospels to be "King of the Jews". Richard Horsley, pointed out, "the Jewish peasantry at the time of Jesus produced several concrete movements led by figures recognized as kings, movements and leaders who actually ruled certain areas of the country for a time."[15] These movements appear to be inspired by Biblical notions of the anointed king (from the line of David)—and therefore often categorised as Messianic. It is important to distinguish these types of movement from broader social movements in Palestine during that period:

> this was not the only possible form that popular social movements could have taken. In the same period of time, in the same general circumstances, there were also other distinctive forms of popular discontent: social banditry, prophetic movements, more general peasant uprisings (i.e., without distinctive "kings" or "prophets" as leaders), and rather amorphous spontaneous urban demonstrations and riots.[16]

Josephus described several Messianic movements around the first century. These occur at two main time points—the uprising after the death of Herod and the first great revolt against Rome (66–70 CE). During these periods, Simon the former Herodian servant (4 BCE), Simon bar Giora (68 CE), Athronges, Judas son of Ezekias, and Menahem (66 CE) briefly made claims to be King of the Jews. All were successfully subdued by the Romans.

Simon bar Giora's large force was able to seize back control of Jerusalem and may have been formally recognized as king by the citizen body and

---

14. Wright, *Resurrection*, 700.
15. Horsley, *Messianic*, 472.
16. Horsley, *Messianic*, 494.

chief priests.[17] However, like all other similar movements, Simon finally surrendered:

> Taken together the manner of his surrender, clad in the symbolic robes of the king of the Jews, the ceremonial event in Rome provides a significant manifestation the way in which Simon bar Giora had assumed the role of the anointed of his people, the recognized leader of a messianic movement among the Judean peasantry in the midst of their assertion of independence from Roman rule.[18]

Simon bar Giora's defeat was followed by perhaps the most famous Messianic candidate during this period (except for Jesus)—Simon bar Kochba. The influential Rabbi Akiva pronounced him the Messiah. His followers took control over various regions in Judea—before inevitable defeat by the Romans.[19]

As Wright notes, there is a common pattern in this period:

- a Messianic candidate drew a following;
- they experienced some initial success;
- the uprising was crushed by the Romans;
- a new Messianic candidate emerged.

These examples suggest that a situational cause for regulating dissonance was common. Members abandoned their group when their previous beliefs conflicted with the reality of their founder's death.

23.4.3 Dositheans

Dositheus is probably the only exception, along with Jesus, in this period where a Messianic claimant's following extended long after his death. He probably lived in the first century CE (likely after the time of Jesus),[20] and his sect lasted until at least the sixth century.

However, information about the Dositheans is highly uncertain. For example, there is disagreement over whether Dositheus was Jewish or Samaritan. There is also debate whether these sources describe one, two,

---

17. Horsley, Messianic, 490.
18. Horsley, Messianic, 491.
19. Horsley, Messianic, 493–94.
20. Origen, *Contra Celsum*, I:57.

Cognitive Dissonance Theory

or three men named Dositheus.[21] None of their writings (if they ever existed) are extant—the earliest sources come from the church father's writings on heresies.

They appear to have been a relatively small sect within Samaritanism, stigmatized as heretics by mainstream Samaritans.[22] They believed Dositheus was the Messiah,[23] modelled on the prophet like Moses (Deuteronomy 18) rather than the Davidic king. Their size, and less political focus, probably posed less threat to the Roman authorities—which may explain their survival.

Traditions about Dositheus's death also conflict. According to the Pseudo-Clementine literature,[24] dated from second to fourth century, there was fierce rivalry between him and Simon of Magus.[25] After a fight, Simon deposed him as leader of the sect—Dositheus died shortly after.

Origen (third century) may have had knowledge of the Pseudo-Clementine literature.[26] He related a tradition from the Dositheans that their founder "did not taste death, but is alive somewhere."[27] But since he wrote approximately two hundred years later, it is unclear when these reports began to emerge.

Epiphanus (approximately fourth century) outlined a conflicting tradition, that Dositheus died in a cave after too much fasting. "After a while people came to visit him, found his body reeking with decay and breeding worms, and a cloud of flies swarming on it."[28]

In summary, accounts of Dositheus's death, and the early developments of the Dosithean sect, are lacking in detail and contradictory. There is insufficient data to conclude why, or how, this group continued to exist after his death.

---

21. Isser, *Dositheans*, 3.
22. Isser, *Dositheans*, 109.
23. Origen, *Contra Celsum*, I:57.
24. Pseudo Clementine, *Recognitions*, Book II: 10-12; Pseudo Clementine, *Homilies*, Homily II:24.
25. He is the magician mentioned in Acts 8:9-25.
26. Since he quipped about the Dositheans struggling to have thirty disciples—the total number of disciples mentioned in the Pseudo Clementine literature. Although it is possible he did not know these works.
27. Origen, *Commentary on John*, 102-3.
28. Epiphanus, *Panarion*, I:13.

PART FIVE: NATURALISTIC EXPLANATIONS

23.5 CDT AND FAILED PROPHECY?

The previous section looked at applications of CDT to certain religious movements. This section now assesses NT scholar, Fernando Bermejo-Rubio's, argument that CDT accounts for the origins of Christianity.

23.5.1 Reinterpreting Prophecy

The New Testament's now and not yet understanding of the Messianic kingdom was a Christian innovation. There is no indication that any pre-Christian group interpreted the Messiah's mission in this way. Was this new belief, due to the response of Jesus' disciples to unexpected circumstances—his resurrection and ascension? Did they search the Hebrew Bible to make sense of these events? Was their belief in the now and not yet kingdom a justified response to their experience? If so, Jesus' death, resurrection, and ascension were the situational causes of this belief.

Bermejo-Rubio proposes an alternative dispositional cause for this new belief. The disciples reinterpreted passages in the Hebrew Bible to overcome cognitive dissonance. He quips that, "emotional needs very often lead to exegetical gymnastics and tours de force."[29] Bermejo-Rubio does not elaborate on what he thinks these "exegetical gymnastics" and "emotional needs" were. Although dispositional attributions about outgroup (Jesus' disciples) beliefs can seem obvious, we need to be careful that this confidence is driven by the data.

23.5.2 Spiritualising Response?

Bermejo-Rubio argues Jesus' disciples spiritualised Messianic prophecies. This enabled their movement to continue and reduced cognitive dissonance:

> According to this reconceptualization, the believers state not that the prophecy was wrong, but that they had merely misunderstood it in a material, earthly way. At the same time, the original prophesied event becomes an invisible and spiritual—and accordingly unfalsifiable—event: non-empirical items cannot be proven wrong. Such a process is clearly perceived in the fact that the material, socio-political features of Jesus' status as an earthly

---

29. Bermejo-Rubio, *Dissonance*, 138.

messiah and the correlative Kingdom of God were toned down and reframed in spiritual categories.[30]

There are various reasons to challenge Bermejo-Rubio's spiritualising claims. An obvious physical and empirical omission is Jesus' resurrection (Acts 17:31). The apostle Paul did not appear to think Jesus' resurrection was unfalsifiable. Would this not provide a situational cause for their change in beliefs? Was it testable? To produce Jesus' dead body would have been a straightforward empirical refutation of the disciples claim.

Additionally, the New Testament consistently affirms that Jesus' disciples interacted with him. Not as a ghostly apparition, but physically. Jesus' disciples also continued to proclaim the coming of the new heaven and the new earth (Romans 8:18–30; Second Peter 3:12–14; Revelation 21:1–3) at the heart of Messianic prophecy (e.g. Isaiah 65:17–18, 66:22–24). Therefore, there is no evidence that they abandoned the earthly for the spiritual.

23.6 CONCLUSION

CDT is a well-established theory within psychology. But there are significant limitations associated with sceptics, and atheist scholars, attempting to apply this theory to explain the disciples' beliefs. Social psychological theories predict we attribute dispositional causes to the beliefs of others. So attribution biases are one potential explanation for why sceptics find naturalistic explanations persuasive.

We also tend to overemphasise overlaps between outgroups (e.g., first century Jews, nineteenth century Americans, and twenty-first century British Hasidic Jews) without spotting key differences. Assessment of first century Messianic movements provide little support that cognitive dissonance was common after the death of their leader.

A third challenge is that applying CDT as an explanatory framework requires evidence of a cognitive dissonance state. Attempts to explain the disciples' beliefs focus on the evolution of their beliefs ("regulation")— without demonstrating that they were experiencing cognitive dissonance.

---

30. Bermejo-Rubio, *Dissonance*, 139.

Chapter 24

A Summary of Alternative Explanations

24.1 INTRODUCTION

I HAVE CONSIDERED A range of naturalistic explanations for reports about Jesus' empty tomb and postmortem appearances. I will summarise the findings from these chapters and make judgments on how likely this evidence would occur if Jesus was not resurrected. At this stage, I will stick to qualitative judgments unless there are empirical estimates available. This chapter sets out to summarise the following:

- naturalistic explanations of the empty tomb;
- naturalistic explanations of Jesus' postmortem appearances;
- combinations of naturalistic explanations (Ehrman, Ludemann, Allison).

24.2 NATURALISTIC EXPLANATIONS OF THE EMPTY TOMB

In chapter 19, I argued there are eight categories of naturalistic explanation for Jesus' empty tomb (summarised in Table 8). I judged it unlikely that the early church would invent a story where Jesus' female disciples were the primary witnesses to this event.

A Summary of Alternative Explanations

Explanation/theory	Judgment (probability)
Escape	Extremely unlikely
Apparent death	Extremely unlikely
Remain buried	Very unlikely
Unburied	Unlikely
Non-agent removal	Very unlikely
Removal by friends	Very unlikely
Removal by enemies	Very unlikely
Removal neither friends nor enemies (e.g. tomb robbers)	Slightly unlikely

Table 8. Alternative explanations for empty tomb

All naturalistic explanations struggle to account for these data. Escape and apparent death theories have the further improbability of claiming that Jesus did not die by crucifixion, now accepted by almost all scholars. Despite some scholars (such as Ludemann) proposing that Jesus' body remained buried, I also judged this explanation very unlikely. Resurrection in the first century related to the body, not simply "life after death" (see chapters 12 and 15 for further details).

A common[1] naturalistic explanation for the empty tomb, is that Jesus' body was not buried. Either his body was left on the cross to be eaten by scavengers, or his body was thrown into a shared grave for criminals. This explanation reflects usual practice for the disposal of executed criminals' bodies. However, there is good evidence that Roman authorities were willing to allow burial on request. Therefore, this explanation was judged unlikely. The removal of Jesus' body was considered unlikely to very unlikely—due to testimony from Jesus' female disciples and testimony about guards at the tomb.

24.3 NATURALISTIC EXPLANATIONS FOR POSTMORTEM APPEARANCES

Explanation/Theory	Judgement and/or probability
Apparent death	Very unlikely
Escape	Very unlikely

---

1. But still minority opinion, as acknowledged by Ehrman.

PART FIVE: NATURALISTIC EXPLANATIONS

Explanation/Theory	Judgement and/or probability
No experience	Very unlikely
Legend	Unlikely
Mistaken identity/distorted memories	Slightly unlikely to slightly likely
Hallucinations/visions experienced by individuals	Prevalence of bereavement hallucination/vision: 0.045 (tactile), 0.133 (visual or audio), or 0.166 (verbal)
	Prevalence of bereavement multi-modal hallucination/ vision
	(visual and auditory): 0.064
Hallucinations/visions experienced by small groups	Prevalence of group visions: range from 0.007 to 0.042
Hallucination/vision experienced by Paul	Incidence of hallucinations/delusions in non-clinical population: 0.02
Hallucination/vision experienced by James	Prevalence of bereavement hallucination/vision: 0.045 (tactile), 0.133 (visual or audio), or 0.166 (verbal)
	Prevalence of bereavement multi-modal hallucination/ vision
	(visual and auditory): 0.064
Hallucination/vision experienced by the 500	Unlikely
Mass hysteria/mass psychogenic illness	Extremely unlikely
Cognitive dissonance	Unlikely

Table 9. Alternative explanations for postmortem appearances

As above, I judged apparent death and escape hypotheses as very unlikely (see Table 9). I also judged it very unlikely that Jesus' disciples and Paul had no experience. In Part Four, I argued the legend hypothesis is unlikely since the key details are complementary and consistent in sources over time. It was also judged unlikely that distorted memories explain the diversity and magnitude of testimony on Jesus' postmortem appearances.

Many sceptics have applied research on hallucinations, in people without a mental health condition, to explain the experiences of Jesus' disciples. I derived median estimates from this literature (see chapter 20) to estimate the prevalence and incidence of these experiences. I also considered the plausibility of mass hysteria or mass psychogenic illness as an explanation for Jesus's postmortem appearance to the 500 in chapter 21. In both cases,

A Summary of Alternative Explanations

I judge these explanations unlikely. Cognitive dissonance was also considered unlikely to account for these data (see chapter 23).

24.4 COMBINATIONS OF NATURALISTIC EXPLANATIONS

No single naturalistic explanation fully explains evidence for Jesus' resurrection. Therefore, many naturalistic theories (e.g., Ehrman, Allison, and Ludemann) combine options.

24.4.1 Ehrman

Ehrman proposed that a small number of disciples (Peter and Mary), and later Paul, experienced visions. He argued since "some doubted" (Matthew 28:17), we should not assume all disciples experienced visions:

> The reason this question is so pressing is that, as we will see, modern research on visions has shown that visions are almost always believed by the people who experience them. When people have a vision—of a lost loved one, for example—they really and deeply believe the person has been there. So why were the visions of Jesus not always believed? Or rather, why were they so consistently doubted?[2]

There are two main issues with this argument. First, Ehrman puts a lot of weight on "doubt narratives" in the Gospels. The Gospels and First Corinthians make clear that doubt was temporary. The creed in First Corinthians (the earliest record) contradicts Ehrman's theory. It states that Jesus appeared to the twelve (First Corinthians 15:5). His argument from the bereavement hallucination literature is also problematic. As argued in chapter 20, many who experience hallucinations or visions are aware these perceptions do not reflect reality.

It is understandable why Ehrman wanted to reduce the number of "visions." For example, Tim and Lydia McGrew[3] pointed out, there is an incredibly low probability (p=10–39) that eleven or twelve people in a group all experienced a vision or hallucination.[4] Reducing the number

---

2. Ehrman, *Jesus*, 190.
3. McGrew and McGrew, *Resurrection*, 628.
4. I'm in favor of a slightly higher estimate than that proposed by the McGrews: they assume the probability of a hallucination is 0.001—whereas the literature gives us

of visions to three or four (including Paul and possibly James) reduces the implausibility of a naturalistic explanation. But even then, the probability of these hallucinations co-occurring is low (approximately p=0.001 for three visions, p=0.0001 for four visions).[5] Three visions is equivalent to Swinburne's probability estimate for a naturalistic explanation for Jesus' resurrection, four visions is even lower.[6]

Ehrman must also account for testimony on the empty tomb. He argued, contrary to many scholars, that Joseph Arimathea was a legendary figure (see chapters 15 and 19 for further discussion). In addition, he posited that Jesus' body may have been deposited in a shared grave.

24.4.2 Ludemann

Ludemann argued that Jesus' body remained in the ground. Therefore there was no empty tomb. In common with Ehrman, claims of postmortem appearances are accounted for by visions or hallucinations. Peter first experienced a bereavement hallucination.[7] This led to contagion and MPI among the disciples (visions of the twelve and 500).[8] Ludemann's thesis is inspired by the nineteenth century orientalist Ernest Renan. However, colonialist interpretations of "religious hysteria" have been criticised by leading experts like Bartholomew (see chapter 21 for further details).

Ludemann offers a psychodynamic explanation for Paul's hallucination. He posited that Paul experienced inner conflict, "a radical sense of guilt and unworthiness combined with an exalted self-image that results in the need to be an authority figure."[9] Paul's conversion was the breakthrough in his emotional conflict. He "fled from his painful situation into the world

---

anywhere between 4–16% (0.04 to 0.16). So to steelman the hallucination hypothesis I would start with a higher figure. However, even assuming a higher prevalence for hallucinations still leads us to conclude the hallucination hypothesis is incredibly unlikely. Further, if we conservatively assume after the index (first) hallucination each vision was twice as likely, such a combination of experiences even then remains very unlikely (see chapters 25 and 26 for further details).

5. Three multimodal visions (assuming prevalence of 6.4% and that each subsequent hallucination is twice as likely than average due to expectation): $(0.064 \times (0.064 \times 2) \times (0.064 \times 2)$, p=0.001 or four visions: $(0.064 \times (0.064 \times 2) \times (0.064 \times 2) \times (0.064 \times 2))=0.0001$.

6. Swinburne, *Resurrection*, 215.
7. Ludemann, *Resurrection*, 163–66.
8. Ludemann, *Resurrection*, 175.
9. Ludemann, *Resurrection*, 170.

A Summary of Alternative Explanations

of hallucination."[10] This is highly imaginative but has little basis in either Paul's writings or in an evidence-based understanding of hallucinations.

24.4.3 Allison's "Skeptical Scenario"

Allison does not identify as a sceptic, but he considered the following "skeptical scenario"[11] a plausible option:

- a tomb robber stole Jesus' body; no one accepted responsibility as they feared recrimination for illegal activity;
- Mary Magdalene and Peter experienced bereavement hallucinations;
- Paul experienced a religious vision that led to his conversion;
- appearances to the twelve are too uncertain on historical grounds, and the doubt narratives add further uncertainty;
- appearance to the 500 explained by "mass hysteria" or pareidolia.

24.5 CONCLUSION

This chapter has considered three influential naturalistic explanations. There is a lot of overlap between these theories—for example, they all posit hallucinations in a few key individuals (bereavement hallucinations for Peter and/or Mary Magdalene, and hallucination for Paul). Only Ludemann seeks to account for the appearance to the twelve (through "mass hysteria"). In my view, Allison's explanation of the empty tomb is the most compelling (tomb robbers) and, overall, his "skeptical scenario" is the most plausible of the three. But we have found the probability of these naturalistic explanations extremely low. Biblical scholar, Peter J. Williams, points out the unenviable task faced:

> a wide range of people believed they had seen Jesus risen from the dead, not only in the Gospel accounts, which focus on the visit of women to the tomb, even though women's testimony was not legally acceptable, but also in the overall variety of claimed resurrection appearances within the New Testament. The resurrected Jesus is recorded as appearing in Judaea and in Galilee, in town

---

10. Ludemann, *Resurrection*, 171.
11. Allison, *Resurrection*, 339.

Part Five: Naturalistic Explanations

and countryside, indoors and outdoors, in the morning and in the evening, by prior appointment and without prior appointment, close and distant on a hill and by a lake, to groups of men and groups of women, to individuals and groups of up to five hundred, sitting, standing, walking, eating, and always talking. Many are explicitly close-up encounters involving conversations. It is hard to imagine this pattern of appearances in the Gospels and early Christian letters without there having been multiple individuals who claimed to have seen Jesus risen from the dead.[12]

In most contexts, the very low probabilities associated with these naturalistic explanations would strongly favour their rejection. These theories can only be maintained by virtually certain prior probabilities for naturalism. Ludemann is transparent about this assumption.[13] Alternatively, some may have very different judgments about the plausibility of these explanations. The next chapter will draw from the previous sections of the book to construct a model on the probability of Jesus' resurrection.

---

12. Williams, *Gospels*, 134–35.
13. Ludemann, *Resurrection*, 69–73.

PART SIX

Modelling Resurrection Evidence

PART FIVE ASSESSED SEVERAL *naturalistic explanations. Most scholars agree no single explanation can account for all data.*

I considered three influential approaches that seek to combine naturalistic explanations: proposed by Ehrman, Allison, and Ludemann. Their main challenge is the need to assume several very unlikely events co-occurred. Therefore, any naturalistic hypothesis must posit an extremely strong prior against Jesus' resurrection. Alternatively, they could argue evidence for the resurrection is even weaker than for these naturalistic explanations.

INTRODUCTION TO PART SIX

Part Six will integrate data and judgments considered in Parts One to Five (see Box 14). This requires proposing prior probabilities for Jesus' resurrection, based on Parts Two and Three. I will then combine these priors with evidence for Jesus' resurrection (Part Four) and evidence for Allison's sceptical scenario (Part Five). This enables a comparison of the resurrection hypothesis with probably the best available naturalistic hypothesis, whilst considering relevant background knowledge.

Evidence from ancient history has many uncertainties; how we evaluate these will depend on our perspective of reality and other factors. Chapter 26 will assess how sensitive our estimates are to various assumptions.

PART SIX: MODELLING RESURRECTION EVIDENCE

> **BOX 14. SUMMARY OF PART SIX**
>
> *Chapter 25.* Resurrection model (pulling together data from Parts Two to Five: the prior probability of Jesus' resurrection; evidence that he was raised from the dead; and evidence supporting naturalistic explanations);
>
> *Chapter 26.* Exploring assumptions (this is a "stress test" of the assumptions in the model including the prior probability of Jesus' resurrection, and strength of evidence for the resurrection);
>
> *Chapter 27.* Conclusion (this chapter argues that the Bible's storyline and evidence for Jesus' resurrection are mutually supportive).

Chapter 25

Resurrection Model

25.1 INTRODUCTION

MANY THINK FRANCIS WATSON and James Crick discovered DNA in the 1950s, but this breakthrough happened much earlier—in the 1860s.[1] Almost ninety years later, they discovered DNA's double helix structure. Watson and Crick's realization was "made possible by recent advances in model building."[2] In those days, this meant actual cardboard cutouts! These models helped them to visualize a structure that best accounted for all the data:

> Using cardboard cutouts representing the individual chemical components of the four bases and other nucleotide subunits, Watson and Crick shifted molecules around on their desktops, as though putting together a puzzle.[3]

The challenge of seeing how a complex set of data fits together is shared by researchers in all disciplines. Probability theory and graph theory often do that job now. Despite technological advances, the goal is much the same. As Judea Pearl, a pioneer of probabilistic modelling, points out, "probability is not really about numbers; it is about the structure of reasoning."[4]

---

1. Pray, *DNA*, §1.
2. Pray, *DNA*, §4.
3. Pray, *DNA*, §4.
4. Pearl, *Reasoning*, 15.

Part Six: Modelling Resurrection Evidence

Of course, putting together the data on Jesus' resurrection is a unique puzzle. This evidence cuts across disparate disciplines like philosophy, psychology, history, biblical studies, physics, religious studies, and theology. So it is unsurprising that debates on the resurrection frequently get lost in translation. For example, atheists are often convinced that the prior probability for resurrection is close to impossible. In contrast, Christian philosophers, like Richard Swinburne, point out the strength of the prior depends on the probability of God's existence:

> If there is no God, then the laws of nature are the ultimate determinants of what happens. But if there is a God, then whether and for how long and under what circumstances laws of nature operate depends on God. And evidence that there is a God, and in particular evidence that there is a God of a kind who might be expected to intervene occasionally in the natural order, will be evidence leading us to expect occasional violations of laws of nature. Any evidence that God might be expected to intervene in a certain way will be evidence supporting historical evidence that he has done so.[5]

But, of course, atheists and Christians often come to conflicting conclusions on the probability of theism or Christianity. For this reason, some scholars suggest we avoid talking about the prior. However, since Hume, most atheists have insisted on taking several steps back from the data, since "extraordinary claims require extraordinary evidence."[6]

In addition, the bipolar world of theists and atheists, that many of our parents grew up in, no longer exists in the West. Atheists are not alone in denying the existence of a creator God—Buddhists, Hindus, and animists agree. Rabbinic Jews concur with atheists that it is close to impossible Jesus is the Messiah. Of course, Rabbinic Jews and Muslims are as likely as Christians to believe in a creator God.

The aim of this chapter is to explore whether modelling helps us to better navigate this complex territory—and will focus on the following themes:

- converting our judgments into probabilities;
- setting out model assumptions;
- model results.

---

5. Swinburne, *Resurrection*, 25.
6. Sagan, *Broca*, 75.

25.2 JUDGMENTS AND PROBABILITIES

Most of the judgments made in this book have been qualitative. But as Richard Swinburne points out, probabilities allow us to reflect the nuances of these judgments with greater precision. Surely an advantage where misunderstanding abounds:

> I have assumed that "natural theology makes it as probable as not that there is a God", and there is evidence which "it would not be too improbable to find", and that "it is far more probable" that Jesus did certain things than that any other prophet did, and so on. Let us see if we can give a sharper, more nearly numerical form to the argument. The tool for doing so is the traditional probability calculus, developed since the seventeenth century and given axiomatic form by Kolmogorov in the nineteenth century. The maximum probability for an event is 1, the minimum 0, and if something is as probable as not it has a probability of ½.

One of the advantages of probability theory is its "ability to express useful qualitative relationships among beliefs and to process these relationships in a way that yields intuitively plausible conclusions."[7] As argued in Part One, this reflects the plurality and unity of reality, probability theory applies as well to our qualitative judgments as it does to formal and empirical investigation of the world. We will use a rule of thumb for converting qualitative judgments into probabilities listed below:[8]

- Close to impossible: 0.000001 (one in a million)
- Extremely unlikely: 0.01 (one in a hundred)
- Very unlikely: 0.05 (one in twenty)
- Unlikely: 0.2 (one in five)
- Slightly unlikely: 0.4 (two in five)
- Unknown 0.5 (fifty-fifty)
- Slightly likely 0.6 (three in five)
- Likely 0.8 (four in five)
- Very likely 0.95 (nineteen in twenty)
- Extremely likely 0.99 (ninety-nine in a hundred)

7. Pearl, *Reasoning*, 15.
8. Adapted from Blais, *Statistics*, 227.

PART SIX: MODELLING RESURRECTION EVIDENCE

Some may protest that it is inappropriate to articulate judgments in probabilities. For example, meteorologists were concerned the public would resist the use of probabilities in weather forecasts. However, worries were unfounded, and the use of probabilities is now the norm.[9] Bookmakers have calculated probabilities (and odds) for numerous sporting events for hundreds of years. I take the pragmatic approach that we can benefit from probability theory whilst acknowledging the obvious limitations. For further discussion of this probabilistic approach, see Part One.

25.3 MODEL ASSUMPTIONS

Figure 6[10] sets out the key factors informing evidence for Jesus' resurrection. The model consists of nodes and links. The rectangle boxes are nodes predicted by the model (e.g., if God raised Jesus from the dead), oval shaped nodes (e.g., evidence for Jesus' resurrection) are the main evidence informing these predictions. Links are arrows indicating relationships between nodes.

The model begins with competing assumptions about the foundational nature of reality:

- physical-first (necessary e.g., a necessary naturalist universe);
- physical-first (contingent e.g., a naturalist universe from nothing);
- unipersonal theism (e.g., Islam, Judaism);
- Triune God (i.e., Christianity);
- mind-first (e.g., most schools of Buddhism, animistic religions like Shintoism).

Whether Jesus is the Messiah or not, depends on the nature of reality and evidence that he fulfilled the Messianic prophecies (arrows illustrate these dependencies). Probability of Jesus' resurrection depends on if he is the Messiah, evidence for Jesus' resurrection, and evidence that he is the Messiah.

---

9. Ripberger, *Probability*, 485.

10. The models described in this paper were created using the GeNIe Modeler, available free of charge for academic research and teaching use from BayesFusion, LLC, https://www.bayesfusion.com/.

Resurrection Model

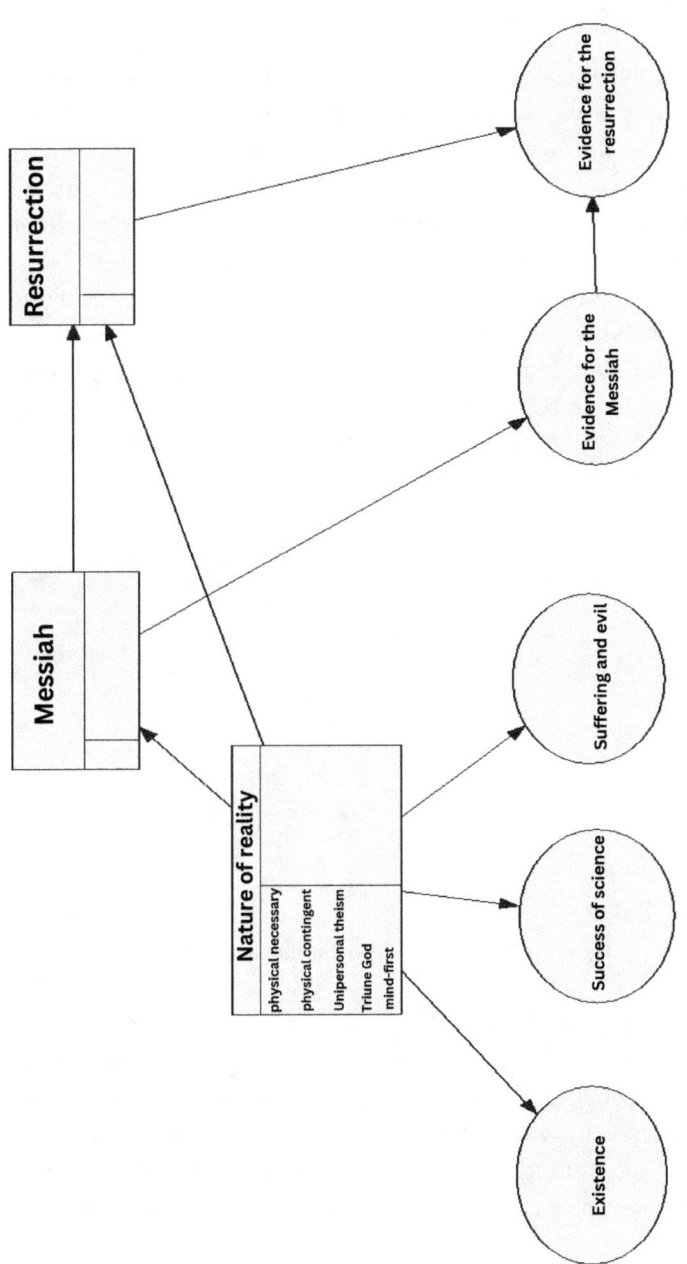

Figure 6. Model of evidence for the resurrection

PART SIX: MODELLING RESURRECTION EVIDENCE

25.4 NATURE OF REALITY

25.4.1 Prior Probability

I proposed five categories of worldview in chapter 3 (physical-first (necessary), physical-first (contingent), unipersonal theism, Christianity, and mind-first). Following Swinburne, I assume worldviews on the nature of reality, "purport to explain so much that there are no "neighbouring fields" outside their scope."[11] Therefore there is no prior information to account for other than the evidence considered in the model.[12]

So we could start out with each worldview having the same prior (initial probability). However, by convention, simpler models are favored over complex ones. I have reflected this principle by assigning higher prior probabilities to simpler models which penalises more complex ones (see Figure 7).[13] We will explore in the next chapter the impact of varying these prior probabilities.

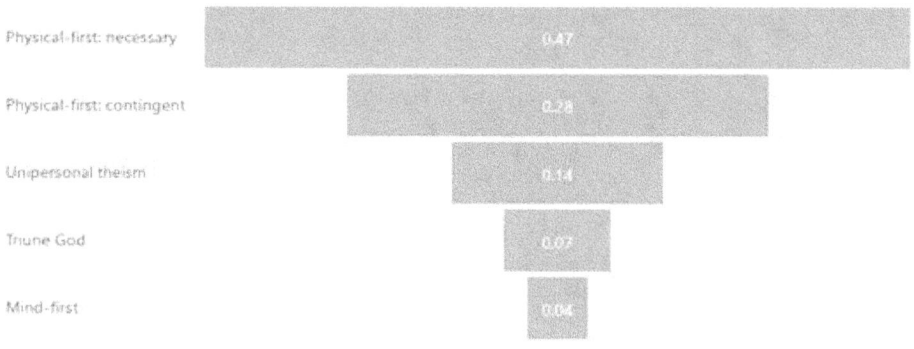

Figure 7. Prior probabilities for the nature of reality

To illustrate the logic, imagine you are watching a race between five horses who may differ on a range of factors (e.g., age, past performance, weight of the jockey). In a handicapped race, horses with a greater advantage carry extra weight (which slows them down) so that each has a fair chance of winning. Let's say I have 100lbs to distribute between the five horses. If none have an initial advantage—I will distribute that weight

---

11. Swinburne, *Resurrection*, 207.
12. Swinburne, *Resurrection*, 207.
13. Swinburne, *Existence*, 65–72.

Resurrection Model

evenly (20lbs each). If a horse is older, or their jockey is heavier, to even up the race I give them less weight to carry.

Most statistical models work on a similar principle. More complex models have an advantage since, all things being equal, the more parameters we include the better it will explain the data.[14] Therefore, we want to penalise more complex models (the equivalent of putting more weight on the horse's back) to give them all a fair chance. As we saw in chapter 8, there is significant debate about which views are more complex. In the literature, there are far more complicated methods for penalising complexity, but for our purposes this isn't necessary—since we are not attempting to estimate objective probabilities. But it is still worth reflecting these principles in an approximate way.

To be conservative against my own view, Christianity, I have assumed physical-first views (e.g., naturalism) are simplest.[15] Following Oppy, necessary versions are assumed simpler than contingent versions.[16] The next simplest is unipersonal theism (e.g., Islam and Judaism). Followed by Christianity. Finally, mind-first views are assumed to be the most complex (see Part One for further discussion).

I have assigned lower prior probabilities to more complex models, so they must "work harder" to be the superior model—they require more supportive evidence. For example, assigning a prior probability of 0.47 for the physical-first (necessary) view gives it a significant advantage over my favored option (Christianity)—for which I have assigned a prior probability of 0.07. Using our horse race analogy, Christianity is carrying just under seven times more weight, so is substantially disadvantaged, at the start of the race (i.e. before we have looked at any evidence). To sum up, these prior probabilities are derived from the following principles:

- probabilities must vary from 0 to 1—0 is impossible, 1 is certain;
- the probabilities from these five categories must add up to 1;
- simpler views are given precedence, and therefore higher prior probability, compared with more complex ones;
- physical first views are assumed simplest;

14. Spiegelhalter, *Model Complexity*, 584.
15. I think Swinburne's definition is far more intuitive than Oppy's. Yet, I have based my judgments of simplicity on Oppy's criteria, which favors physical first views over Christianity, and therefore is more conservative towards my favored option.
16. Oppy, *Naturalistic*, 10.

- a necessary universe is assumed simpler than a contingent universe (hence a slight decrement to the prior for physical-first (contingent));
- unipersonal theism is the next simplest view, and assigned a probability half the magnitude of physical-first (contingent);
- the Triune God of Christianity is more complex than unipersonal theism, and assigned half the probability of the previous category;
- mind-first views are assumed the most complex.

25.4.2 Likelihood Function

25.4.2.1 *Existence of Our Universe*

Part Two reviewed natural theological arguments for these worldviews. The first assumption is that the universe exists. Judgments on the probability of the universe's existence for each category are summarised below (for further discussion, see chapter 4):

- physical-first (necessary): the probability of our universe's existence, given this view, is *unlikely*; evidence that the universe may not be past infinite is inconsistent with a necessary universe;
- physical-first (contingent): the probability of our universe's existence given this view (e.g., our universe is founded on one contingent substance) is *extremely unlikely*; narrow physical constants observed in our universe make the probability of our universe's existence extremely unlikely in this context;[17]
- unipersonal theism: the probability of our universe if unipersonal theism is true is *slightly likely* since reality is ultimately impersonal (or semi-personal) but God has the power to bring it about;
- Christianity: the probability our universe, if the Triune God exists, is *likely* given that personality and relationship is foundational, and God has the power to make it happen;
- mind-first: the probability of our universe's existence, given this view, is *unlikely*; evidence that the universe may not be past infinite is inconsistent with this view.

---

17. Barnes, *Fine Tuning*, 6:42.

Resurrection Model

25.4.2.2 Intelligibility and the Success of Science

The universe is intelligible therefore science is possible. The likelihood of this type of universe for each worldview is summarised below (see chapter 5 for further justification):

- physical-first (necessary): *unlikely* since there is no reason to think impersonal reality would be intelligible;
- physical-first (contingent): as above;
- unipersonal theism: God is rational and ordered, therefore it is likely that creation is also ordered and rational; therefore intelligibility is *likely*;
- Christianity: given that God is rational and ordered, and God is relational, the intelligibility of the universe is *likely*;
- mind-first: given the existence of multiple finite gods the likelihood of our universe being intelligible is *very unlikely* since reality is more chaotic than ordered.

25.4.2.3 Suffering and Evil

It is assumed there is evil and suffering in our universe for further details (see chapters 6 and 7). The likelihood of these data for each worldview is:

- physical-first (necessary): in an indifferent universe we expect suffering, however evil is more difficult for this view to explain; therefore suffering and evil is *likely*, but not certain;
- physical-first (contingent): *likely*, for the reasons above;
- unipersonal theism: given a loving God, the likelihood of suffering and evil is *slightly unlikely*;
- Christianity: given a loving God, suffering and evil is unexpected; but only *slightly unlikely*;
- mind-first: given the existence of multiple finite gods the presence of suffering and evil was judged *likely*.

PART SIX: MODELLING RESURRECTION EVIDENCE

25.5 IS JESUS THE MESSIAH?

25.5.1 Prior Probability

The nature of reality (the previous node) impacts the probability that Jesus is the Messiah. If the *Triune God* exists, then it is certain Jesus is the Messiah. But to be conservative, I will assume *50–50*. However, if our reality is *physical-first* it is *close to impossible* that Jesus is the Messiah and Jesus' resurrection *certainly did not happen*. If reality is *mind-first*, it is possible Jesus was resurrected but still *extremely unlikely*.

Unipersonal theism is more complicated. Muslims consider Jesus to be *al-Masih* (the Messiah) but reject that he is divine or that he died by crucifixion. Followers of Judaism also reject the New Testament understanding of the Messiah. Therefore, if unipersonal theism is true, it is *close to impossible* that Jesus is the Messiah as claimed in the New Testament.[18]

25.5.2 Likelihood Function

25.5.2.1 Evidence Jesus is the Messiah

- no one else in history has fulfilled the Messianic mission like Jesus;
- no one else in history has met the range of Messianic prophecies compared with Jesus;
- no other Messianic claimant has met the requirement of a worldwide following except Jesus.

25.5.2.2 Probability of the Evidence That Jesus is the Messiah

The model then considers the probability of observing this evidence in two scenarios: if Jesus is the Messiah or not:

- if Jesus is the Messiah: it is *slightly likely* he would meet these criteria;
- if Jesus is not the Messiah: the likelihood of a worldwide following is *extremely unlikely*, although not impossible.[19]

---

18. Of course, Jehovah's witnesses would be one example of an exception to this rule. For the sake of streamlining the model I have not considered their worldview here, but future models should seek to accommodate their views.

19. An exact estimate of the number of religions in history is probably impossible,

Resurrection Model

25.6 EVIDENCE FOR JESUS' RESURRECTION

25.6.1 Prior Probability

The prior probability is determined by sections 25.4 and 25.5 above:

- nature of reality;
- if Jesus is the Messiah.

25.6.2 Likelihood function

25.6.2.1 Evidence for Empty Tomb

Part Four considered evidence from the Gospels and First Corinthians 15. There is a consensus among the Gospels that Jesus was buried and that later his tomb was found empty. First Corinthians 15:3–8 does not mention the empty tomb (only that he was buried and resurrected). However, many scholars conclude (although not all) that this early creed assumes the empty tomb.

25.6.2.2 Evidence for Jesus' Appearances

The Gospels and First Corinthians 15 record a range of postmortem appearances of Jesus to individuals and groups. In addition, First Corinthians 15 records an appearance to 500 people.

25.6.2.3 Probability of This Evidence if Jesus Was Resurrected

Testimonial evidence on the empty tomb and the wide range of people who claimed to see Jesus in physical form provides support for Jesus' resurrection. Taken together, if Jesus was raised from the dead, it is conservatively assumed this type of evidence is *slightly likely*.[20]

---

or at least very difficult, due to the magnitude of the task and the disputed nature of the term (see Holland, *Dominion*, 399–404). However, it is uncontroversial that there are: a) many thousands of religions, and; b) very few religions in history that have had a worldwide following matching Christianity.

20. Of course, as Christians because the Word of God states clearly that Jesus was raised from the dead we know this with certainty. Yet, since this is unlikely to be compelling for non-Christians, I will use a much more conservative estimate.

PART SIX: MODELLING RESURRECTION EVIDENCE

25.6.2.4 *Probability of This Evidence if Jesus Was Not Raised*

Part Five considered various naturalistic explanations for the probability of this evidence if Jesus was not raised from the dead. Allison's "skeptical scenario" was considered the most compelling (see chapter 24), although still extremely unlikely:

- *empty tomb*: tomb robbers (*slightly unlikely*: p=0.4);
- *Paul*: hallucination non-clinical population (0.02x0.5x2, potential insight not real (p=0.5) but also allowing the possibility empty tomb triggers hallucination (multiplied by 2));
- *Peter*: bereavement hallucination (0.064x0.5x2);
- *Mary*: bereavement hallucination (0.064x0.5x2);
- *the 500*: pareidolia (*unlikely*, p=0.2);
- total probability: p=0.000007 (just under 1/140,000);
- *does not account for group appearances—therefore probably even less likely.*

To be conservative against the resurrection explanation, I have rounded up the probability to p=0.00001 (1/100,000).

25.7 RESULTS (POSTERIOR PROBABILITY)

Applying Sobel's criteria for extraordinary (or sufficient evidence), Jesus' resurrection meets this stringent standard (see section 1.2).[21] The prior probability of Jesus resurrection (p=0.02)[22] is greater than the probability of this evidence if he was not resurrected (p=0.00001).

Based on the inputs above, the model estimated Jesus' resurrection to be extremely likely[23] compared with Allison's "skeptical scenario" (see Figure 8). More surprisingly, starting with a low prior for the Triune God,[24] evidence from natural theology and Jesus' resurrection suggests it is

---

21. i.e. p(A) > p(a&~A) where A=miracle, a=testimony about a miracle, ~A=a miracle did not happen.

22. Prior for the Triune God (p=0.07) multiplied by the prior that the Triune God would send a Messiah (p=0.5), multiplied by the probability the Messiah would be resurrected (p=0.6)=0.02.

23. p=0.999.

24. p=0.07.

Resurrection Model

extremely likely the Triune God exists[25] compared to a very low probability for all other categories (unipersonal theism, physical-first (necessary), physical-first (contingent), mind-first). It is also extremely likely that Jesus is the Messiah.[26]

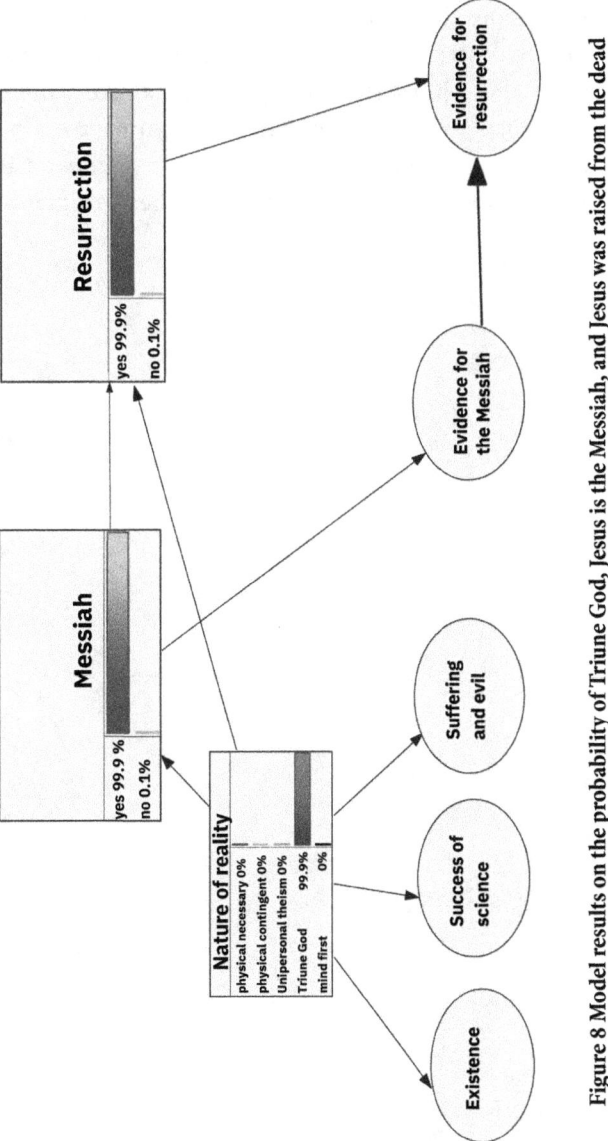

Figure 8 Model results on the probability of Triune God, Jesus is the Messiah, and Jesus was raised from the dead

---

25. p=0.999.
26. p=0.999.

25.8 CONCLUSION

This chapter has outlined a model that compares the evidence for two main options—Allison's "skeptical scenario" and the Christian view that Jesus was raised from the dead. We have also estimated the prior probability for these options by considering the nature of reality, and the extent to which Jesus' mission (as described in the Gospels) reflects the promised Messiah.

Of course, these judgments are made under great uncertainty. For example, naturalists may consider a necessary universe more probable. Most sceptics are also likely to question my judgments on the evidence for Jesus' resurrection. The impact of varying these estimates is explored in the next chapter.

Chapter 26

Exploring the Robustness of the Model

26.1 INTRODUCTION

WHEN DISCUSSING THE RESURRECTION, we can sometimes end up debating issues that have little impact on conclusions. Stubbornness on both sides, no doubt, plays a part. Yet I think it is more than that. As we have seen, judgments on Jesus' resurrection are complex. This is where modelling can help. There are established methods for identifying key issues that drive our estimates. This can prevent us getting bogged down in trivial details.

We will vary several assumptions in the model, whilst keeping all other factors constant. If these sensitivity analyses have no impact on our conclusions, then debating them wastes time. I will assess the robustness of these estimates to a range of different assumptions including:

- varying priors;
- varying evidential judgments about nature of reality (our universe is certain if physical-first or mind-first views are true; physical-first (necessary) is very likely; Christianity or unipersonal theism are extremely unlikely given the existence of suffering);
- varying evidential judgments that Jesus is the Messiah and the probability of observing this evidence if he was either resurrected or not resurrected.

PART SIX: MODELLING RESURRECTION EVIDENCE

26.2 VARYING PRIORS

In the main model, to be conservative, I set the prior for the Triune God (p=0.07) much lower than physical-first (necessary, p=0.47) and physical-first (contingent, p=0.28). Yet many naturalists may feel these differences in priors are insufficient—particularly for a necessary universe. However, the intrinsic plausibility of all other worldviews would have to be incredibly low (1 in 4 million), and physical-first (necessary) virtually certain (p=0.9999992), to change conclusions on Jesus' resurrection.

Similarly, some mind-first approaches are monist (reality is characterised by oneness), and compatible with our universe being necessary. Therefore, arguably the prior for this view should be similar to physical-first (necessary). But as we saw above, for conclusions to change, a virtually certain prior for this view (1 in 4 million) is needed.

Recall in Part One, Oppy argues simplicity should only be employed to differentiate equally well supported models. Since a prior of that magnitude would place far more weight on simplicity than evidence, it is inappropriate. Therefore, these sensitivity analyses show that *our conclusions are very unlikely to be impacted by choice of priors.*

26.3 VARYING EVIDENTIAL JUDGMENTS ABOUT NATURE OF REALITY

The main model assumes a potential inconsistency between a necessary universe and evidence that the universe may have had a beginning. This makes physical-first (necessary) views unlikely. Proponents of this view may counter that this entails our universe is certain. Yet assuming our universe is necessary (p=1) makes no difference to conclusions (see Table 10).

Another potential criticism is that evidence for physical-first (necessary) or mind-first views are underestimated. In response, I have run scenarios that assume evidence from natural theology indicates physical-first (necessary) is extremely likely. This has negligible impact on conclusions. Implausibly strong evidence, at least in my view, for physical-first (necessary) is required to overturn these conclusions (see Table 10). Similar conclusions apply in sensitivity analyses related to mind-first views.

Finally, some may think the impact of evil and suffering on the likelihood of Christianity are underestimated. However, to overturn conclusions about Jesus' resurrection, Christianity would have to be virtually impossible if evil and suffering exist (see Table 10). This effectively assumes the logical argument for evil (i.e., the existence of a loving God is logically incompatible with the existence of evil and suffering). However, few atheist philosophers are now willing to express that level of certainty.[1]

Sensitivity analyses	Value needed to change conclusion*
Assume our universe is certain (p=1) if physical-first (necessary) is true.	Does not change conclusion.
Probability of physical-first (necessary) after considering all natural theology evidence[2]	Physical-first (necessary): $p=0.99992$ based on natural theology evidence. It is virtually certain physical-first (necessary) is true, and $p=0.000002$ (1 in 500,000) chance another view is true.
Suffering and evil extremely unlikely if Christianity true	Suffering and evil if Christianity true: $p=0.0000005$ (1 in 2 million)

Table 10. Varying natural theology judgments
*Value needed to change probability of Jesus' resurrection to p≤.50 (at best no more likely than not)

To sum up this section, sensitivity analyses on our judgments about the nature of reality show that the model's conclusions are robust to a range of plausible assumptions.

26.4 VARYING EVIDENTIAL JUDGMENTS THAT JESUS IS THE MESSIAH AND WAS RESURRECTED

Table 11 summarizes the sensitivity analyses (varying estimates in the model). As we saw in chapter 20, prevalence estimates for bereavement hallucinations vary widely, so this is important to explore further. In the main model, I used an estimate of 4.6% (p=0.046) based on data on multimodal hallucinations. However, some sceptics may argue it is possible the disciples had a unimodal hallucination. The median (50th percentile) for visual (14%) or auditory (15%) hallucinations alone is substantially higher. The 75th percentile offers an even more generous estimate (i.e., 75% of estimates

---

1. See for example, Oppy, *Evil*, 75.

2. This is tested by setting "virtual evidence" for the nature of reality node to various values for physical-first (necessary) and reducing the probability for other views proportionally.

Part Six: Modelling Resurrection Evidence

are lower than this value) of visual (25%) or auditory hallucinations (28%). Rounding the estimate up, my sensitivity analyses assumes a 30% probability (p=0.3) that the disciples experienced a bereavement hallucination. This increases the probability of Allison's skeptical scenario from 0.000007 to 0.0001. However, as we see in Table 11, using this more generous estimate (for a naturalistic explanation) has no impact on conclusions.

There are only two scenarios where conclusions about Jesus' resurrection could change (see Table 11). First, if it was close to impossible to expect this type of evidence if Jesus was raised from the dead. It seems obvious this is the type of evidence (reports of empty tomb, postmortem appearances) we would expect, so this scenario is implausible.

Second, if Jesus was not raised from the dead, the evidence that Jesus is the Messiah[3] would have to be relatively *unlikely* (p=0.15) *and* the evidence for Jesus' resurrection[4] would also have to be relatively *unlikely* (p=0.15). But since only two religions (Islam and Christianity) of thousands in history, have achieved anything like a worldwide following, the probability of this happening is far lower than one in seven (p=0.15). Similarly, Allison, Ludemann, and Ehrman's naturalistic theories posit a series of events far less probable than one in seven (see table 11). Therefore, the chances of both these scenarios happening is even lower.

Therefore, it is clear, our *conclusions are robust to reasonable assumptions about the evidence.*

Sensitivity analyses	Value needed to change conclusion*
Probability of evidence if Jesus is not Messiah	Does not impact conclusions.
Alternative naturalistic theories: Bart Ehrman (Unburied + Experience of Mary + Experience of Peter + Experience of Paul)[5]	Ehrman's scenario (p=0.000008)[6] is less probable than the estimate used in the main model (p=0.00001) so using this scenario has no impact on results.

3. That he met the criteria better than anyone in history and had a worldwide following as predicted in the Hebrew Bible and New Testament.

4. Reports of witnessing empty tomb, and post-mortem appearances.

5. Ehrman, Jesus, 192, also mentions the possibility that James may have had a vision. But for the sake of maximising the probability for this naturalistic explanation, I will not include this in the estimate as this would make it less probable.

6. *Empty tomb*: Jesus was not buried (p=0.2); *Mary*: bereavement hallucination (p=0.064x0.5x2, potential insight not real (p=0.5) but also allowing the possibility empty tomb triggers hallucination (multiplied by 2)); *Peter*: bereavement hallucination

Sensitivity analyses	Value needed to change conclusion*
Gerd Ludemann's scenario (Remain buried + Experience of Peter + MPI + Experience of James+ Experience of Paul)	Ludemann's scenario (p=0.0000003)[7] is also a lower probability than the main model so has no impact on results.
Allison's scenario (used in main model, chapter 25): but assuming a 30% prevalence for bereavement hallucinations	Has no impact on estimates for the probability of Christianity, probability of Jesus being the Messiah, or probability of Jesus' resurrection.
Varying probability of evidence if Jesus is not Messiah and Jesus was not raised	Probability of Jesus meeting more Messianic criteria than any one in history and having a worldwide following as predicted (p=0.15) and probability of evidence for his resurrection (p=0.15).
Probability of evidence if Jesus was raised	It is virtually impossible that there would be this lack of evidence if Jesus was raised from the dead (p=0.00001, 1 in 100,000).

Table 11. Varying judgments about the evidence
*Value needed to change probability of Jesus' resurrection
to p≤.50 (at best no more likely than not)

26.5 LIMITATIONS

This model is a work in progress, further development is needed. For example, arguments for competing views on the nature of reality (existence of the universe, the success of science, and suffering and evil), have been considered to inform the prior probability of Jesus' resurrection. However, the focus of this book has not been on the existence of God so a more comprehensive model in future is needed that will consider a wider range of data including consciousness, intentionality, psychophysical harmony, divine hiddenness, multiplicity of religions.

(p=0.064x0.5x2), *Paul*: hallucination non-clinical population (p=0.02x0.5): p=0.000008 but does not account for group appearances.

7. *Empty tomb*: Jesus remained buried (p=0.05); *Peter*: bereavement hallucination (p=0.064x0.5x2); Gr*oup appearances*: mass psychogenic illness among disciples (p=0.01), *Paul*: hallucination (p=0.02x0.5): p=0.0000003.

PART SIX: MODELLING RESURRECTION EVIDENCE

26.6 CONCLUSIONS

Evidence for Jesus' resurrection meets formal criteria for extraordinary evidence. His resurrection is also a far better explanation of the evidence than Allison's "skeptical scenario", or the naturalistic theories of Bart Ehrman and Gerd Ludemann. The model gives us insight into the framework through which evidence should be interpreted. The Biblical framework that the Triune God exists, and that Jesus is the Messiah promised in the Hebrew Bible, is by far the best explanation of these data. All other options have a negligible possibility in comparison.

Chapter 27

Resurrection and Redemption

27.1 INTRODUCTION

I BEGAN WITH SAGAN's famous retort, "extraordinary claims require extraordinary evidence". *Part One* argued this position is founded on strong assumptions about the *prior probability* of miracles. *Parts Two to Three* challenged Hume and Sagan's argument that the prior probability for Jesus' resurrection is close to impossible. *Parts Four to Six* integrated evidence for the resurrection with earlier sections on the prior probability. Estimates from the model (see chapters 25 and 26), robust to a wide range of scenarios, show that:

- evidence for Jesus' resurrection meets Hume and Sagan's criteria for *extraordinary*;
- Jesus' resurrection accounts for the data much better than several influential naturalistic theories;
- Christianity far better accounts for the nature of reality than the four alternative worldviews considered;
- the data suggests it is much more likely Jesus is the Messiah than not.

This final chapter summarises a central argument of the book. We cannot understand Jesus' resurrection in isolation from the rest of Scripture, or the nature of reality. The following themes are discussed below:

- Triune God as the foundation for reality;
- resurrection and defeat of death;

- heavenly enthronement of Jesus;
- ascension of Jesus and the descent of the Holy Spirit;
- hope of the new heavens and new earth.

27.2 THE TRIUNE GOD AS THE FOUNDATION FOR REALITY

"The God who made the world and everything in it is the Lord of heaven and earth" (Acts 17:24).

Physical-first (e.g., naturalism) and mind-first (e.g., Hinduism, Buddhism, and animism) views deny the existence of a creator God. In contrast, Christians and unipersonal theists believe the universe, and us, are dependent on God for our existence. Jesus' resurrection separates Christianity from all other theisms. God who raised Jesus from the dead is the creator of our world:

> Jesus and the resurrection presupposed the doctrine of creation. Jesus and the resurrection implied the doctrine of judgment to come. It was the Son of God who had made the world and who was to come as judge of men at the end of the history of the world, who died and rose again from the dead in His human nature.[1]

27.3 DEATH, RESURRECTION, AND ASCENSION

After Adam and Eve sinned, their descendants were condemned to death (Genesis 3:19). Furthermore, cherubim guarded the entrance into the garden of Eden, keeping people from the presence of God (Genesis 3:24). After the exodus, God once more dwelt with Israel in the tabernacle/temple. The day of atonement, the most important event in Israel's calendar, pointed to a day when humanity will dwell with God—like in Eden:

> By cleansing the sanctuary they permit the holy God to dwell among an unholy people (vv16–17; cf. Isa. 6:3ff.; Ps. 15; 24:3ff.) . . . [Leviticus 16:7] underlines the fact that only one man, the high priest, may enter into the holy of holies. Under both testaments there is but one mediator between God and man (cf. 1 Tim 2:5).[2]

---

1. Van Til, *Paul*, 10.
2. Wenham, *Leviticus*, 233.

The New Testament proclaims Jesus' death, resurrection, and ascension as fulfilment of these tabernacle rituals:

> They [the priests] serve at a sanctuary that is a copy and shadow of what is in heaven. This is why Moses was warned when he was about to build the tabernacle: "see to it that you make everything according to the pattern shown you on the mountain." [Exodus 25:40] But in fact the ministry Jesus has received is as superior to theirs as the covenant of which he is mediator is superior to the old one, since the new covenant is established on better promises (Hebrew 8:5–6).

Jesus' death (as fulfilment of the tabernacle sacrifices) cleanses us from our sins, so that we, an unholy people, may dwell with God. Jesus' resurrection signals his victory over death on our behalf:

> the last word once again lies not with death—undeniably grievous though it is—but with life. Given the reality and potency ascribed to death throughout the Hebrew Bible, what overcomes it is nothing short of the most astonishing miracle, the Divine Warrior's eschatological victory.[3]

On the day of atonement, the high priest went behind the curtain into the holy of holies (a symbol of heaven). Jesus' ascension was "an entrance into the temple of the Father's house through his sacrificial death."[4] His final words, before his ascension, were to bless his people as both priest (Luke 24:50–51) and king (e.g., Psalms 24, 110; Daniel 7).

27.4 THE DESCENT OF THE SPIRIT AND THE MISSION TO THE NATIONS

Jesus' entrance into heaven was necessary for the next phase of mission, the descent of the Holy Spirit. He unites Jesus with his people, from all nations: "Jesus ascended for the sake of the Spirit's descent; without the Spirit's descent, God's people cannot ascend. Apart from the outpoured Spirit, there is no new access to God the Father's heavenly abode."[5] Therefore, the New Testament does not end with Jesus' resurrection and ascension:

---

3. Levenson, *Resurrection*, 216.
4. Morales, *Ascend*, 265.
5. Morales, *Ascend*, 279.

Part Six: Modelling Resurrection Evidence

Christ's threefold office of prophet, priest, and king continues into his state of exaltation. As prophet he teaches disciples in the forty days, and by the Holy Spirit sent at Pentecost, he makes known to the world all the treasures of wisdom and knowledge hidden in him. In the same manner, as the Epistle to the Hebrews points out, he continues as our High Priest to intercede for us. And, finally, he is our eternal King who rules us by his Word and Spirit and equips us to be victorious over sin and Satan.[6]

27.5 THE HOPE OF THE NEW CREATION

By the Spirit, Jesus now dwells in our hearts through faith (Ephesians 3:17). Yet he is also absent from us, seated on the throne of heaven and therefore not on earth. The Holy Spirit "tantalizes us with a real presence [of Christ] so that we may discover what real absence is, thus learning to love and long for Jesus' appearing."[7]

Revelation 21 and 22 look forward to the time when Christ will return: "And I heard a loud voice from the throne saying, "Look! God's dwelling place is now among the people, and he will dwell with them. They will be his people, and God himself will be with them and be their God" (Revelation 21:3). The Bible began with humanity dwelling with God in Eden, the first temple.[8] The end of Revelation looks to when "God's presence fills the new heavens and new earth as his temple at the consummation of history."[9]

Jesus' resurrection and the Bible's storyline are mutually supportive. Viewed through the lens of naturalism, or any other worldview (except Christianity), the evidence is insufficient for such an extraordinary claim. Yet together they account for our reality far better than all other competing worldviews. In the words of the apostle Paul: "he [God the Father] has fixed a day on which he will judge the world in righteousness by a man whom he has appointed; and of this he has given assurance to all by raising him from the dead." (Acts 17:31)

---

6. Bavinck, *Dogmatics*, 3:420–421.
7. Farrow, *Ascension*, 271.
8. Beale and Kim, *God Dwells*, 17–28.
9. Beale and Kim, *God Dwells*, 147.

Appendix 1

Summary of Major Rabbinic Jewish Writings on Isaiah 52:13—53:12

IT IS OFTEN ARGUED the traditional Jewish view of Isaiah 52:13—53:12 (Isaiah 53) had nothing to do with the Messiah. Rabbi Tovia Singer is a prominent spokesman:

> Despite strong objections from conservative Christian apologists, the prevailing rabbinic interpretation of Isaiah 53 ascribes the "servant" to the nation of Israel who silently endured unimaginable suffering at the hands of its gentile oppressors.[1]

A1.1 SOURCES

Debates on Isaiah 53 often descend into selective citations by Christians and Rabbinic Jews alike. To avoid this tendency, we need to be as consistent and transparent as possible. I have focused on two sources (freely available online) so readers can go back and check for themselves:

- *The Fifty-Third Chapter of Isaiah: According to the Jewish Interpreters.* This is an English translation of Jewish sources on Isaiah 53 identified by Samuel Driver (Regus Professor of Hebrew) and Adolf Nebauer (Associate Professor of Hebrew and manuscript expert) at the University of Oxford up to 1877.

---

1. Singer, *Biblical*, 116.

APPENDIX 1

- *Sefaria*: a Jewish website that aims to be a "living library of Torah texts"

These two sources encompass a relatively comprehensive collection of Jewish literature on Isaiah 53. Driver and Nebauer, in their academic quest for comprehensiveness, included a wide range of sources. As Rabbi Moshe Shulman points out, some of this literature is more important than others.[2] He argues major Rabbinic works should be given more weight than the writings of less influential figures. Similarly, Shulman notes that Driver and Neubauer included Karaite and other literature commonly judged outside the boundaries of "orthodox Judaism". I think Shulman's critique is fair, sometimes Christians can apply a false equivalency across these sources. Therefore, I will focus on the most relevant literature.

A1.2 INCLUSION CRITERIA

All Rabbinic literature from Driver and Nebauer, Sefaria, and additional hand searching that met the following criteria were included in this review.

1. Rabbinic Judaism's "Canon" outside the Hebrew Bible

My Jewish Learning (myjewishlearning.com) provides a standard summary of sources that constitute Jewish [Rabbinic] literature:

- Talmud
- Zohar
- Midrash: to narrow this down to most relevant Rabbinic works I included literature from Sefaria only

2. Targums and Major rabbis

Targums are early Aramaic paraphrases of the Hebrew Bible (for example Targum of Jonathan). They provide key insights into early Jewish interpretations of Scripture.

As a Christian, my assessment of who qualifies as a major rabbi in Jewish history is of little consequence. Therefore, I have used the list proposed by Rabbi Moshe Shulman:

- Rabbi Solomon ben Isaac (Rashi)

---

2. Schulman, *Rabbinic*, §2.

Summary of Major Rabbinic Jewish Writings

- Rabbi Abraham ibn Ezra
- Rabbi David Kimhi (Radak)
- Rabbi Yechiel Hillel ben David
- Rabbi Meir Leibish Malbim
- Rabbi Moshe Al Sheich
- Rabbi Moshe ben Nachman (Nachmanides/Ramban)
- Rabbi Moshe Maimonides (Rambam)
- Rabbi Yosef Kara
- Rabbi Don Isaac Abrabanel[3]

A1.3 EXCLUSION CRITERIA

To focus on the most relevant literature, my review will also exclude the following sources:

1. Anonymous works included in Driver and Nebauer
2. Minor or obscure Rabbis included in Driver and Nebauer (according to Shulman):[4]

    - Rabbi Jacob bar Reuben
    - Rabbi Yeshaya m'Trani
    - Nizzahon Vetus
    - Rabbi Shem Tov ibn Shaprut
    - Rabbi Moshe Cohen of Tordesilla
    - Rabbi Shlomo Astruc
    - Rabbi Yom Tov Lipmann Muhlhausen
    - Rabbi Avraham Farisol
    - Rabbi Meir Aramah
    - Rabbi Samuel ben Avraham Laniado
    - Rabbi Naftali ben Asher Altshuler

3. Shulman, *Rabbinic*, §4.
4. Shulman, *Rabbinic*, §5.

Appendix 1

- Rabbi Solomon ben Isaac de Marini
- Rabbi Menasha ben Yisroel
- Judah ben Balaam
- Eliezer of Beaugenci
- Yosef ben Nathan
- Rabbi Yitzchok Eli Kohen
- Rabbi David de Rocca Martini
- Rabbi Saadiah ibn Danan
- Rabbi Solomon ben Melekh
- Gershom ben Nathan
- Rabbi Solomon ben Isaac Levi
- Rabbi Avraham the Proselyte
- Avraham ben Judah Hazan
- Rabbi Isaac Lopez
- Rabbi Joshua Segre
- Rabbi Joseph Passini

3. Karaite and non-orthodox Jewish literature included in Driver and Neubauer (according to Shulman[5])

   - Yaphet ben Ali
   - Jacob ben Reuben
   - Aaron Ben Yosef the Elder
   - Moshe Ibn Crispin
   - Isaac Troki
   - Herz Homberg
   - Samuel David Luzzato

---

5. Shulman, *Rabbinic*, §6.

A1.4 SUMMARY OF RABBINIC LITERATURE BEFORE 1000CE

According to several major rabbis, Sanhedrin 98b shows the Talumdic sages believed Isaiah 53 was Messianic (Table 12). There is also an intriguing reference to Moses in the Talmud citing Isaiah 53:12 (b. Sotah 14a). This may suggest a link between Moses, the servant of the Lord (e.g. Numbers 12:7–8, Deuteronomy 34:5, Joshua 1:1), and the servant of Isaiah 53, picked up in an early midrash:

> This verse refers to the Messiah, the descendant of David. Why was he called a great mountain? Because he will be greater than the patriarchs, as is said: Behold, My servant shall prosper, he shall be exalted and lifted up, and shall be very high (Isa. 52:13). He shall be exalted above Abraham; lifted up above Isaac; and shall be very high above Jacob. He shall be exalted above Abraham, concerning whom it is said: I have lifted up my hand unto the Lord (Gen. 14:22); lifted up above Moses. (Tanchuma Toldot 14:1)

The other three citations relate to Rabbi Akiva (a first century Jewish leader), "the one the Lord delights in", and a citation that appears to have little connection to the original text (not uncommon in midrash!). No Rabbinic sources during this period claimed Israel was the servant. The writings of Origen (a third century Christian—and therefore outside the scope of this review), constitute the earliest claim Jews believed the servant alone was Israel.

Source	Date	Individual	Messiah	Israel	Vicarious suffering	Reference
Talmud	c. 300–600 CE	Yes*	No	No	No	Shekalim 5:1[6]
Talmud	c. 300–600 CE	Yes	Yes	No	Yes	Sanhedrin 98b:14
Talmud	c. 300–600 CE	No**	No	No	No	Berakhot 5a:11
Talmud	c. 300–600 CE	No	No	No	No	Berakhot 57b
Talmud	c. 300–600 CE	Yes***	No	No	Yes	Sotah 14a:7–10
Targum of Jonathan on Isaiah	c.150 BCE— c.350 CE	Yes	Yes	No	No	Targum Jonathan on Isaiah 52:13
Tanchuma Toldot	c.500–800 CE	Yes	Yes	No	Unclear	Tanchuma Toldot 14:1

6. Driver and Neubauer, *Isaiah*, 7.

APPENDIX 1

Source	Date	Individual	Messiah	Israel	Vicarious suffering	Reference
Peshikta	c.600–900 CE	Yes	Yes	No	Yes	Driver and Neubauer[7]
Midrash Ruth Rabbah	c.700–950 CE	Yes	Yes	No	Unclear	Midrash Rabbah Ruth 2:14

Table 12. Summary of major Rabbinic literature
on Isaiah 52:13—53:12 before 1000 CE
*Rabbi Akiva **The one who the Lord delights in ***Moses

A1.5 SUMMARY OF RABBINIC LITERATURE AFTER 1000 CE

Table 13 shows a clear shift in Rabbinic interpretation during this period. Leading commentators such as Rashi, Radak, and Ibn Ezra concluded Israel was the subject of Isaiah 53.

However, the Messianic interpretation did not disappear. The Zohar, Nachmanides, and Maimonides continued to associate Isaiah 53 with the Messiah. In common with the Talmud and earlier midrash, Moses also continued to be associated with the servant of Isaiah 53.

Source	Date	Individual	Messiah	Israel	Vicarious suffering	Reference
Rashi	1075–1105 CE	No	No	Yes	No	Commentary on Isaiah 52:13—53:12
Rabbi Yosef Kara	1090–1135 CE	No	No	Yes	No	Driver and Neubauer[8]
Yalkut Shimoni	1100 CE	Yes*	No	No	Yes	2:338[9]
Yalkut Shimoni	1100 CE	Yes	Yes	No	Unclear	2:620[10]

7. Driver and Neubauer, *Isaiah*, 11.
8. Driver and Neubauer, *Isaiah*, 42.
9. Driver and Neubauer, *Isaiah*, 9.
10. Driver and Neubauer, *Isaiah*, 9.

Summary of Major Rabbinic Jewish Writings

Source	Date	Individual	Messiah	Israel	Vicarious suffering	Reference
Midrash Lekach Tov	1105–1115 CE	Yes	Yes	No	Unclear	Commentary on Numbers 24:7
Rabbi David Kimchi (Radak)	1118–1235 CE	No	No	Yes	No	Commentary on Isaiah 52:13—53:12.
Rabbi Abraham Ibn Ezra	1155–1165 CE	No	No	Yes	No	Commentary on Isaiah 52:13—53:12
Maimonides (Rambam)	1173–1174 CE	Yes	Yes	No	Unclear	Epistle to Yemen
Midrash Rabbah Numbers	1200 CE	No	No	Yes	No	Commentary on Numbers 13:2
Nachmanides (Ramban)	1220–270 CE	Yes	Yes	Yes	No	Driver and Neubauer[11]
Zohar	1300 CE	Unclear	Unclear	No	No	Driver and Neubauer[12]
Zohar	1300 CE	Yes	Yes	No	Yes	Driver and Neubauer[13]
Zohar	1300 CE	Yes	No	No	Yes	Driver and Neubauer[14]
Zohar	1300 CE	Yes	No	No	Yes	Driver and Neubauer[15]
Zohar	1300 CE	Unclear	Unclear	No	Yes	Driver and Neubauer[16]
Zohar	1300 CE	No	No	No	No	Driver and Neubauer[17]
Zohar	1300 CE	Yes	No	No	Yes	Driver and Neubauer[18]
Zohar	1300 CE	No	No	Yes	No	Driver and Neubauer[19]

11. Driver and Neubauer, Isa*iah*, 78–85.
12. Driver and Neubauer, Isa*iah*, 13–14.
13. Driver and Neubauer, Is*aiah*, 14–15.
14. Driver and Neubauer, *Isaiah*, 15.
15. Driver and Neubauer, *Isaiah*, 15.
16. Driver and Neubauer, *Isaiah*, 16.
17. Driver and Neubauer, *Isaiah*, 16.
18. Driver and Neubauer, *Isaiah*, 16.
19. Driver and Neubauer, *Isaiah*, 16.

APPENDIX 1

Source	Date	Individual	Messiah	Israel	Vicarious suffering	Reference
Rabbi Don Isaac Abarbanel	1483–1513 CE	No	No	Yes	Yes	Commentary of Isaiah 52:13—53:12
Rabbi Moshe Alshich	1540–590 CE	Yes	Yes	No	Yes	Driver & Neubauer[20]
Rabbi David Altschuler	1740–780 CE	No	No	Yes	Yes	Driver & Neubauer[21]
Rabbi Nachman of Breslov	1772–1810	Yes	Yes	No	Yes	Likutei Moharan 118:4-6.
Rabbi Meir Leibish Malbim	1844–1874 CE	No	No	Yes	Unclear	Commentary of Isaiah 52:13—53:12

Table 13. Summary of major Rabbinic literature on Isaiah 52:13—53:12 from 1000 CE
*Moses

A1.6 WHAT MIGHT EXPLAIN THIS CHANGING TREND?

One explanation is Rashi—probably the most influential scholar in Jewish history. He likely pioneered the claim that the servant of Isaiah was Israel alone. Jewish persecution during this period may have impacted Rashi.[22] In 1096, he witnessed the death of many friends and family by Crusaders seeking a source of income for their travels.

Reinterpretation of Isaiah 53 had several benefits. It delegitimized the arguments of Christendom that Jesus was the Messiah of Isaiah 53. How could that be true, if the Jewish people had all along concluded the passage was about Israel? It also encouraged suffering Jews.

---

20. Driver and Neubauer, *Isaiah*, 258–74.
21. Driver and Neubauer, *Isaiah*, 367–72.
22. Driver and Neubauer, *Jewish*, xliv–xlvi.

A1.7 CONCLUSION

Rabbi Singer's view that Israel is the servant of Isaiah 53 held limited influence in early (and therefore most authoritative) Rabbinic Jewish tradition. However, an abrupt shift to the "collectivist" view (the servant as Israel) occurred from approximately 1100 CE. It is not hard to empathise with Rashi in his response to the hostile environment imposed on Jewish people. However, the Messianic interpretation never left Judaism. The early testimony of Jewish tradition was too strong.

Appendix 2

Studies Included in Bereavement Hallucination Estimates

Included (Table 14) and excluded (Table 15) studies are summarised below. The following inclusion and exclusion criteria were applied to studies reported in the three reviews consulted.[1]

- focus on estimating the incidence and/or prevalence of bereavement hallucinations or visions;
- rates of hallucinations or visions reported separately from "sense of presence" or other phenomena;
- ≥ 40 participants included in study;
- reported by the person with the experience (e.g., not doctors or nurses reporting experiences of patients).

---

1. Castelnovo, *Hallucinatory*, 266–74; Kamp, *Bereavement*, 1367–1381; Streithorn, *After-Death*.

Studies Included in Bereavement Hallucination Estimates

Study	N	Recruitment	Definition of hallucination	Visual hallucination (median: 14%)	Auditory hallucination (median: 15%)	Tactile hallucination (median: 5%)	Verbal hallucination (median: 12%)	Multisensory (median: insufficient data)
Arcangel 2005	827	International survey: US, Canada, Mexico, Australia, New Zealand and others. Participants recruited at grief workshops, through healthcare professionals etc	Unvalidated	14% (114/827)	2% (16/827)	1% (10/827)	NR	Visual and auditory: 9% (76/827) Visual and tactile: 0.2% (2/827) Auditory and tactile: 0.2% (2/827) Visual, auditory, tactile: 3% (21/827)
Barbato 1999	47	Next of kin	Specific APA criteria	2% (1/47)	13% (6/47)	4% (2/47)	NR	NR
Byrne 1994	57	Widowers	Unvalidated	NR*	NR	NR	NR	NR
Carlson 2007	45	Spouses	Unvalidated	13% (6/45)	29% (13/45)	NR	4% (2/45)	NR
Datson 1997	87	Family member: parent, child, or spouse (99%)	Unvalidated	10% (9/87)	11% (10/87)	6% (5/87)	NR	NR

Appendix 2

Study	N	Recruitment	Definition of hallucination	Visual hallucination (median: 14%)	Auditory hallucination (median: 15%)	Tactile hallucination (median: 5%)	Verbal hallucination (median: 12%)	Multisensory (median: insufficient data)
Grimby 1993	50	Spouses	Unvalidated	22% (11/50)	26% (13/50)	6% (3/50)	26% (13/50)	Combines sense of presence with more specific hallucinations
Houck 2005	162	clinical case managers, nursing staff, and social workers from various hospice, suicide support groups, and HIV/AIDS agencies to recruit volunteers for the study.	Vague and unvalidated	10% (16/162)	19% (30/162)	3% (5/162)	NR	4% (6/162) (auditory + visual)
Jahn 2014	1301	Suicide bereavement, close family member: parent, child, spouse/partner (57.8%), Friend (8.6%), Sibling (18.1%)	Unvalidated	117/1301 9%	114/1301 9%	NR	NR	Combines various experiences with more specific hallucinations

Studies Included in Bereavement Hallucination Estimates

Study	N	Recruitment	Definition of hallucination	Visual hallucination (median: 14%)	Auditory hallucination (median: 15%)	Tactile hallucination (median: 5%)	Verbal hallucination (median: 12%)	Multisensory (median: insufficient data)
Kalish 1973	434	Community population in Los Angeles, USA.	Vague and unvalidated	Unclear**	NR	3% (12/434)	Unclear	NR
Kamp 2023	310	Spouse	Clear distinction between types of hallucination	7% full figure person (22/310)	7%*** (22/310)	12% (38/310)	5% conversation (17/310)	NR
Kamp 2018	175	Spouse	Unclear	27% (48/175)	23% (41/175)	NR	17% (29/175)	NR
Klugman 2006	202	Parent (39.4%), Grandparent (22%), Friend (8.7%), Spouse (7.9%), Sibling (7.1%), Child (3.2%)	Unvalidated	38% (76/202) (vision or image)	35% (71/202) (voice)	25% (51/202) (touch)	70% (141/202) (converse with them)	NR
Longman 1988	97	Majority were spouses, followed by parents	Unvalidated (26% of experiences when asleep)	15% (15/97)	16% (16/97)	5% (5/97)	NR	NR
Olson 1985	46	Spouse	Unvalidated	48% (22/46)	30% (14/46)	13% (6/46)	11% (5/46)	NR

APPENDIX 2

Study	N	Recruitment	Definition of hallucination	Visual hallucination (median: 14%)	Auditory hallucination (median: 15%)	Tactile hallucination (median: 5%)	Verbal hallucination (median: 12%)	Multisensory (median: insufficient data)
Rees 1971	293	Spouse	Distinction made between hallucination, sense of presence, and dreams.	14% (41/293)	13% (39/293)	3% (8/293)	12% (34/293)	NR
Schuchter 1993	350	Spouse	Vague and unvalidated	NR	NR	NR	39%	NR
Zisook 1985	300	Spouse	Vague and unvalidated	NR****	NR	NR	11%	NR
Zisook 1986	61	Spouse	Vague and unvalidated	NR****	12% (7/61)	NR	NR	NR

Table 14. Summary of studies used to estimate median prevalence of bereavement hallucinations *seen, heard, or felt as touched, **appeared or spoke, ***auditory-verbal occurring outside the head, ****visual image of the deceased was judged insufficiently precise to be included, NR=not reported, N=number of participants

Studies Included in Bereavement Hallucination Estimates

Ref	Reason
Field 2010	Not a prevalence study
Field 2013	Number of participants <40
Lindstrom 1995	Number of participants <40
Palmer 1979	No specific data on bereavement hallucinations
Greeley 1975	Only asked about contact with dead people
Kohr 1980	Survey of member of Association of Research and Enlightenment—a psychic non-profit. Unlikely to be representative of all experiences.
Mack 2005	Only asked about post-death communication
Haraldson 1977	Exact question unclear—related to apparition of the dead
Marris 1958	Exact question unclear—primarily sense of presence
Osis 1977	Deathbed observations by doctors and nurses
MacDonald 1992	Asked if they were in touch with the dead
Haraldson 1985, 1991	Asked if they were in touch with the dead
Greeley 1987	Asked if they were in touch with the dead
Luke 2005	Too broad: experience of communication with dead person or spirit
McClenon 1988	Asked if they were in touch with the dead
Sidgwick 1894	Not assessing bereavement hallucinations
Kelly 2002	Sense of presence—not specifically visual, auditory, tactile experience
Osis 1977	Deathbed observations by doctors and nurses
Sormanti 1997	Not a prevalence or incidence study
Simon-Buller 1988	Sense of presence
Burton 1982	Psychic research groups and classes
Hobson 1964	Sense of presence—unclear what question asked
Parkes 1970	Number of participants <40
Silverman 1996	Unclear what questions asked
Yamamoto 1969	Number of participants <40
Parkes 1965	Number of participants <40
Ball 1977	Sense of presence and hallucinations not separated
Nichols 2001	Sense of presence only
Epstein 2006	No prevalence data on hallucinations
Laroi 2006	Non-bereaved and also no specific prevalence data on hallucinations
Lee 2005	Not a prevalence study

APPENDIX 2

Ref	Reason
Simon 2011	Not a prevalence study
Bennett 2000	Not a prevalence study
Chan 2005	Not a prevalence study
Conant 1996	Not a prevalence study
Doran 2006	Not a prevalence study
Gondar-Portasany 1989	Not a prevalence study
Hayes and Leuder 2016	Not a prevalence study
Keen 2013	Not a prevalence study
Nowatzki and Kalischuk 2009	Not a prevalence study
Steffen and Coyle 2011	Not a prevalence study
Troyer 2014	Not a prevalence study
Parker 2005	Not a prevalence study

Table 15. Studies excluded with reasons

BIBLIOGRAPHY OF INCLUDED STUDIES

Arcangel, Dianne. *Afterlife encounters: Ordinary people, extraordinary experiences.* Charlottesville, VA: Hampton Roads, 2005.

Barbato, Michael., et al. Parapsychological Phenomena near the Time of Death. *Journal of Palliative Care* 15 (1999) 30–37.

Byrne, G.J., and Raphael, B. A longitudinal study of bereavement phenomena in recently widowed elderly men. *Psychological Medicine* 24 (1994) 411–21.

Carlson, Maria E., and Nilsson, I.M. Bereaved spouses' adjustment after the patients' death in palliative care. *Palliative and Supportive Care* 5 (2007) 397–404.

Datson, S.L., and Marwit, S.J. Bereaved spouses' adjustment after the patients' death in palliative care. *Death Studies* 21 (1997) 131–46.

Grimby, A. Bereavement among elderly people: grief reactions, post-bereavement hallucinations and quality of life. *Acta Psychiatrica Scandinavica* 87 (1993) 72–80.

Houck, James A. The universal, multiple, and exclusive experiences of after-death communication. *Journal of Near-Death Studies* 24 (2005) 117–27.

Jahn, Danielle R., and Spencer-Thomas, S. Continuing Bonds Through After-Death Spiritual Experiences in Individuals Bereaved by Suicide. *Journal of Spirituality in Mental Health* 16 (2014) 311–24.

Kalish, Richard A., and Reynolds, David. K. Phenomenological reality and post-death contact. *Journal for the Scientific Study of Religion*, 12 (1973) 209–21.

Kamp, Karina et al. Bereavement hallucinations after the loss of a spouse: Associations with psychopathological measures, personality and coping style. *Death Studies* 43 (2019) 260–269.

Studies Included in Bereavement Hallucination Estimates

———. Prevalence and phenomenology of sensory experiences of a deceased spouse: A survey of bereaved older adults. *OMEGA* 87 (2023) 103–25.

Klugman, Craig. Dead Men Talking: Evidence of Post Death Contact and Continuing Bonds. *OMEGA* 53 (2006) 249–62.

Longman, A.J., et al. Sensory-perceptual experiences of bereaved individuals. additional cues for survivors. *American Journal of Hospice Care* 5 (1988), 42.

Olson, P.R., et al. Hallucinations of widowhood. *Journal of the American Geriatric Society* 33 (1985), 543–47.

Rees, Dewi. The Hallucinations of Widowhood. *BMJ* 4 (1971) 39–41.

Schuchter, Stephen R., and Zisook, Sidney. "The course of normal grief." In *Handbook of Bereavement*, edited by Margaret S. Stroebe et al., 23–43. Cambridge: Cambridge University Press, 1993.

Zisook, S., Schuchter, S. The first four years of widowhood. *Psychiatric Annals* 16 (1986), 288–94.

Zisook, S., Shuchter, S. Time course of spousal bereavement. *General Hospital Psychiatry* 7 (1985), 95–100.

Bibliography

Adams, Douglas. *The Salmon of Doubt*. London: Pan Macmillan, 2003.
Ahmed, Arif, and Habermas, Gary. "Debate: Did Jesus Rise from the Dead?" University of Cambridge, 2008. YouTube Video, 1:28:51. https://www.youtube.com/watch?v=Mg7rYJxHA4Y [accessed 08/03/2024]
Allison, Dale. *The Resurrection of Jesus*. London: Bloomsbury, 2023.
Anderson, Amanda et al. A Systematic Review of the experimental induction of auditory perceptual experiences. *Journal of Behavior Therapy and Experimental Psychiatry* 71 (2021) 101635.
Anderson, James. If Knowledge Then God: The Epistemological Theistic Arguments of Plantinga and Van Til. *Calvin Theological Journal* 40:1 (2005).
Aybeck, Selma and David L. Perez. Diagnosis and management of functional neurological disorder. *BMJ* 376 (2022) 064.
Baddeley, Alan D. Is the study of memory unduly preoccupied with its sins? *Memory* 30 (2022) 55– 59.
Balfour, G.W., and J.G. Piddington. Case of Haunting at Ramsbury, Wilts. *Journal of the Society of Psychical Research* 27 (1932) 297–304.
Barnes, Luke. A reasonable little question: a formulation of the fine-tuning argument. *Ergo* 6:42 (2019–2020).
Barrett, David et al. *The World Christian Encyclopaedia: A Comprehensive Survey of Church and Religions in the Modern World (Second edition), volume 2*. Oxford: Oxford University Press, 2001.
Bartholomew, Robert. Tarantism, dancing mania and demonopathy: the anthro-political aspects of "mass psychogenic illness." *Psychological Medicine* 24 (1994) 281–306.
Bauckham, Richard. *Gospel Women: Studies of the Named Women in the Gospels*. London: T&T Clark International, 2002.
Bavinck, Herman. *Reformed Dogmatics, volume 3*, edited by John Bolton. Translated by John Vriend. Grand Rapids, MI: Baker Academic, 2006.
Beale, G.K. "Revelation". In *Commentary on the New Testament Use of the Old Testament*, edited by G.K. Beale and D.A. Carson, 1081–1162. Grand Rapids, MI: Baker Academic, 2007.

Bibliography

Beale, G.K., and Mitchell Kim. *God Dwells Among Us: Expanding Eden To The Ends Of The Earth.* London: IVP, 2015.

Beale, G.K., and D.A. Carson. "Introduction." In *Commentary on the New Testament Use of the Old Testament,* edited by G.K. Beale and D.A. Carson, xxiii–xxviii. Grand Rapids, MI: Baker Academic, 2007.

Bergeron, Joseph, and Gary Habermas. The Resurrection of Jesus: A Clinical Review of Psychiatric Hypotheses for the Biblical Story of Easter. *Irish Theological Quarterly* 80 (2015) 157–72.

Bermejo-Rubio, Fernando. The Process of Jesus' Deification and Cognitive Dissonance Theory. *Numen* 64 (2017) 119–52.

Berntsen, Dorthe and Dorthe Thomsen. Personal Memories for Remote Historical Events: Accuracy and Clarity of Flashbulb Memories Related to World War II. *Journal of Experimental Psychology: General* 134 (2005) 242–57.

Blais, Brian. *Statistical inference for everyone.* Save the Broccoli Publishing, 2020.

Bock, Darrell. "The Parables of Enoch and Mark 14:53–73: Blasphemy and Exaltation." In *Reading Mark in Context: Jesus and Second Temple Judaism,* edited by Ben C. Blackwell, et al., 231–37. Grand Rapids, MI: Zondervan, 2018.

Bourget, David, and David Chalmers. The 2020 PhiPapers Survey. https://survey2020.philpeople.org/ [accessed 06/15/2024]

Boyarin, Daniel. *Borderlines.* Philadelphia, PA: University of Pennsylvania Press, 2004.

———. *The Jewish Gospels: the Story of Jesus Christ.* New York: New Press, 2013.

———. "Logos a Jewish Word." In *Annotated Jewish New Testament,* edited by Amy-Jill Levine and Marc Zvi Brettler, 688–90. Oxford: Oxford University Press, 2017.

Brewin, Chris R. Impact on the legal system of the generalizability crisis in psychology. *Behavioral and Brain Sciences* 45 (2022) e7.

Brewin, Chris R., et al. Regaining Consensus on the Reliability of Memory. *Current Directions in Psychological Science* 29 (2020) 121–25.

Brown, Michael. *Answering Jewish Objections to Jesus, Volume 3: Messianic Prophecy Objections.* Ada, MI: Baker, 2003.

Bruce F.F. *Book of Acts.* New International Commentary on the New Testament. Grand Rapids, MI: William Eerdmans, 1988.

Bryson, Bill. *A Short History of Nearly Everything.* London: Transworld Digital, 2010. Overdrive.

Bultmann, Rudolf, et al. *Kerygma and Myth, volume 1,* edited by Hans Werner Bartsch. New York: Harper & Row, 1961.

Carrier, Richard. "The Spiritual Body of Christ and the Legend of the Empty Tomb." In *The Empty Tomb: Jesus Beyond the Grave,* edited by Jeffery Jay Lowder and Robert Price, 105–232. Amherst, NY: Prometheus Books, 2005.

Carson, DA. *Gospel According to John.* Leicester: Apollos, 1991.

———. *Matthew.* Grand Rapids, MI: Zondervan Academic, 2017.

Castelnovo, Anna, et al. Post bereavement hallucinatory experiences: A critical overview of population and clinical studies. *Journal of Affective Disorders* 186 (2015) 266–74.

Chester, Tim and Jonny Woodrow. *The Ascension.* Fearn: Christian Focus, 2013.

Christian Jr., William, A. *Visionaries.* London: University of California Press, 1996.

Clowney, Edmund P. *The Unfolding Mystery Discovering Christ in The Old Testament.* Philipsburg, NJ: Presbyterian &Reformed, 2013.

Collerton, Daniel., et al. Understanding visual hallucinations: A new synthesis. *Neuroscience and Biobehavioral Reviews* 150 (2023) 105208.

Cook, John Granger. Crucifixion and Burial. *New Testament Studies* 57 (2011) 193–213.

Bibliography

Cortez, Marc. *Theological Anthropology*. London: T&T Clark, 2009.

Craig, William Lane. *Problem of Dwindling Probabilities*. https://www.reasonablefaith.org/writings/question-answer/problem-of-dwindling-probabilities [accessed 06/15/2024]

———. *Reasonable Faith*. Wheaton, IL: Crossway, 2008.

Darwiche, Adnan. *Modeling and reasoning with Bayesian Networks*. Cambridge: Cambridge University Press, 2009.

Dawes, Gregory W. In defense of naturalism. *International Journal for Philosophy of Religion* 70 (2011) 3–25.

Diamond, Nicholas B., et al. The Truth Is Out There: Accuracy in Recall of Verifiable Real-World Events. *Psychological Science* 31 (2020) 1544–1556.

Draper, Paul. "God, Science, and Naturalism." In *The Oxford Handbook of Philosophy of Religion*, edited by William J. Wainwright, 272–303. Oxford: Oxford University Press, 2005.

———. "Pain and Pleasure: An Evidential Problem for Theists." In *The Problem of Evil*, edited by Michael L. Peterson, 553–75. Notre Dame, IN: University of Notre Dame Press, 2017.

———. "Seeking but not Believing: Confessions of a Practicing Agnostic." In *Divine Hiddenness*, edited by Daniel Howard-Snyder and Paul K Moser, 197–214. Cambridge: Cambridge University Press, 2009.

Duguid, Iain. "Messianic Themes in Zechariah." In *The Lord's Anointed: Interpretation of Old Testament Messianic Texts*, edited by Phillip Satterthwaite et al., 265–80. Eugene, OR: Wipf & Stock, 1995.

Ehrman, Bart. *The Apostolic Fathers*. The Loeb classical library. Cambridge, MA: Harvard University Press, 2003.

———. *How Jesus Became God*. Boulder, CO: Bravo, 2015.

———. *Jesus Before the Gospels*. New York: Harper Collins, 2016.

———. *Triumph of Christianity: How a Forbidden Religion Swept the World*. London: Oneworld Publications, 2018.

Einstein, Albert. Physics and Reality. *Journal of the Franklin Institute* 221 (1936) 349–82.

Ellis, George. "Does the Multiverse Really Exist?" https://www.scientificamerican.com/article/does-the-multiverse-really-exist/ [accessed 06/15/2024]

———. "Issues in the Philosophy of Cosmology." https://arxiv.org/abs/astro-ph/0602280 [accessed 06/15/2024]

Epiphanius. *The Panarion of Epiphanius of Salamis: Book I*. Translated by Frank Williams. Leiden: Brill, 2009.

Er, Nurhan. A new flashbulb memory model applied to the Marmara earthquake. *Applied Cognitive Psychology* 17 (2003) 503–17.

Etheridge, John Wesley. *Targums of Onkelos and Jonathan Ben Uzziel on the Pentateuch*. Piscataway, NJ: Gorgias, 2005.

Evans, Craig A. *Word and Glory: On the exegetical and theological background of John's Prologue*. Sheffield: Sheffield Academic Press, 1993.

Farrow, Douglas. *Ascension and Ecclesia*. London: T&T Clark International, 1999.

Fee, Gordon D. *Pauline Christology*. Peabody, MA: Hendrickson, 2007.

The Fifty-Third Chapter of Isaiah: According to the Jewish Interpreters. Translated by Samuel Rolles Driver and Adolf Neubauer. London: James Parker, 1877. https://www.academia.edu/45097518/_The_Fifty_Third_Chapter_of_Isaiah_According_to_the_Jewish_Interpreters_Translations_eds_Samuel_Rolles_Driver_and_

Bibliography

Adolf_Neubauer_Oxford_and_London_James_Parker_and_Co_1877_ [accessed 06/15/2024]

Flammarion, Camille. *Death and its Mystery at the Moment of Death*. Translated by Latrobe Carroll. New York: The Century, 1922.

Frame, John and Joseph E. Torres. *Apologetics: A Justification of Christian Belief*. Phillipsburg, NJ: P&R, 2015.

France, R.T. *The Gospel of Mark: The New International Greek Testament Commentary*. Grand Rapids, MI: William. B. Eerdmans, 2002.

Garfield, Jay. *Engaging Buddhism: why it matters to philosophy*. Oxford: Oxford University Press, 2015.

Garrison, Jane R., et al. Paracingulate Sulcus Morphology and Hallucinations in Clinical and Nonclinical Groups. *Schizophrenia Bulletin* 45 (2019) 733–41.

———. Testing continuum models of psychosis: No reduction in source monitoring ability in healthy individuals prone to auditory hallucinations. *Cortex* 91 (2017) 197–207.

Goff, Philip. "Can you prove a miracle?" https://conscienceandconsciousness.com/2022/04/20/can-you-prove-a-miracle/ [accessed 06/15/2024]

———. Is the Fine-Tuning Evidence for a Multiverse? *Synthese* 204 (2024) 1–22.

Grant, Edward. *The Foundations of Modern Science in the Middle Ages: Their Religious, Institutional and Intellectual Contexts*. Cambridge: Cambridge University Press, 1996.

Gregory, Richard L. Putting illusions in their place. *Perception* 20 (1991) 1–4.

Gupta, Gopal. *Māyā in the Bhāgavata Purāṇa*. Oxford: Oxford University Press, 2020.

Habermas, Gary, and Michael Licona. *The Case for the Resurrection of Jesus*. Grand Rapids, MI: Kregel, 2004.

Hájek, Alan, "Interpretations of Probability", *The Stanford Encyclopedia of Philosophy* (Winter 2023 Edition), Edited by Edward N. Zalta and Uri Nodelman. https://plato.stanford.edu/archives/win2023/entries/probability-interpret/. [accessed 06/15/2024]

Harrison, Peter. Review of The Fall of Man and the Foundations of Science, by Ian Shaw. *Foundations* 72 (2017) 107–13.

———. Naturalism and the success of science. *Religious Studies* 56 (2020) 274–91.

———. *The Fall of Man and the Foundations of Science*. Cambridge: Cambridge University Press, 2007.

Hartke M. "An Unshakable Kingdom: How Cognitive Dissonance Explains Christianity." https://mlhartke.wordpress.com/2022/11/21/an-unshakable-kingdom-how-cognitive-dissonance-explains-christianity/ [accessed 06/15/2024]

Hawthorne, John and Yoaav Isaacs. "Fine-Tuning." In *Knowledge, Belief and God*, edited by M. Benton, et al., 136–68. Oxford: Oxford University Press, 2018.

Harvey, Peter. *Buddhism and Monotheism*. Cambridge: Cambridge University Press, 2019.

Heilig Christoph. "What Bayesian Reasoning Can and Can't Do for Biblical Research." https://www.uzh.ch/blog/theologie-nt/2019/03/27/what-bayesian-reasoning-can-and-cant-do-for-biblical-research/ [accessed 06/15/2024]

Hengel, Martin, and Anna Maria Schwemer. *Jesus and Judaism*. Translated by Wayne Coppins. Reprint, Waco, TX: Baylor University Press, 2019.

Himmelfarb, Martha. *Jewish Messiahs in a Christian Empire: A History of the Book of Zerubbabel*. Cambridge, MA: Harvard University Press, 2017.

Bibliography

Hogg, Michael, and Graham Vaughn. *Social Psychology (Ninth Edition)*. London: Pearson, 2021.

Holland, Tom. *Dominion*. Little, Brown, and Company; 2019.

Horgan, John. "Physicist George Ellis Knocks Physicists for Knocking Philosophy, Falsification, Free Will." https://www.scientificamerican.com/blog/cross-check/physicist-george-ellis-knocks-physicists-for-knocking-philosophy-falsification-free-will/ [accessed 5th February, 2024]

Horsley, Richard A. Popular Messianic Movements around the Time of Jesus. *Catholic Bible Quarterly* 46 (1984) 471–94.

Hume David, *An Enquiry concerning Human Understanding*, https://davidhume.org/texts/e/ [accessed 5th February, 2024]

Hutchings, David, and David Wilkinson. *God, Stephen Hawking and the Multiverse*. London: SPCK, 2020.

Ibn Ezra. *On Isaiah*. https://www.sefaria.org/Ibn_Ezra_on_Isaiah?tab=contents [accessed 06/15/2024]

Isser, Stanley Jerome. *The Dositheans: a Samaritan Sect in Late Antiquity*. Leiden: Brill, 1976.

Jones E.E., and V.A. Harris. The Attribution of Attitudes. *Journal of Experimental Social Psychology* 3 (1967) 1–24.

Jordan, James. *Through New Eyes*. Portland, OR: Wipf and Stock, 1999.

Kalish, Richard A., and David K. Reynolds. Phenomenological Reality and Post-Death Contact. *Journal for the Scientific Study of Religions* 12 (1973) 209–21.

Kallgard A. Masshysterin på Pitcairn märkligt exempel på psykogen smitta. *Lakartidningen* 94 (1997) 4722.

Kamp, Karina S., et al. Sensory and Quasi-Sensory Experiences of the Deceased in Bereavement: An Interdisciplinary and Integrative Review. *Schizophrenia Bulletin* 46 (2020) 1367–1381.

Kay, Peter. "Missed the bus." YouTube Video, 0.24 https://www.youtube.com/watch?v=ZBvFM3JpTUs [accessed 06/15/2024]

Keener, Craig. *Acts*. Cambridge: Cambridge University Press, 2020.

Keown, Damien. *A very short introduction to Buddhism (second edition)*. Oxford: Oxford University Press, 2013.

Komarnitsky, Kris. "Cognitive Dissonance and the Resurrection of Jesus." https://www.westarinstitute.org/editorials/cognitive-dissonance-resurrection-jesus [accessed 06/15/2024]

Knohl, Israel. *The Messiah Before Jesus: The Suffering Servant of the Dead Sea Scrolls*. California: University of California Press, 2000.

Knott, Kim. *Hinduism: a very short introduction (2nd edition)*. Oxford: Oxford University Press, 2016.

Lee, Raymond L., S.E. Ackerman. The sociocultural dynamics of mass hysteria. *Psychiatry* 43 (1980) 78–88.

Lennox, John. *God's Undertaker: Has Science Buried God?* Kidderminster: Lion Books, 2009.

Levenson, Jon. *Resurrection and the Restoration of Israel*. New Haven, CO: Yale University Press, 2006.

Licona, Michael. *Why Are There Differences in the Gospels?* Oxford: Oxford University Press, 2016.

Loke, Andrew. *Investigating the Resurrection of Jesus Christ*. London: Routledge, 2020.

Bibliography

———. *Studies on the Origin of Divine and Resurrection Christology*. Eugene, OR: Cascade, 2023.

Longman III, Tremper. *Psalms*. Tyndale Old Testament Commentaries. Leicester: IVP, 2014.

Lowder, Jeffery Jay. The Evidential Argument from the History of Science (AHS), 2012. https://secularfrontier.infidels.org/2012/06/the-evidential-argument-from-the-history-of-science-ahs/ [accessed 06/15/2024]

Ludemann, G. *The Resurrection of Christ*. Amherst, NY: Prometheus, 2004.

MacKenzie, Andrew. *The Unexplained*. London: Arthur Barker, 1966.

Madigan, David, and Jon Levenson. *Resurrection: The Power of God for Christians and Jews*. New Haven, CO: Yale University Press, 2008.

Maimonides, Moses. *The Guide for the Perplexed*. Translated by M. Friedlander, Fourth Edition. New York: Dutton, 1904.

Marshall, I. Howard. *Gospel of Luke*. The New International Greek Testament Commentary. Exeter: Paternoster, 1978.

Martin, Michael. Why the resurrection is initially improbable. *Philo* 1 (1998) 63–73.

McDowell, Sean. "A Historical Evaluation of the Evidence for the Death of the Apostles as Martyrs For Their Faith." PhD Diss., Southern Baptist Theological Seminary, 2014.

McGrew, Timothy, and Lydia McGrew. "The Argument from Miracles: A Cumulative Case for the Resurrection of Jesus of Nazareth." In *The Blackwell Companion to Natural Theology*, edited by William Lane Craig and J. P. Moreland, 593–662. Oxford: Blackwell, 2009.

McNamara, Martin. *Targum Neofiti 1: Genesis, Translated with Apparatus and Notes*. Collegeville, MN: Liturgical Press; 1992.

McWhirter, Laura and Alan Carson. Pseudohallucinations as functional cognitive disorders—Authors' reply. *Lancet Psychiatry* 7 (2020) P230.

Metcalf, Thomas. "Ethical Realism, or Moral Realism." https://1000wordphilosophy.com/2015/11/05/ethical-realism/ [accessed 06/15/2024]

Metzudad David [Rabbi Altschuler, David]. *On Daniel*. https://www.sefaria.org/Metzudat_David_on_Daniel?tab=contents [accessed 06/15/2024]

———. *On Isaiah*. https://www.sefaria.org/Metzudat_David_on_Isaiah?tab=contents [accessed 06/15/2024]

Morales, L. Michael. *Who Shall Ascend the Hill of the Lord?* Downers Grove, IL: IVP Academic, 2015.

Morris, Leon. *Gospel According to John*. New International Commentary on the New Testament. Grand Rapids, MI: William Eerdmans, 1995.

———. *Luke*. Tyndale New Testament Commentaries. Leicester: IVP, 1988.

Motyer, Alec. *The Prophecy of Isaiah*. Leicester: IVP, 1994.

Murray, Michael J., and Michael C. Rea. *An Introduction to the Philosophy of Religion*. Cambridge: Cambridge University Press, 2008.

Nagel, Thomas. *Mind and Cosmos*. Oxford: Oxford University Press, 2012.

Neisser, U., and N. Harsch. "Phantom flashbulbs: False recollections of hearing the news about Challenger." In *Affect and accuracy in recall: Studies of "flashbulb" memories*, edited by E. Winograd and U. Neisser, 9–31. Cambridge: Cambridge University Press, 1992.

Neisser, U., et al. Remembering the Earthquake: Direct Experience vs. Hearing the News. *Memory* 4 (1996) 337–57.

Bibliography

O'Connell, Jake. *Jesus' Resurrection and Apparitions: A Bayesian Analysis.* Portland, OR: Resource, 2016.

Ono, Sokyo. *Shinto: the Kami Way.* Rutland, Vermont: Charles E. Tuttle, 1983.

Open Science Collaboration. Estimating the reproducibility of psychological science. *Science* 349 (2015) 493.

Oppy, Graham. *Arguing About Gods.* Cambridge: Cambridge University Press, 2009.

———. "Problems of Evil". In *The Problem of Evil: Eight Views in Dialogue* edited by N.N. Tratzakis. Oxford: Oxford University Press, 2018.

———. "Ultimate Naturalistic Explanation." In in T. Goldschmidt (ed.) *Why is there Something rather than Nothing?*, 46-63. London: Routledge, 2013. https://philarchive.org/rec/OPPUNC [accessed 06/15/2024]

Origen. *Commentary on the Gospel of John: Books 13-32.* Translated by Ronald Heine. Washington DC: Catholic University of America, 2006.

———. "Contra Celsum." https://www.newadvent.org/fathers/0416.htm [accessed 06/15/2024]

Page, Don, N. "Susskind's challenge to the Hartle-Hawking no boundary proposal and possible resolutions." https://arxiv.org/abs/hep-th/0610199 [accessed 06/15/2024]

Palmer, J. A community mail survey of psychic experiences. *Journal of the American Society for Psychical Research* 73 (1979) 221-51.

Pao, David W., and Eckhard J. Schnabel. "Luke." In *Commentary on the New Testament Use of the Old Testament,* edited by G.K. Beale and D.A. Carson, 251-414. Grand Rapids, MI: Baker Academic, 2007.

Pearl, Judea. *Probabilistic Reasoning in Intelligent Systems.* San Franscisco, California: Morgan Kaufmann, 1988.

Pearl, Judea and Dana Mackenzie. *The Book of Why: The New Science of Cause and Effect.* London: Penguin, 2014.

Peyroux, Elodie, and Nicolas Franck. "An Epistemological Approach: History of Concepts and Ideas About Hallucinations in Classical Psychiatry." In *Neuroscience of hallucinations,* edited by Renaud Jardri et al., 3-20. New York, NY: Springer, 2012.

Pirkei DeRabbi Eliezer. https://www.sefaria.org/Pirkei_DeRabbi_Eliezer?tab=contents [accessed 06/15/2024]

Plantinga, Alvin. "A Christian life partly lived." In *Philosophers Who Believe,* edited by Kelly James Clark, 45-81. Downer's Grover, IL: Intervarsity, 1997.

———. *Warranted Christian Belief.* Oxford: Oxford University Press, 2000.

———. *Where the Conflict Really Lies: Science, Religion, and Naturalism.* Oxford: Oxford University Press, 2012.

Poythress, Vernon. *Chance and the Sovereignty of God: A God-Centered Approach to Probability and Random Events.* Wheaton, IL: Crossway, 2014.

Pray, Leslie A. Discovery of DNA Structure and Function: Watson and Crick. *Nature Education* 1 (2008) 100.

Pseudo Clement. *Clementine Homilies.* https://www.newadvent.org/fathers/0808.htm [accessed 06/15/2024]

———. *Recognitions of Clement.* https://www.newadvent.org/fathers/0804.htm [accessed 06/15/2024]

Radak [Rabbi Kimchi, David]. *On Isaiah.* https://www.sefaria.org/Radak_on_Isaiah?tab=contents [accessed 06/15/2024]

Ramachandra, Vinoth. *Faiths in Conflict.* Leicester: IVP, 1999.

Bibliography

Rambam [Maimonides]. *On Mishnah Sanhedrin.* https://www.sefaria.org/Rambam_on_Mishnah_Sanhedrin.10.1.15?lang=bi&with=About&lang2=en [accessed 06/15/2024]

Ramban [Nachmanides]. *On Genesis.* https://www.sefaria.org/Ramban_on_Genesis?tab=contents [accessed 06/15/2024]

Ramos Diaz, Antonio. "Mind and Formal Structures. On the Kripke-Ross Argument Against Naturalizing Formal Understanding." PhD diss. KU Leuven, 2019.

Rashi [Rabbi Shlomo ben Yitzchak]. *On Daniel.* https://www.sefaria.org/Rashi_on_Daniel?tab=contents [accessed 06/15/2024]

———. *On Genesis.* https://www.sefaria.org/Rashi_on_Genesis?tab=contents [accessed 06/15/2024]

———. *On Leviticus.* https://www.sefaria.org/Rashi_on_Leviticus?tab=contents [accessed 06/15/2024]

Reeves, Michael. *The Glory of God: The Christological Anthropology of Irenaeus of Lyons and Karl Barth.* PhD Diss., Kings College London, 2005.

———. *The Good God.* Exeter: Paternoster; 2012.

Ridderbos, Herman. *Gospel According to John.* Grand Rapids, MI: William Eerdmans, 2018.

Ripberger, Joseph, et al. Communicating Probability Information in Weather Forecasts: Findings and Recommendations from a Living Systematic Review of the Research Literature. *Weather, Climate, and Society* 14 (2022) 481–95.

Sagan, Carl. *Broca's Brain.* London: Hodder & Stoughton, 1980.

Sailhamer, John. *Pentateuch as Narrative.* Grand Rapids, MI: Zondervan Academic, 1995.

Sanneh, Lamin. "The Changing Face of Christianity: The Cultural Impetus of a World Religion." In *The Changing Face of Christianity: Africa, the West, and the World*, edited by Lamin Sanneh and Joel Carpenter, 3–18. Oxford: Oxford University Press, 2005.

Scrivener, Glen. "THIS argument is weak. No wonder Joe Rogan and Alex O'Connor are NOT convinced". Speak Life, 2024. YouTube Video, 31:43. https://www.youtube.com/watch?v=oyIh73GF_rE [accessed 06/15/2024]

Seale-Carlisle, Travis, M., et al. New Insights on Expert Opinion About Eyewitness Memory Research. *Perspectives on Psychological Science* (2024) 1–22.

Seamon, John G., et al. Do you remember proposing marriage to the Pepsi machine? False recollections from a campus walk. *Psychonomic Bulletin and Review* 13 (2006) 752–56.

Segal, Alan, F. *Two Powers in Heaven.* Leiden: Brill, 1977.

Sforno. *On Genesis.* https://www.sefaria.org/Sforno_on_Genesis?tab=contents [accessed 06/15/2024]

Shulman, Moshe. "Rabbinic Commentators after Rashi on Isaiah 53." https://jewsforjudaism.org/knowledge/articles/rabbinic-commentators-rashi-isaiah-53 [accessed 06/15/2024]

Sidgwick, Henry. Report on the Census of Hallucinations', *Proceedings of the Society for Psychical Research*, 10 (1894) 25–401.

Singer, Tovia. *Let's Get Biblical! Why Doesn't Judaism Accept the Christian Messiah? Volume 1.* RNBN, 2014.

Smith, James K.A. *How (Not) to be Secular: Reading Charles Taylor.* Grand Rapids, MI: William Eerdmans, 2014.

Bibliography

Sobel, Jordan Howard. Hume's Theorem on Testimony Sufficient to Establish a Miracle. The *Philosophical Quarterly* 41 (1991) 229–37.

Spiegelhalter, David, J., et al. Bayesian measures of model complexity and fit. *Journal of the Royal Statistical Society, Series B*, 64 (2002) 583–639.

Spurgeon, C.H. *The Treasury of David, Volume 2*. London: Marshall Brothers. https://ccel.org/ccel/spurgeon/treasury2/treasury2.i.html [accessed 06/15/2024]

Staines, Lorna, et al. Incidence and Persistence of Psychotic Experiences in the General Population: Systematic Review and Meta-Analysis. *Schizophrenia Bulletin* 49 (2023) 1007–1021.

Streit-Horn, Jenny. "A systematic review of research on after-death communication." PhD Diss., University of North Texas, 2011.

Strobel, Lee. *The Case for Easter*. Grand Rapids, MI: Zondervan, 2018.

Stump, Eleonore. "The problem of evil." In *Philosophy of Religion: A Reader and Guide*, edited by William Lane Craig, et al., 394–424. Edinburgh: Edinburgh University Press, 2001.

Swinburne, Richard. *Existence of God: Second Edition*. Oxford: Oxford University Press, 2003.

———. *Resurrection of God Incarnate*. Oxford: Oxford University Press, 2009.

Taleb, Nicholas. *The Black Swan: The Impact of the Highly Improbable*. London: Penguin, 2010.

Targum of Jonathan. *On Isaiah*. https://www.sefaria.org/Targum_Jonathan_on_Isaiah?tab=contents [accessed 06/15/2024]

Taylor C. *Secular Age*. Cambridge: Harvard University Press, 2007.

The Meaning of the Holy Qur'an. Translated by Yusuf Ali. Beltsville, MD: Amana, 2016.

Thiselton, Anthony. *The First Epistle to the Corinthians*. The New International Greek Testament Commentary. Grand Rapids, MI: William B Eerdmans, 2013.

Tipton, Lane G. "Resurrection, Proof, and Presuppositionalism." In *Revelation and Reason: New Essays in Reformed Apologetics*, edited by K. Scott Oliphint and Lane Tipton, 41–66. Phillipsburg, NJ: P&R, 2007.

Toh, Wei Lin, et al. Characteristics of non-clinical hallucinations: A mixed-methods analysis of auditory, visual, tactile and olfactory hallucinations in a primary voice-hearing cohort. *Psychiatry Research* 289 (2020) 112987.

Tratzakis, N.N. "Reply." In *The Problem of Evil: Eight Views in Dialogue* edited by N.N. Tratzakis, 85–87. Oxford: Oxford University Press, 2018.

Trueman, Carl. Luther's Theology of the Cross. *The Theologian* (2005) http://www.theologian.org.uk/churchhistory/lutherstheologyofthecross.html#:~:text=Carl%20Trueman%20is%20Professor%20of,and%20English%20Reformers%201525%E2%80%931556. [accessed 06/15/2024]

Torrance, Thomas F. *Space, Time, and Resurrection*. London: T & T Clark International, 1998.

Vaidis, D.C., and A. Bran. Respectable Challenges to Respectable Theory: Cognitive Dissonance Theory Requires Conceptualization Clarification and Operational Tools. *Frontiers in Psychology* 10 (2019) 1189.

Van Til, Cornelius. *A Christian Theory of Knowledge*. Grand Rapids, Michigan: Baker, 1969.

———. *Paul in Athens*. Phillipsburg, NJ: P&R,1959.

———. *Who Do You Say I Am?* Phillipsburg, NJ: P&R, 1975.

Bibliography

Vilenkin, Alexander. The Beginning of the Universe. *Inference* 1 (2015). https://inference-review.com/article/the-beginning-of-the-universe [accessed 06/15/2024]

Vroegop, Mark. *Dark Clouds, Deep Mercy: Discovering the Grace of Lament*. Wheaton, IL: Crossway, 2019.

Ware, James. The Resurrection of Jesus in the Pre-Pauline Formula of 1 Cor 15.3–5. *New Testament Studies* 60 (2014) 475–98.

Wenham, Gordon J. *Book of Leviticus*. Grand Rapids, MI: William B. Eerdmans, 1979.

Wessely, Simon. Mass hysteria: two syndromes? *Psychological Medicine* 17 (1987) 109–20.

Wigner, Eugene. The Unreasonable Effectiveness of Mathematics in the Natural Sciences. *Communications in Pure and Applied Mathematics* 13 (1960) 1–14.

Williams, Peter J. *Can We Trust the Gospels?* Wheaton, IL: Crossway, 2018.

Wixted, John T., et al. Rethinking the Reliability of Eyewitness Memory. *Perspectives on Psychological Science* 13 (2018) 324–35.

Wright, David P. "Azazel." The Anchor Yale Bible Dictionary, vol. 1, edited by Daniel N. Freedman, 536–37. New Haven, CT: Yale University Press, 1992.

Wright, NT. *The Resurrection of the Son of God*. London: SPCK, 2003.

Yoneyama, Shoko. Miyazaki Hayao's Animism and the Anthropocene. *Theory, Culture & Society* 38 (2021) 251–66.

Young, Edward J. *Daniel*. Edinburgh: Banner of Truth, 1973.

Young, Rosalind. *Mutiny of the Bounty and story of Pitcairn Island 1790–894*. Mountain View, CA: Pacific Press, 1894.

Subject Index

Allison, Dale, 15–16, 125–28, 134, 136–37, 148, 155, 157–59, 161, 162, 167–69, 175–79, 205, 220–22, 226–28
Animism, 22–23, 27, 30, 33, 35, 62, 65, 68, 210, 212, 230
apparitions. *See* Visions
appearances of Jesus
    Cleopas, 137–39
    female disciples, 130, 134, 137, 142, 146–48, 155, 161, 177, 200–201
    the 500, 123, 126, 129, 149, 178–79, 202, 204, 205–6, 219, 220
    James, brother of Jesus, 126, 128–29, 149, 170, 202, 204, 226
    Mary Magdelene, 141, 142–43, 170, 178, 203–5, 220, 226
    Paul, 123, 127–29, 149, 170, 172, 177, 202, 203–4, 204–5, 206, 220, 226, 227
    the twelve, 123, 126–28, 147, 148, 149, 157, 168, 203, 204, 205
ascension
    Holy Spirit and mission, 141,149, 230–231
    Luke-Acts, 137, 140, 146, 149, 230
    Other Gospels, 140–41
    Paul, 125
    Priest-King, 104–6, 114

Son of Man, 106–10
spiritual, 127, 160
temple, 105, 113, 230–31
Bayesian models
    Barnes, Luke, 40, 216
    Bayesian networks, 8–9, 212–22, 223–27
    Bayes's rule, 3, 4, 6–8, 12, 14
    Bayes theorem. *See* Bayes's rule.
    likelihood, 6–7, 216, 217, 218, 219
    McGrew, Tim and Lydia, 8, 19, 20, 21, 203
    objections, 15–19
    posterior probability 6–7, 9, 14, 19, 220–21
    prior probability 4–5, 6, 7–10, 11–12, 19–21, 22, 23, 31, 33–34, 36, 53, 65–67, 74, 77, 83, 98, 111, 117, 119–20, 151–52, 206, 207–8, 210, 214–16, 218, 219, 220, 222, 223, 224, 227, 229
    Sobel J.H., 4, 220
    Swinburne, Richard, 11, 19, 20–21, 77, 83, 204, 210, 211, 214
Big Bang theory, 37
Boyarin, Daniel, 24–25, 78–81, 83, 90–91, 107

Subject Index

Buddhism, 22, 23, 27, 30, 33, 34, 51, 59, 62, 64, 65, 68, 212, 230
burial of Jesus
   First Corinthians 15, 123–24,
   Gospel accounts, 130–32, 134, 137, 141–42, 146, 147–48
   historical context, 98, 156, 158
   Joseph of Arimathea, 124, 130, 134, 142, 146, 147–48, 157–58, 204
   sceptical arguments, 124, 157–58, 201, 204

cognitive bias
   Bayesian approaches, reduction of, 15
   correspondence bias, 190–91, 199
   fundamental attribution error. *See* correspondence bias.
   homogeneity bias, 192, 194, 199
   selection bias, 194
   ultimate attribution error, 191
cognitive dissonance
   Bermejo-Rubio, 191, 198–99
   Cognitive Dissonance Theory, 189, 192–93
   first century movements 194–97
   Leon Festinger, 192
   Millerites, 193–94
contradictions in resurrection accounts, alleged, 130–32, 136–37, 137–38, 139, 140–41, 142, 145–49, 150
conversion disorder. *See* Functional Neurological Symptom Disorder.

death of Jesus, 55, 56, 76–77, 90, 92, 96, 98, 104, 108, 109–10, 113, 114–15, 120–21, 122, 123, 131–32, 133, 134, 141, 142, 146, 147, 149, 187–88, 189, 198, 201–2, 231
Draper, Paul, 34, 39, 44–48, 53, 57–58, 60, 69

Ehrman, Bart, 11, 15, 90, 122–25, 148, 152, 157–58, 162, 166, 170, 180–84, 186, 188, 200, 201, 203–4, 207, 226, 228

empty tomb
   female disciples' testimony 134, 142, 146
   First Corinthians 15, 124, 219–20
   Gospel accounts, 131–32, 134–35, 137–38, 141–42, 146, 147, 148, 152, 219–20
   sceptical challenges, 153, 155–61, 178, 187, 200–201, 204, 205, 226

fine tuning, 39–41
Frame, John, 10, 15, 41, 54, 62, 63, 69, 72, 111, 113, 116, 117
Functional Neurological Symptom Disorder, 172–73, 179

Habermas, Gary, 11, 20, 162, 173
hallucinations
   application to New Testament, 169—70
   bereavement, 152, 164–65, 202–4, 205, 206, 220, 225–27, 242–49
   cognitive dissonance and, 189–90
   definition, 163
   experimental induction 165–66
   general population, 164, 202, 220
   group. *See* visions.
   illusions, definition, 164,
   insight, 166–67, 203
Harrison, Peter, 44–47, 50
Hartle-Hawking model, 37–39
Hinduism, 22–23, 27, 29–30, 33, 51, 59, 62, 64, 65, 68, 230
Hume, David, 3–6, 7–10, 14, 17, 20, 22, 33, 62, 65, 72, 74, 119–20, 152, 210, 229

Islam, 2, 23, 27–28, 30–31, 33, 46, 50, 56, 65, 74, 78, 90, 188, 210, 212, 215, 218, 226

Judaism
   early, 76, 78–79, 80–81, 90–91, 97, 98, 106, 124, 160, 193, 195–96, 234
   modern, 2, 23, 27–28, 30, 33, 50, 56, 65, 97, 98, 212, 215, 218, 234

Subject Index

legendary embellishments, alleged, 121, 124, 136–37, 144, 155, 163, 178, 202, 204
Licona, Mike, 20, 131, 132, 152, 162
logic, 47, 48–49, 50–51, 73
Loke, Andrew, 152, 156, 159, 160, 163, 167, 176, 185, 188
Ludemann, Gerd, 136, 144, 154, 160, 162, 171, 172, 200, 201, 203, 204–5, 206, 207, 226, 227, 228

mass hysteria. *See* mass psychogenic illness.
mass psychogenic illness, 172, 174, 178–79, 202, 204, 227
memory
    confidence and accuracy, 183
    false memories, 181–83
    flashbulb memories, 184
    real world vs lab experiments, 182–83
    reliability, 180–81
Messiah
    divinity of, 23–25, 77, 78–83, 93, 99, 107, 109, 111–12, 113, 218
    early Judaism, 75, 79, 80, 81–82, 90–91, 94, 96, 97, 98–99, 102, 194–96
    Hebrew Bible, 79–81, 84–85, 85–88, 92–95, 99–102,
    Isaiah 53, 95, 101–2, 233–41
    modern Judaism, 75, 78, 84–85, 97,
    New Testament and the, 75, 78, 82, 90, 95,
    resurrection of the, 77, 98,
    son of David, 96, 105–6, 114, 133,
    son of Joseph, 92, 93, 94, 96,
    son of Ephraim. *See* son of Joseph.
    suffering of the, 90–96,
minimal facts approach, 11, 20
morality, 23, 28, 61–64, 69–70, 72, 74
Muslim. *See* Islam.

naturalism
    assumption of, 20, 21, 33, 43, 232
    ethics, evil and, 23, 60, 61–62, 64
    evidential argument for, Draper's, 57–58
    life-permitting universe and, 40
    metaphysical, 46, 47
    methodological, 41, 46, 47
    non-reductive physicalism, 28, 33
    prior probability of, 20–21, 206, 215,
    reason (or logic) and, 48–49
    reductive physicalism, 28, 33
    simplicity, 66–67, 68–69
    success of science and, 43–49, 70
    testability, 7–10, 46–47, 152
    ultimate reality, 22–23, 27–29, 230
naturalistic theories of Jesus' resurrection
    Allison, 205, 207, 220, 222, 226, 228
    Ehrman, 203–4, 207, 226, 228
    Ludemann, 204–5, 207, 226, 228

Oppy, Graham, 28–29, 39, 57, 60, 63, 66, 66–67, 68–69, 215, 224, 225

pareidolia, 176
parsimony. *See* simplicity.
Pearl, Judea, 8, 209, 211
persecution of disciples, 185–88
Plantinga, Alvin, 17–19, 21, 50, 60
Probability, types of, 13–14
problem of evil or suffering
    Buddhist perspectives on suffering and evil, 58–59, 62–63, 70–71, 217
    Christian perspectives on suffering and evil, 53–54, 63–64, 69, 70–71, 71–72, 217
    evidential argument, 57–58
    Hindu perspectives on suffering and evil, 58–59, 70–71, 217
    logical argument, 56–57
    naturalist perspectives on suffering and evil, 56–58, 62, 69, 70–71, 217
    resurrection model, impact, 217, 224–25
    Unipersonal theist perspective, 56, 63–64, 69, 71–72, 217

quasi-sensory experiences. *See* hallucinations, visions.

reason. *See* logic.

Subject Index

Sagan, Carl, 1, 3, 4, 17, 22, 210, 229
the scientific method
   Buddhism and, 51
   Christianity and, 50
   god-of-the-gaps and, 45
   Hinduism and, 51
   history of, 45–46, 47
   intelligibility of the universe and, 43–44
   Islam and, 46
   logic and reason, 48–49
   mathematics, 44
   natural and supernatural distinction in, 44–45
   naturalism and, 48–49
   subtraction stories, 34, 43, 44, 45, 178
   success of science and naturalism, 44–48
   Unipersonal theism and, 50
Shintoism, 30, 35, 62, 212
simplicity, 66–69, 215, 224
Singer, Rabbi Tovia, 56, 84–85, 233, 241
Son of Man
   ascension, 104–6
   Daniel 7, 106–8, 135, 140, 141, 149
   First Enoch, 106
   New Testament, 106, 108–9, 140, 141, 149
   suffering, 95, 108
suffering. *See* problem of evil.

theism. *See* Triune God, Unipersonal theism.
third day, resurrection, 102
Trinity. *See* worldviews, Triune God.

universe, existence of, 23–24, 27, 30, 31, 33, 34, 35–42, 54, 65, 68, 69, 70, 71, 72, 73–74, 119–20, 216, 227

visions
   application to New Testament, 177–79, 220, 227
   group, 163, 167–70, 172, 174
   Mary, of, 174–75

William Lane Craig, 15, 18, 19, 20, 21, 155, 187

the Word
   early Judaism, 24–25, 26, 79–81, 81–82, 83, 111–12
   Gnosticism, alleged, 78
   Hebrew Bible, 23–24, 79–81, 111–12
   the image of God, 26
   Logos, 78–79, 81–82
   Memra. *See* early Judaism.
   New Testament, 26, 78–80, 82, 112
   Philo, 81–82
Worldviews
   Animism. *See* mind-first.
   Buddhism. *See* mind-first.
   Christianity. *See* Triune God.
   Hinduism. *See* mind-first.
   Islam. *See* Unipersonal theism.
   Judaism. *See* Unipersonal theism.
   mind-first, 23, 29–30, 31, 33, 34, 36, 41–42, 51, 60, 64, 65, 69–71, 72, 73–74, 212, 213–17, 218, 220–221, 223–24, 230
   naturalism. *See* physical-first (contingent), physical-first (necessary).
   physical-first (contingent), 23, 28–29, 31, 33, 34, 36, 41–42, 51, 60, 64, 65, 67, 69–71, 72, 73–74, 212, 213–17, 218, 220–21, 223–24, 230
   physical-first (necessary), 23, 28–29, 31, 33, 34, 36, 41–42, 51, 60, 64, 65, 67, 69–71, 72, 73–74, 212, 213–17, 218, 220–21, 223–24, 225, 230
   Triune God, 21, 23, 27–28, 31, 33, 41, 50, 51, 53, 60, 64, 65, 67–68, 69–72, 73–74, 119–20, 212, 213–17, 218, 220–21, 223–24, 228, 229, 230
   Unipersonal Theism, 23, 27–28, 30–31, 33– 34, 41, 43, 50, 51, 56, 63–64, 65, 67, 68, 69–72, 73–74, 119–20, 212, 213–14, 215–17, 218, 220–21, 223–24, 230
Wright, N.T., 98, 99, 122, 124, 125, 126, 130, 131, 132, 133, 135, 136, 137, 138, 139, 145, 150, 169, 176, 191, 193, 195, 196

www.ingramcontent.com/pod-product-compliance
Lightning Source LLC
Chambersburg PA
CBHW050841230426
43667CB00012B/2096